Jakarta EE Cookbook
Second Edition

Practical recipes for enterprise Java developers to deliver large scale applications with Jakarta EE

Elder Moraes

BIRMINGHAM - MUMBAI

Jakarta EE Cookbook
Second Edition

Copyright © 2020 Packt Publishing

Commissioning Editor: Kunal Chaudhari
Acquisition Editor: Denim Pinto
Content Development Editor: Tiksha Lad
Senior Editor: Afshaan Khan
Technical Editor: Sonam Pandey
Copy Editor: Safis Editing
Project Coordinator: Francy Puthiry
Proofreader: Safis Editing
Indexer: Pratik Shirodkar
Production Designer: Shankar Kalbhor

First published: June 2019
Second edition: May 2020

Production reference: 1280520

Published by Packt Publishing Ltd.
Livery Place
35 Livery Street
Birmingham
B3 2PB, UK.

ISBN 978-1-83864-288-4

www.packt.com

To Jesus Christ, my only source of eternal life and purpose.

To my beloved wife, Erica—thanks for your love and for sharing your life with me.

To my adorable daughter, Rebeca—if this book helps a single person, maybe it could help to turn the world into a better place for you.

To the memory of my mother, Matilde, who I miss every day.

To my brother, Marco, who introduced me to this incredible world of computers and software.

To my friend and guru, Bruno "Javaman" Souza—I would probably never have written this book if I hadn't met you.

To the amazing team at SouJava—you folks really live the community thing.

To my peers at TCDB for all encouragement, tips, sharing, and feedback. Thank you!

Packt.com

Subscribe to our online digital library for full access to over 7,000 books and videos, as well as industry leading tools to help you plan your personal development and advance your career. For more information, please visit our website.

Why subscribe?

- Spend less time learning and more time coding with practical eBooks and Videos from over 4,000 industry professionals

- Improve your learning with Skill Plans built especially for you

- Get a free eBook or video every month

- Fully searchable for easy access to vital information

- Copy and paste, print, and bookmark content

Did you know that Packt offers eBook versions of every book published, with PDF and ePub files available? You can upgrade to the eBook version at www.packt.com and as a print book customer, you are entitled to a discount on the eBook copy. Get in touch with us at customercare@packtpub.com for more details.

At www.packt.com, you can also read a collection of free technical articles, sign up for a range of free newsletters, and receive exclusive discounts and offers on Packt books and eBooks.

Foreword

(Foreword from the previous edition)

It is a measure of the penetration, longevity, and quality of Java EE technology that, in 2018, my friend Elder Moraes asked me to write the foreword for his book about Java EE 8. My personal involvement with Java EE goes back to the days preceding J2EE 1.4 in 2001. Since then, I have had the great honor of leading or co-leading the community teams that have developed JavaServer Faces and, later, Servlet, two of the technologies Elder covers in this book. During that time, I tried to follow the model of servant-leader, and I think the result has been a very engaged community that has a real stake in the continued success of Java EE.

When writing this foreword, I want to focus on four Cs: **curation**, **cohesion**, **current**, and **completeness**. So much has been written about Java EE over the years, and continues to be written, that the task of writing a book, particularly one in the useful cookbook format, involves a lot of **curation**. From the range of all possible things that people are doing with Java EE, which is vast, Elder has presented a curation of what he thinks are the most useful and essential things. Elder is well positioned to decide what goes in and what stays out. Elder has been consulting and working with Java EE for nearly as long as I have, but from the more practical perspective of the user.

Technical books that follow the cookbook pattern frequently suffer from a feeling of disjointedness. Not this book. Elder has put a great deal of effort into ensuring **cohesion**. Over the years, the technologies of Java EE have sometimes been criticized for not being cohesive enough with each other. This is something Sun made a conscious effort to address, starting with Java EE 6, and which Oracle continued working on in Java EE 8. Elder has leveraged this effort to seek out and present the best way to leverage the synergy of all the technologies of Java EE 8 to maximum effect.

The world outside Java EE has continued to evolve, and this has changed the way people use Java EE dramatically. The challenge for any architect on a multiyear software effort, with a service lifetime of at least a decade, is how to keep it maintainable even while the surrounding technology landscape changes. Elder has accounted for this with two excellent chapters about microservices and Docker. These two technologies provide a great complement to the power of Java EE, but also have numerous pitfalls. Elder helps you avoid the pitfalls while getting the most out of these **current** trends.

Finally, **completeness**. Many technology cookbooks stop short of providing complete reference sort of material, but Elder goes much deeper. It's almost to the point that the term cookbook does not do this book justice. Perhaps a more correct label would be complete restaurant management with supply chain logistics and a cookbook on top. Elder covers the current popular app servers on which people are running Java EE, continuous integration and pipelines, reactive programming, and more. Coming back to the curation point, it's all there, and in depth.

I hope you have success with Java EE and with its successor, Jakarta EE from the Eclipse Foundation.

Ed Burns

Consulting Member of Technical Staff at Oracle

Specification Lead of JSF and Servlet

Contributors

About the author

Elder Moraes helps Jakarta EE developers build and deliver secure, fast, and available applications so that they are able to work on great projects. He is passionate about content sharing; he does it by speaking at international events, blogging, and writing articles. He has been working with Java since 2002 and has developed applications for different industries. As a board member at SouJava, he led the *Java EE 8 - The Next Frontier* initiative, interviewing some world-class Java EE experts.

> *First, I have to thank my wife and daughter, Erica and Rebeca, respectively, for all the time they allowed me to put into writing this book. It was not easy for any of us. Also, thank you to my friends, Lucas and Mari, for all the support and encouragement since day one. Last but not least, thank you to all the Packt team (Isha, Sreeja, Jason, Prajakta, and others that I haven't talked to personally). You folks rock!*

About the reviewer

Deepak Vohra is a consultant and a principal member of the NuBean.com software company. He is a Sun Certified Java Programmer and Web Component Developer and has worked in the fields of XML, Java programming and Java EE for ten years.

Deepak is the co-author of the Apress book, Pro XML Development with Java Technology and is also the author of the Packt Publishing books JDBC 4.0 and Oracle JDeveloper for J2EE Development, Processing XML Documents with Oracle JDeveloper 11g, EJB 3.0 Database Persistence with Oracle Fusion Middleware 11g, and Java EE Development in Eclipse IDE, and Advanced Java EE Development with WildFly.

Packt is searching for authors like you

If you're interested in becoming an author for Packt, please visit `authors.packtpub.com` and apply today. We have worked with thousands of developers and tech professionals, just like you, to help them share their insight with the global tech community. You can make a general application, apply for a specific hot topic that we are recruiting an author for, or submit your own idea.

Table of Contents

Preface

Jakarta EE is a mature platform that's widely used around the world. It is also a standard that has evolved through the hard work of individuals, vendors, groups leaders, and communities. It has a whole market and ecosystem around it, with millions of users, which also means a big and active community that is always willing to help it move forward.

For those reasons, the purpose of this book is to meet the needs of those professionals who depend on Jakarta EE to deliver really awesome enterprise solutions, not only talking about real solutions to real problems but also showing how to implement those solutions in a practical way.

The book starts with a quick overview of what Jakarta EE is and the improvements in version 8. Then, it takes you on a hands-on journey through the most important APIs.

You will learn how to use Jakarta EE for server-side development, web services, and web applications. You will also take a look at how you can properly improve the security of your enterprise solutions.

No Jakarta EE application is good enough if it doesn't follow the standards, and for that, you can count on the Jakarta EE application servers. This book will teach you how to use the most important servers on the market and get the best that they have to offer for your project.

From an architectural point of view, the book will cover microservices, cloud computing, and containers. Also, it will not forget to give you all the tools you need to build a reactive Jakarta EE application using not only Jakarta EE features, but also Java core features such as lambdas and completable futures.

The whole Java world is all about the community, so we will also show you how community-driven professionals can improve the results of their projects and even go to higher levels in their careers.

This book was based on a concept that I call *The Five Mistakes That Keep Jakarta EE Professionals Away From Great Projects*. I am ruining my career when I don't do the following things:

- Keep myself up to date
- Know the APIs (having an overview of all of them and a mastery of the most important ones)
- Know the most commonly used Jakarta EE application servers
- Know advanced architectures
- Share what I know

So, the book is a straightforward, practical, and helpful solution to each one of these mistakes. I can say with confidence that dealing with them properly can change the careers and lives of many developers around the world. I know because they've changed mine, for good.

Who this book is for

This book is made for developers who would like to learn how to meet real enterprise application needs using Jakarta EE 8. They should be familiar with application development and need to have knowledge of at least basic Java, some minimal knowledge of Jakarta EE, the basic concepts of cloud computing, and web services.

You should want to learn how to combine a bunch of APIs in a secure and fast solution, and for this, you need to know how the APIs work and when to use each one.

If when you got this book in your hands we already have Jakarta EE 9 released, please read the *To get the most out of this book* section ahead, for directions on how to make 100% of the code of this book work without any issues.

What this book covers

Chapter 1, *New Features and Improvements*, explains the main changes to the Jakarta EE 8 specification and what you can do with them. It also shows the new features and briefly explores the benefits of them. All these topics are supported by code examples.

Chapter 2, *Server-Side Development*, deep-dives into the most important APIs and the most commonly used features for server-side development. You will go through real recipes for solving real problems.

Chapter 3, *Building Powerful Services with JSON and RESTful Features*, creates web services for different enterprise scenarios. You will go deep into the JAX-RS, JSON-P, and JSON-B APIs.

Chapter 4, *Web- and Client-Server Communication*, deals with the communication generated by web applications in a fast and reliable way using the latest Jakarta EE 8 features, such as HTTP2 and Server Push.

Chapter 5, *Security of Enterprise Architecture*, gives you information on various tools using the best Jakarta EE features to create secure architectures.

Chapter 6, *Reducing the Coding Effort by Relying on Standards*, describes the services and features that Jakarta EE application servers give to the applications they host. Those features not only enable you to rely on a standard and build your application based on it, but also allow you to write less code, as you don't need to implement features that have already been implemented by the server.

Chapter 7, *Deploying and Managing Applications on Major Jakarta EE Servers*, describes the use of each of the most commonly used Jakarta EE application servers on the market, giving special attention to the way you deploy and manage them.

Chapter 8, *Building Lightweight Solutions Using Microservices*, helps you to understand how microservice architectures work and how you can easily use Jakarta EE 8 to build microservices and/or break down your monoliths in order to implement this paradigm.Continuous delivery and continuous deployment are also described, as no successful microservice project is complete without a mature building and deployment process.

Chapter 9, *Using Multithreading on Enterprise Context*, describes the use of multithreading and concurrency when building enterprise applications.

Chapter 10, *Using Event-Driven Programming to Build Reactive Applications*, describes the use of Jakarta EE 8 and core Java to create low-latency, efficient, and high-throughput applications.

Chapter 11, *Rising to the Cloud – Jakarta EE, Containers, and Cloud Computing*, describes how to combine Jakarta EE and containers to run applications on the cloud.

Appendix, *The Power of Sharing Knowledge*, describes how the community is vital for the whole Jakarta EE ecosystem (even if you don't know about it), and looks at how you can improve your own daily work by joining the Adopt a JSR initiative.

The chapter also describes how sharing knowledge is a powerful tool for improving your career and explains what it has to do with Jakarta EE (it has everything to do with Jakarta EE!).

To get the most out of this book

You should be familiar with application development and you need to have at least basic knowledge of Java and Jakarta EE. Basic knowledge of cloud computing and web services is also assumed.

Software/hardware covered in the book	OS requirements
Open JDK 8 or superior	Linux/macOS/Windows
Maven 3.5	Linux/macOS/Windows
Eclipse GlassFish 5.1	Linux/macOS/Windows
Docker CE 18	Linux/macOS/Windows
Git SCM 2.16	Linux/macOS/Windows

If when trying to run any of the code in this book you got a message saying that the "address is already in use" or something like it, you probably have an other service/application using the same port that the example is trying to use. Closing it will fix this issue.

Jakarta EE 9 is on the way – what now?

By the time this second edition is released, we will just be a few months away from the release of Jakarta EE 9! Because of this, you may be wondering, "*why not publish the book when 9 is alive and kicking?*".

Good question! And the answer is equally clear: because no APIs/features will be changing in this release. So, what's changed that would justify a new release?

Because of one thing in the Jakarta EE field known as *big bang*. If you've been following Jakarta EE for a while now, you should be aware of it. If not, let me quickly explain it to you.

Due to Java EE being transferred from Oracle to Eclipse Foundation, it was rebranded to Jakarta EE, and due to this, we had the Jakarta EE 8 release. That's why we have the second edition of this book!

As part of the branding and intellectual property process, another thing needed to be changed: the `javax` namespaces.

The following examples have been taken from this very book, and all of them use the `javax` namespace:

```
import javax.ws.rs.core.Application;
import javax.ws.rs.container.AsyncResponse;
import javax.ejb.EJB;
import javax.validation.constraints.Size;
```

So, all the APIs under Jakarta EE have to change their namespaces from `javax` to `jakarta`. This same list in Jakarta EE 9 will look like this:

```
import jakarta.ws.rs.core.Application;
import jakarta.ws.rs.container.AsyncResponse;
import jakarta.ejb.EJB;
import jakarta.validation.constraints.Size;
```

Since this book was written to help you deliver the most incredible applications using Jakarta EE 8, I need to answer the following, and most important, question: *how does this change affect you and/or your code if you migrate from 8 to 9?*

The simple and quick answer is that your code/project will break. Period.

This isn't as bad as it sounds. At the end of the day, Jakarta EE has a huge community of developers around the world (probably one of the biggest communities), and most of them are developers like you that will face these same problems if there's no way out.

So, yes, you'll need to change the *imports* for all the classes in your project that use the `javax` namespace. And no, you won't need to do this manually (unless you want to).

While I'm writing this, there is already one tool that is being developed by the Apache Tomcat folks. You can try it out and follow the project for more information at `https://github.com/apache/tomcat-jakartaee-migration`.

I'm pretty sure that even more tools will become available soon. Stay tuned!

For more information about the *big bang*, you can read this amazing blog post by Mike Milinkovich: `https://eclipse-foundation.blog/2020/01/16/moving-forward-with-jakarta-ee-9/`.

Download the example code files

You can download the example code files for this book from your account at `www.packtpub.com`. If you purchased this book elsewhere, you can visit `www.packtpub.com/support` and register to have the files emailed directly to you.

You can download the code files by following these steps:

1. Log in or register at www.packtpub.com.
2. Select the **SUPPORT** tab.
3. Click on **Code Downloads & Errata**.
4. Enter the name of the book in the **Search** box and follow the onscreen instructions.

Once the file is downloaded, please make sure that you unzip or extract the folder using the latest version of:

- WinRAR/7-Zip for Windows
- Zipeg/iZip/UnRarX for Mac
- 7-Zip/PeaZip for Linux

The code bundle for the book is also hosted on GitHub at https://github.com/eldermoraes/javaee8-cookbook. In case there's an update to the code, it will be updated on the existing GitHub repository.

We also have other code bundles from our rich catalog of books and videos available at https://github.com/PacktPublishing/. Check them out!

Download the color images

We also provide a PDF file that has color images of the screenshots/diagrams used in this book. You can download it here: https://static.packt-cdn.com/downloads/9781838642884_ColorImages.pdf .

Conventions used

There are a number of text conventions used throughout this book.

CodeInText: Indicates code words in text, database table names, folder names, filenames, file extensions, pathnames, dummy URLs, user input, and Twitter handles. Here is an example: "Then, two key methods from SseResource do their work."

A block of code is set as follows:

```
<dependency>
    <groupId>javax</groupId>
    <artifactId>javaee-api</artifactId>
    <version>8.0</version>
```

```
    <scope>provided</scope>
</dependency>
```

Any command-line input or output is written as follows:

```
Info:    destroy
```

Bold: Indicates a new term, an important word, or words that you see onscreen. For example, words in menus or dialog boxes appear in the text like this. Here is an example: "We defined the security rules and roles through our code (the program). There's another approach called **declarative security**."

 Warnings or important notes appear like this.

 Tips and tricks appear like this.

Sections

In this book, you will find several headings that appear frequently (*Getting ready, How to do it..., How it works..., There's more...*, and *See also*).

To give clear instructions on how to complete a recipe, use these sections as follows.

Getting ready

This section tells you what to expect in the recipe and describes how to set up any software or any preliminary settings required for the recipe.

How to do it...

This section contains the steps required to follow the recipe.

How it works...

This section usually consists of a detailed explanation of what happened in the previous section.

There's more…

This section consists of additional information about the recipe in order to make you more knowledgeable about the recipe.

See also

This section provides helpful links to other useful information for the recipe.

Get in touch

Feedback from our readers is always welcome.

General feedback: Email `feedback@packtpub.com` and mention the book title in the subject of your message. If you have questions about any aspect of this book, please email us at `questions@packtpub.com`.

Errata: Although we have taken every care to ensure the accuracy of our content, mistakes do happen. If you have found a mistake in this book, we would be grateful if you would report this to us. Please visit `www.packtpub.com/submit-errata`, selecting your book, clicking on the Errata Submission Form link, and entering the details.

Piracy: If you come across any illegal copies of our works in any form on the internet, we would be grateful if you would provide us with the location address or website name. Please contact us at `copyright@packtpub.com` with a link to the material.

If you are interested in becoming an author: If there is a topic that you have expertise in and you are interested in either writing or contributing to a book, please visit `authors.packtpub.com`.

Reviews

Please leave a review. Once you have read and used this book, why not leave a review on the site that you purchased it from? Potential readers can then see and use your unbiased opinion to make purchase decisions, we at Packt can understand what you think about our products, and our authors can see your feedback on their book. Thank you!

For more information about Packt, please visit `packtpub.com`.

1
New Features and Improvements

Jakarta EE 8 is a big release, desired and anticipated by the global community for many years. More than ever before, the whole platform is now even more robust, mature, and stable.

This chapter will cover the main APIs that we can highlight for Jakarta EE 8. Not that they are the only topics covered by this release—far from it—but they have a big role in the enterprise context and are worthy of a careful look inside.

Also, this chapter (as the whole book) will work perfectly with Jakarta EE 9.

In this chapter, we will cover the following recipes:

- Running your first Jakarta Bean Validation 2.0 code
- Running your first Jakarta CDI 2.0 code
- Running your first JAX-RS 2.1 code
- Running your first JSF 2.3 code
- Running your first JSON-P 1.1 code
- Running your first JSON-B 1.0
- Running your first Jakarta Servlet 4.0 code
- Running your first Jakarta Security 1.0
- Running your first MVC 1.0 code

Running your first Jakarta Bean Validation 2.0 code

Jakarta Bean Validation is a Java specification that basically helps you to protect your data. Through its API, you can validate fields and parameters, express constraints using annotations, and extend your customs validation rules.

It can be used both with Java SE and Jakarta EE.

In this recipe, you will have a glimpse of Jakarta Bean Validation 2.0. It doesn't matter whether you are new to it or are already using version 1.1; this content will help to familiarize you with some of its new features.

Getting ready

First, you need to add the right Jakarta Bean Validation dependency to your project, as follows:

```
<dependencies>
    <dependency>
        <groupId>junit</groupId>
        <artifactId>junit</artifactId>
        <version>4.12</version>
        <scope>test</scope>
    </dependency>
    <dependency>
        <groupId>org.hibernate.validator</groupId>
        <artifactId>hibernate-validator</artifactId>
        <version>6.0.15.Final</version>
    </dependency>
    <dependency>
        <groupId>org.glassfish</groupId>
        <artifactId>javax.el</artifactId>
        <version>3.0.1-b11</version>
    </dependency>
</dependencies>
```

How to do it...

We need to perform the following steps to try this recipe:

1. First, we need to create an object with some fields to be validated:

```
public class User {

    @NotBlank
    private String name;
    @Email
    private String email;
    @NotEmpty
    private List<@PositiveOrZero Integer> profileId;

    public User(String name, String email, List<Integer> profileId)
{
        this.name = name;
        this.email = email;
        this.profileId = profileId;
    }
}
```

2. Then, we create a UserTest class to validate those constraints:

```
public class UserTest {

    private static Validator validator;

    @BeforeClass
    public static void setUpClass() {
        validator = Validation.buildDefaultValidatorFactory()
        .getValidator();
    }

    @Test
    public void validUser() {
        User user = new User(
            "elder",
            "elder@eldermoraes.com",
            asList(1,2));

            Set<ConstraintViolation<User>> cv = validator
            .validate(user);
            assertTrue(cv.isEmpty());
    }

    @Test
```

```
        public void invalidName() {
            User user = new User(
                "",
                "elder@eldermoraes.com",
                asList(1,2));

                Set<ConstraintViolation> cv = validator
                .validate(user);
                assertEquals(1, cv.size());
        }

    @Test
    public void invalidEmail() {
        User user = new User(
        "elder",

        "elder-eldermoraes_com",
        asList(1,2));

        Set<ConstraintViolation<User>> cv = validator
        .validate(user);
        assertEquals(1, cv.size());
    }

    @Test
    public void invalidId() {
        User user = new User(
            "elder",
            "elder@eldermoraes.com",
            asList(-1,-2,1,2));

            Set<ConstraintViolation<User>> cv = validator
            .validate(user);
            assertEquals(2, cv.size());
    }
}
```

After this, let's see how the recipe works.

How it works...

Our `User` class uses four of the new constraints introduced by Jakarta Bean Validation 2.0:

- `@NotBlank`: This ensures that the value is not null, empty, or an empty string (it trims the value before evaluation, to make sure there aren't spaces).
- `@Email`: This allows only a valid email format. Forget those crazy JavaScript functions!
- `@NotEmpty`: This ensures that a list has at least one item.
- `@PositiveOrZero`: This guarantees that a number is equal to or greater than zero.

Then, we create a test class (using JUnit) to test our validations. It first instantiates `Validator`, as follows:

```
@BeforeClass
public static void setUpClass() {
    validator = Validation.buildDefaultValidatorFactory().getValidator();
}
```

`Validator` is an API that validates beans according to the constraints defined for them.

Our first `test` method tests a valid user, which is a `User` object that has the following:

- Name not empty
- Valid email
- A `profileId` list only with integers greater than zero

This is shown in the following code snippet:

```
User user = new User(
    "elder",
    "elder@eldermoraes.com",
    asList(1,2));
```

And finally, we have the validation:

```
Set<ConstraintViolation<User>> cv = validator.validate(user);
```

The `validate()` method from `Validator` returns a set of constraint violations found, if any, or an empty set if there are no violations at all.

So, for a valid user, it should return an empty set:

```
assertTrue(cv.isEmpty());
```

For the other methods that work with variations around this model, we have the following:

- `invalidName()`: Uses an empty name
- `invalidEmail()`: Uses a malformed email
- `invalidId()`: Adds some negative numbers to the list

Note that the `invalidId()` method adds two negative numbers to the list:

```
asList(-1,-2,1,2));
```

So, we expect two constraint violations:

```
assertEquals(2, cv.size());
```

In other words, `Validator` checks not only the constraints violated, but how many times they are violated.

See also

- You can check the Jakarta Bean Validation 2.0 specification at `http://beanvalidation.org/2.0/spec/`.
- The full source code of this recipe is at `https://github.com/eldermoraes/javaee8-cookbook/tree/master/chapter01/ch01-beanvalidation/`.

Running your first Jakarta CDI 2.0 code

Jakarta **Contexts and Dependency Injection (CDI)** is certainly one of the most important APIs for the Jakarta EE platform. In version 2.0, it also works with Java SE.

Nowadays, CDI has an impact on many other APIs in the Jakarta EE platform as said in an interview for *Java EE 8 – The Next Frontier* project:

> *"If there was CDI by the time we created JSF, it would be made completely different."*
> *– Ed Burns, JSF Spec Lead*

There are a lot of new features in CDI 2.0. This recipe will cover observer ordering to give you a quick start.

Getting ready

We need to add the right CDI 2.0 dependency to your project. To make things easier at this point, we are going to use CDI SE, the dependency that allows you to use CDI without a Jakarta EE server:

```
<dependency>
    <groupId>org.jboss.weld.se</groupId>
    <artifactId>weld-se-shaded</artifactId>
    <version>3.1.0.Final</version>
</dependency>
```

How to do it...

This recipe will show you one of the main features introduced by CDI 2.0: ordered observers. Now, you can turn the observer's job into something predictable:

1. First, let's create an event to be observed:

```
public class MyEvent {
    private final String value;
    public MyEvent(String value){
        this.value = value;
    }
    public String getValue(){
        return value;
    }
}
```

2. Now, we build our observers and the server that will fire them:

```
public class OrderedObserver {

    public static void main(String[] args){
        try(SeContainer container =
        SeContainerInitializer.newInstance().initialize()){
            container
                .getBeanManager()
                .fireEvent(new MyEvent("event: " +
                System.currentTimeMillis()));
        }
    }

    public void thisEventBefore(
            @Observes @Priority(Interceptor.Priority
            .APPLICATION - 200)
```

```
                MyEvent event){
        System.out.println("thisEventBefore: " + event.getValue());
    }

    public void thisEventAfter(
            @Observes @Priority(Interceptor.Priority
            .APPLICATION + 200)
            MyEvent event){
        System.out.println("thisEventAfter: " + event.getValue());
    }
}
```

3. Also, don't forget to add the `beans.xml` file to the `META-INF` folder:

```xml
<?xml version="1.0" encoding="UTF-8"?>
<beans xmlns="http://xmlns.jcp.org/xml/ns/javaee"
       xmlns:xsi="http://www.w3.org/2001/XMLSchema-instance"
       xsi:schemaLocation="http://xmlns.jcp.org/xml/ns/javaee
       http://xmlns.jcp.org/xml/ns/javaee/beans_1_1.xsd"
       bean-discovery-mode="all">
</beans>
```

4. Once you run it, you should see a result like this:

```
INFO: WELD-ENV-002003: Weld SE container
353db40d-e670-431d-b7be-4275b1813782 initialized
 thisEventBefore: event -> 1501818268764
 thisEventAfter: event -> 1501818268764
```

Now, let's see how this works.

How it works...

First, we are building a server to manage our event and observers:

```java
public static void main(String[] args){
    try(SeContainer container =
    SeContainerInitializer.newInstance().initialize()){
        container
            .getBeanManager()
            .fireEvent(new ExampleEvent("event: "
            + System.currentTimeMillis()));
    }
}
```

This will give us all of the resources needed to run the recipe as if it were a Jakarta EE server.

Then, we build an observer, as follows:

```
public void thisEventBefore(
        @Observes @Priority(Interceptor.Priority.APPLICATION - 200)
        MyEvent event){
    System.out.println("thisEventBefore: " + event.getValue());
}
```

So, we have three important topics:

- @Observes: This annotation is used to tell the server that it needs to watch the events fired with MyEvent.
- @Priority: This annotation informs in which priority order this observer needs to run; it receives an int parameter, and the execution order is ascendant.
- MyEvent event: This is the event being observed.

In the thisEventBefore method and thisEventAfter, we only changed the @Priority value and the server took care of running it in the right order.

There's more...

The behavior would be exactly the same in a Jakarta EE 8 server. You just wouldn't need SeContainerInitializer and would need to change the dependencies to the following:

```
<dependency>
    <groupId>jakarta.platform</groupId>
    <artifactId>jakarta.jakartaee-api</artifactId>
    <version>8.0.0</version>
</dependency>
```

See also

- You can stay tuned with everything related to the Jakarta CDI specification at http://www.cdi-spec.org/.
- The source code of this recipe is at https://github.com/eldermoraes/javaee8-cookbook/tree/master/chapter01/ch01-cdi

Running your first JAX-RS 2.1 code

Jakarta RESTful Web Service, previously known as JAX-RS, is an API designed to give a portable and standard way of building RESTful web services in Java. This is one of the most widely used technologies for transporting data between different applications that use a network (the internet included) for communication.

One of the coolest features introduced by the 2.1 release is **Server-Sent Events** (**SSE**), which will be covered in this recipe. SSE is a specification created by HTML5, where it has established a channel between server and client, one way only from server to client. It is a protocol that transports a message containing some data.

Getting ready

Let's start by adding the right dependency to our project:

```
<dependencies>
    <dependency>
        <groupId>org.glasstish.jersey.containers</groupId>
        <artifactId>jersey-container-grizzly2-http</artifactId>
        <version>2.28</version>
    </dependency>
    <dependency>
        <groupId>org.glassfish.jersey.inject</groupId>
        <artifactId>jersey-hk2</artifactId>
        <version>2.28</version>
    </dependency>
    <dependency>
        <groupId>org.glassfish.jersey.media</groupId>
        <artifactId>jersey-media-sse</artifactId>
        <version>2.28</version>
    </dependency>
</dependencies>
```

You surely noticed that we are using Jersey here. Why? Because Jersey is one of the reference implementations for JAX-RS, which means that it implements all JAX-RS specifications.

Moreover, with Jersey, we can use Grizzly to start a small local server, which will be useful for this recipe, as we need just a few server features to show the SSE behavior.

Further on in this book, we will use a full GlassFish to build more JAX-RS recipes.

How to do it...

We need to perform the following steps to try this recipe:

1. First, we create a class that will be our server:

```
public class ServerMock {

    public static final URI CONTEXT =
    URI.create("http://localhost:8080/");
    public static final String BASE_PATH = "ssevents";

    public static void main(String[] args) {
        try {
            final ResourceConfig resourceConfig = new
            ResourceConfig(SseResource.class);

            final HttpServer server =
            GrizzlyHttpServerFactory.createHttpServer(CONTEXT,
            resourceConfig, false);
            server.start();

            System.out.println(String.format("Mock Server started
            at %s%s", CONTEXT, BASE_PATH));

            Thread.currentThread().join();
        } catch (IOException | InterruptedException ex) {
            System.out.println(ex.getMessage());
        }
    }
}
```

2. Then, we create a JAX-RS endpoint to send the events to the clients:

```
@Path(ServerMock.BASE_PATH)
public class SseResource {

    private static volatile SseEventSink SINK = null;

    @GET
    @Produces(MediaType.SERVER_SENT_EVENTS)
    public void getMessageQueue(@Context SseEventSink sink) {
        SseResource.SINK = sink;
    }

    @POST
    public void addMessage(final String message, @Context Sse sse)
    throws IOException {
```

```
        if (SINK != null) {
            SINK.send(sse.newEventBuilder()
                .name("sse-message")
                .id(String.valueOf(System.currentTimeMillis()))
                .data(String.class, message)
                .comment("")
                .build());
        }
    }
}
```

3. Then, we create a client class to consume the events generated from the server:

```
public class ClientConsumer {

    public static final Client CLIENT = ClientBuilder.newClient();
    public static final WebTarget WEB_TARGET =
    CLIENT.target(ServerMock.CONTEXT
    + BASE_PATH);
    public static void main(String[] args) {
        consume();
    }

    private static void consume() {

        try (final SseEventSource sseSource =
                    SseEventSource
                            .target(WEB_TARGET)
                            .build()) {

            sseSource.register(System.out::println);
            sseSource.open();

            for (int counter=0; counter < 5; counter++) {
                System.out.println(" ");
                for (int innerCounter=0; innerCounter < 5;
                innerCounter++) {
                    WEB_TARGET.request().post(Entity.json("event "
                    + innerCounter));
                }
                Thread.sleep(1000);
            }
            CLIENT.close();
            System.out.println("\n All messages consumed");
        } catch (InterruptedException e) {
            System.out.println(e.getMessage());
        }
```

```
            }
    }
```

4. For you to try it out, first run the `ServerMock` class and then the `ClientConsumer` class. If everything worked well, you should see something like this:

    ```
    InboundEvent{name='sse-message', id='1502228257736', comment='',
    data=event 0}
    InboundEvent{name='sse-message', id='1502228257753', comment='',
    data=event 1}
    InboundEvent{name='sse-message', id='1502228257758', comment='',
    data=event 2}
    InboundEvent{name='sse-message', id='1502228257763', comment='',
    data=event 3}
    InboundEvent{name='sse-message', id='1502228257768', comment='',
    data=event 4}
    ```

These are the messages sent from the server to the client.

How it works...

This recipe is made up of three parts:

*   The server, represented by the `ServerMock` class
*   The SSE engine, represented by the `SseResource` class
*   The client, represented by the `ClientConsumer` class

So, once `ServerMock` is instantiated, it registers the `SseResource` class:

```
final ResourceConfig resourceConfig = new
ResourceConfig(SseResource.class);
final HttpServer server =
GrizzlyHttpServerFactory.createHttpServer(CONTEXT, resourceConfig, false);
server.start();
```

Then, two key methods from `SseResource` take place. The first one adds messages to the server queue:

```
addMessage(final String message, @Context Sse sse)
```

The second one consumes this queue and sends the messages to the clients:

```
@GET
@Produces(MediaType.SERVER_SENT_EVENTS)
public void getMessageQueue(@Context SseEventSink sink)
```

Note that this one has a media type, SERVER_SENT_EVENTS, introduced in this version for this very purpose. And finally, we have our client. In this recipe, it is both posting and consuming messages.

It consumes here:

```
sseSource.register(System.out::println);
sseSource.open();
```

It posts here:

```
ServerMock.WEB_TARGET.request().post(Entity.json("event " + innerCounter));
```

See also

- You can stay tuned with everything related to JAX-RS at https://github.com/jax-rs.
- The source code of this recipe is at https://github.com/eldermoraes/javaee8-cookbook/tree/master/chapter01/ch01-jaxrs.

Running your first JSF 2.3 code

Jakarta Server Faces (JSF) is the Java technology made to simplify the process of building UIs.

With JSF, you can build components and use (or reuse) them in the UI in an extensible way. You can also use other powerful APIs, such as Jakarta CDI and Jakarta Bean Validation, to improve your application and its architecture.

In this recipe, we will use the Validator and Converter interfaces with the new feature introduced by version 2.3, which is the possibility of using them with generic parameters.

Getting ready

We need to add the required dependencies:

```
<dependency>
    <groupId>jakarta.platform</groupId>
    <artifactId>jakarta.jakartaee-api</artifactId>
    <version>8.0.0</version>
</dependency>
```

How to do it...

We need to perform the following steps to try this recipe:

1. Let's create a `User` class as the main object of our recipe:

```
public class User implements Serializable {

    private String name;
    private String email;

    public User(String name, String email) {
        this.name = name;
        this.email = email;
    }
    //DON'T FORGET THE GETTERS AND SETTERS
    //THIS RECIPE WON'T WORK WITHOUT THEM
}
```

2. Now, we create a `UserBean` class to manage our UI:

```
@Named
@ViewScoped
public class UserBean implements Serializable {

    private User user;
    public UserBean(){
        user = new User("Elder Moraes", "elder@eldermoraes.com");
    }

    public void userAction(){
        FacesContext.getCurrentInstance().addMessage(null,
                new FacesMessage("Name|Password welformed"));
    }

    //DON'T FORGET THE GETTERS AND SETTERS
```

```
            //THIS RECIPE WON'T WORK WITHOUT THEM
    }
```

3. Now, we implement the `Converter` interface with a `User` parameter:

```
@FacesConverter("userConverter")
public class UserConverter implements Converter<User> {

    @Override
    public String getAsString(FacesContext fc, UIComponent uic,
    User user) {
        return user.getName() + "|" + user.getEmail();
    }

    @Override
    public User getAsObject(FacesContext fc, UIComponent uic,
    String string) {
        return new User(string.substring(0, string.indexOf("|")),
        string.substring(string.indexOf("|") + 1));
    }

}
```

4. Now, we implement the `Validator` interface with a `User` parameter:

```
@FacesValidator("userValidator")
public class UserValidator implements Validator<User> {

    @Override
    public void validate(FacesContext fc, UIComponent uic,
    User user)
    throws ValidatorException {
        if(!user.getEmail().contains("@")){
            throw new ValidatorException(new FacesMessage(null,
                                         "Malformed e-mail"));
        }
    }
}
```

5. And then, we create our UI using all of them:

```
<h:body>
    <h:form>
        <h:panelGrid columns="3">
            <h:outputLabel value="Name|E-mail:"
            for="userNameEmail"/>
            <h:inputText id="userNameEmail"
            value="#{userBean.user}"
```

```
                converter="userConverter" validator="userValidator"/>
                <h:message for="userNameEmail"/>
            </h:panelGrid>
            <h:commandButton value="Validate"
            action="#{userBean.userAction()}"/>
        </h:form>
    </h:body>
```

Don't forget to run it in a Jakarta EE 8 server.

How it works...

From the code in the preceding section, we see that the `UserBean` class manages the communication between the UI and the server. Once you instantiate the `user` object, it is available for both of them.

That's why, when you run it, `Name | E-mail` is already filled (the `user` object is instantiated when the `UserBean` class is created by the server).

We associated the `userAction()` method from the `UserBean` class with the `Validate` button of the UI:

```
<h:commandButton value="Validate" action="#{userBean.userAction()}"/>
```

You can create other methods in `UserBean` and do the same to empower your application.

The whole core of our recipe is represented by just a single line in the UI:

```
<h:inputText id="userNameEmail" value="#{userBean.user}"
converter="userConverter" validator="userValidator"/>
```

So, our two implemented interfaces used here are `userConverter` and `userValidator`.

Basically, the `UserConverter` class (with the `getAsString` and `getAsObject` methods) converts an object into/from a string and vice versa, according to the logic defined by you.

We have just mentioned it in the preceding code snippet:

```
value="#{userBean.user}"
```

The server uses the `userConverter` object, calls the `getAsString` method, and prints the result using the preceding expression language.

Finally, the `UserValidator` class is automatically called when you submit the form, by calling its `validate` method, and applying the rules defined by you.

There's more...

You could increase the validators by adding a Jakarta Bean Validation on it and, for example, defining the email property from User with an @Email constraint.

See also

- You can stay tuned with everything related to JSF at https://javaserverfaces. github.io/.
- The source code of this recipe is at https://github.com/eldermoraes/javaee8-cookbook/tree/master/chapter01/ch01-jsf.

Running your first JSON-P 1.1 code

Jakarta JSON Processing is the API for JSON processing. By processing, we mean generating, transforming, parsing, and querying JSON strings and/or objects.

In this recipe, you will learn how to use a JSON Pointer to get a specific value from a JSON message very easily.

Getting ready

Let's get our dependency:

```
<dependencies>
    <dependency>
        <groupId>org.eclipse</groupId>
        <artifactId>yasson</artifactId>
        <version>1.0.3</version>
    </dependency>
    <dependency>
        <groupId>org.glassfish</groupId>
        <artifactId>javax.json</artifactId>
        <version>1.1.4</version>
    </dependency>
    <dependency>
        <groupId>jakarta.platform</groupId>
        <artifactId>jakarta.jakartaee-api</artifactId>
        <version>8.0.0</version>
        <scope>runtime</runtime>
```

```
    </dependency>
  </dependencies>
```

How to do it...

You need to perform the following steps to try this recipe:

1. First, we define a JSON message to represent the `User` object:

```json
{
  "user": {
    "email": "elder@eldermoraes.com",
    "name": "Elder",
    "profile": [
      {
        "id": 1
      },
      {
        "id": 2
      },
      {
        "id": 3
      }
    ]
  }
}
```

2. Now, we create a method to read it and print the values we want:

```java
public class JPointer {

    public static void main(String[] args) throws IOException{
        try (InputStream is =
JPointer.class.getClassLoader().getResourceAsStream("user.json");
                JsonReader jr = Json.createReader(is)) {

            JsonStructure js = jr.read();
            JsonPointer jp = Json.createPointer("/user/profile");
            JsonValue jv = jp.getValue(js);
            System.out.println("profile: " + jv);
        }
    }
}
```

3. The execution of this code prints the following:

profile: [{"id":1},{"id":2},{"id":3}]

How it works...

The JSON Pointer is a standard defined by the **Internet Engineering Task Force (IETF)** under **Request for Comments (RFC)** 6901. The standard basically says that a JSON Pointer is a string that identifies a specific value in a JSON document.

Without a JSON Pointer, you would need to parse the whole message and iterate through it until you find the desired value—probably lots of `if` and `else` instances and things like that.

So, a JSON Pointer helps you to decrease the written code dramatically by doing this kind of operation very elegantly.

See also

- You can stay tuned with everything related to JSON-P at `https://javaee.github.io/jsonp/`.
- The source code of this recipe is at `https://github.com/eldermoraes/javaee8-cookbook/tree/master/chapter01/ch01-jsonp`.

Running your first JSON-B 1.0 code

Jakarta JSON Binding is an API for converting Java objects into/from JSON messages in a standardized way. It defines a default mapping algorithm to convert Java classes into JSON and still lets you customize your own algorithms.

With **JSON-B (JSON-Binding)**, Jakarta EE has a complete set of tools to work with JSON, such as the JSON API and **JSON-P (JSON-Padding)**. No third-party frameworks are needed anymore (although you are still free to use them).

This quick recipe will show you how to use JSON-B to convert a Java object into and from a JSON message.

Getting ready

Let's add our dependencies to the project:

```
<dependencies>
    <dependency>
```

```
        <groupId>org.eclipse</groupId>
        <artifactId>yasson</artifactId>
        <version>1.0.3</version>
    </dependency>
    <dependency>
        <groupId>org.glassfish</groupId>
        <artifactId>javax.json</artifactId>
        <version>1.1.4</version>
    </dependency>
</dependencies>
```

How to do it...

You need to perform the following steps to try this recipe:

1. Let's create a `User` class as a model for our JSON message:

    ```
    public class User {

        private String name;
        private String email;

        public User(){
        }

        public User(String name, String email) {
            this.name = name;
            this.email = email;
        }

        @Override
        public String toString() {
            return "User{" + "name=" + name + ", email=" + email + '}';
        }

        //DON'T FORGET THE GETTERS AND SETTERS
        //THIS RECIPE WON'T WORK WITHOUT THEM

    }
    ```

2. Then, let's create a class to use JSON-B to transform an object:

    ```
    public class JsonBUser {
        public static void main(String[] args) throws Exception {
            User user = new User("Elder", "elder@eldermoraes.com");
            Jsonb jb = JsonbBuilder.create();
    ```

```
                    String jsonUser = jb.toJson(user);
                    User u = jb.fromJson(jsonUser, User.class);
                    jb.close();
                    System.out.println("json: " + jsonUser);
                    System.out.println("user: " + u);
            }
        }
```

3. The result printed is as follows:

```
json: {"email":"elder@eldermoraes.com","name":"Elder"}
user: User{name=Elder, email=elder@eldermoraes.com}
```

The first line is the object transformed into a JSON string. The second is the same string converted into an object.

How it works...

It uses the getters and setters defined in the User class to transform both ways and that's why they are so important.

See also

- You can stay tuned with everything related to JSON-B at http://json-b.net/.
- The source code of this recipe is at https://github.com/eldermoraes/javaee8-cookbook/tree/master/chapter01/ch01-jsonb.

Running your first Jakarta Servlet 4.0 code

Jakarta Servlet 4.0 is one the of biggest APIs of Jakarta EE 8. Since the very beginning of the Java EE platform (the old J2EE), the Servlet specification has always played a key role.

The coolest additions of this version are surely HTTP/2.0 and Server Push. Both of them bring performance improvements to your application.

This recipe will use Server Push to do one of the most basic tasks on a web page—load an image.

Getting ready

Let's add the dependencies that we need:

```xml
<dependency>
    <groupId>jakarta.platform</groupId>
    <artifactId>jakarta.jakartaee-api</artifactId>
    <version>8.0.0</version>
</dependency>
```

How to do it...

You need to perform the following steps to try this recipe:

1. We will create a servlet:

```java
@WebServlet(name = "ServerPush", urlPatterns = {"/ServerPush"})
public class ServerPush extends HttpServlet {

    @Override
    protected void doGet(HttpServletRequest request,
    HttpServletResponse
    response) throws ServletException, IOException {

        PushBuilder pb = request.newPushBuilder();
        if (pb != null) {
            pb.path("images/javaee-logo.png")
                .addHeader("content-type", "image/png")
                .push();
        }

        try (PrintWriter writer = response.getWriter();) {
            StringBuilder html = new StringBuilder();
            html.append("<html>");
            html.append("<center>");
            html.append("<img src='images/javaee-logo.png'><br>");
            html.append("<h2>Image pushed by ServerPush</h2>");
            html.append("</center>");
            html.append("</html>");
            writer.write(html.toString());
        }
    }
}
```

2. To try it, run the project in a Jakarta EE 8 server and open this URL:

```
https://localhost:8181/ch01-servlet/ServerPush
```

Let's now see how this works.

How it works...

We use the `PushBuilder` object to send an image to the client before it is requested by the `img src` tag. In other words, the browser doesn't need to do another request (what it usually does with `img src`) to have an image available for rendering.

It might seem as if it doesn't make too much difference for a single image, but it would with dozens, hundreds, or thousands of images. There's less traffic for your client and from your server. That's better performance for all!

There's more...

If you are using JSF, you can get the benefits from Server Push for free! You don't even need to rewrite a single line of your code, as JSF relies on the Server Push specification.

Just make sure that you run it under the HTTPS protocol, as HTTP/2.0 only works under it.

See also

- You can stay tuned with everything related to the Jakarta Servlet specification at `https://github.com/javaee/servlet-spec`.
- The source code of this recipe is at `https://github.com/eldermoraes/javaee8-cookbook/tree/master/chapter01/ch01-servlet`.

Running your first Jakarta Security code

Security is one of the top concerns when you build an enterprise application. Luckily, the Jakarta EE platform now has this API that handles many of the enterprise requirements in a standardized way.

In this recipe, you will learn how to define roles and give them the right authorization based on rules defined in the methods that manage sensitive data.

Getting ready

We start by adding our dependencies to the project:

```
<dependencies>
    <dependency>
        <groupId>junit</groupId>
        <artifactId>junit</artifactId>
        <version>4.12</version>
        <scope>test</scope>
    </dependency>
    <dependency>
        <groupId>org.apache.tomee</groupId>
        <artifactId>openejb-core</artifactId>
        <version>7.0.4</version>
    </dependency>
    <dependency>
        <groupId>jakarta.platform</groupId>
        <artifactId>jakarta.jakartaee-api</artifactId>
        <version>8.0.0</version>
        <scope>provided</scope>
    </dependency>
</dependencies>
```

How to do it...

You need to perform the following steps to try this recipe:

1. We first create a User entity:

```
@Entity
public class User implements Serializable{

    @Id
    private Long id;
    private String name;
    private String email;

    public User(){
    }

    public User(Long id, String name, String email) {
        this.id = id;
        this.name = name;
        this.email = email;
    }
```

```
                //DON'T FORGET THE GETTERS AND SETTERS
                //THIS RECIPE WON'T WORK WITHOUT THEM
        }
```

2. Here, we create a class to store our security roles:

```
public class Roles {
        public static final String ADMIN = "ADMIN";
        public static final String OPERATOR = "OPERATOR";
}
```

3. Then, we create a stateful bean to manage our user operations:

```
@Stateful
public class UserBean {

        @PersistenceContext(unitName = "ch01-security-pu",
        type = PersistenceContextType.EXTENDED)
        private EntityManager em;

        @RolesAllowed({Roles.ADMIN, Roles.OPERATOR})
        public void add(User user){
            em.persist(user);
        }

        @RolesAllowed({Roles.ADMIN})
        public void remove(User user){
            em.remove(user);
        }

        @RolesAllowed({Roles.ADMIN})
        public void update(User user){
            em.merge(user);
        }

        @PermitAll
        public List<User> get(){
            Query q = em.createQuery("SELECT u FROM User as u ");
            return q.getResultList();
        }
```

4. Now, we need to create an executor for each role:

```
public class RoleExecutor {

        public interface Executable {
            void execute() throws Exception;
        }
```

```
@Stateless
@RunAs(Roles.ADMIN)
public static class AdminExecutor {
    public void run(Executable executable) throws Exception {
        executable.execute();
    }
}

@Stateless
@RunAs(Roles.OPERATOR)
public static class OperatorExecutor {
    public void run(Executable executable) throws Exception {
        executable.execute();
    }
}
}
```

5. And finally, we create a test class to try our security rules.

6. Our code uses three test methods: `asAdmin()`, `asOperator()`, and `asAnonymous()`.

7. First, it tests `asAdmin()`:

```
//Lot of setup code before this point

@Test
public void asAdmin() throws Exception {
    adminExecutor.run(() -> {
        userBean.add(new User(1L, "user1", "user1@user.com"));
        userBean.add(new User(2L, "user2", "user2@user.com"));
        userBean.add(new User(3L, "user3", "user3@user.com"));
        userBean.add(new User(4L, "user4", "user4@user.com"));

        List<User> list = userBean.get();

        list.forEach((user) -> {
            userBean.remove(user);
        });

        Assert.assertEquals("userBean.get()", 0,
        userBean.get().size());
    });
}
```

8. Then, it tests `asOperator()`:

```
@Test
public void asOperator() throws Exception {
```

```
    operatorExecutor.run(() -> {
        userBean.add(new User(1L, "user1", "user1@user.com"));
        userBean.add(new User(2L, "user2", "user2@user.com"));
        userBean.add(new User(3L, "user3", "user3@user.com"));
        userBean.add(new User(4L, "user4", "user4@user.com"));

        List<User> list = userBean.get();

        list.forEach((user) -> {
            try {
                userBean.remove(user);
                Assert.fail("Operator was able to remove user " +
                user.getName());
            } catch (EJBAccessException e) {
            }
        });
        Assert.assertEquals("userBean.get()", 4,
        userBean.get().size());
    });
}
```

9. And, finally, it tests `asAnonymous()`:

```
@Test
public void asAnonymous() {

    try {
        userBean.add(new User(1L, "elder",
        "elder@eldermoraes.com"));
        Assert.fail("Anonymous user should not add users");
    } catch (EJBAccessException e) {
    }

    try {
        userBean.remove(new User(1L, "elder",
        "elder@eldermoraes.com"));
        Assert.fail("Anonymous user should not remove users");
    } catch (EJBAccessException e) {
    }

    try {
        userBean.get();
    } catch (EJBAccessException e) {
        Assert.fail("Everyone can list users");
    }
}
```

This class is huge! For the full source code, check the link at the end of this recipe.

How it works...

The whole point in this recipe is to do with the `@RolesAllowed`, `@RunsAs`, and `@PermitAll` annotations. They define what operations each role can do and what happens when a user tries an operation using the wrong role.

There's more...

What we did here is called **programmatic security,** that is, we defined the security rules and roles through our code (the program). There's another approach called **declarative security**, where you declare the rules and roles through application and server configurations.

One good step up for this recipe is to evolve the roles management to a source outside the application, such as a database or a service.

See also

- You can stay tuned with everything related to Jakarta Security at `https://github.com/javaee-security-spec`.
- The source code of this recipe is at `https://github.com/eldermoraes/javaee8-cookbook/tree/master/chapter01/ch01-security`.

Running your first MVC 1.0 code

If you have been following Jakarta EE 8 history for a while, you may now be wondering: *why is MVC 1.0 here if it was dropped from the Jakarta EE 8 umbrella?*

Yes, it is true. MVC 1.0 doesn't belong to the Jakarta EE 8 release. But that doesn't reduce the importance of this great API and I'm sure it will change the way some other APIs work in future releases (for example, JSF).

So, why not cover it here? You will use it anyway.

This recipe will show you how to use a **Controller** (the **C**) to inject a **Model** (the **M**) into the **View** (the **V**). It also brings some Jakarta CDI and JAX-RS to the party.

Getting ready

Add the proper dependencies to your project:

```
<dependencies>
    <dependency>
        <groupId>jakarta.platform</groupId>
        <artifactId>jakarta.jakartaee-api</artifactId>
        <version>8.0.0</version>
        <scope>provided</scope>
    </dependency>
    <dependency>
        <groupId>javax.mvc</groupId>
        <artifactId>javax.mvc-api</artifactId>
        <version>1.0 pr</version>
    </dependency>
</dependencies>
```

How to do it...

You need to perform the following steps to try this recipe:

1. Start by creating a root for your JAX-RS endpoints:

   ```
   @ApplicationPath("webresources")
   public class AppConfig extends Application{
   }
   ```

2. Create a `User` class (this will be your Model):

   ```
   public class User {

       private String name;
       private String email;

       public User(String name, String email) {
           this.name = name;
           this.email = email;
       }
   ```

```
        //DON'T FORGET THE GETTERS AND SETTERS
        //THIS RECIPE WON'T WORK WITHOUT THEM
    }
```

3. Now, create a session bean, which will be injected later in your Controller:

```
@Stateless
public class UserBean {
    public User getUser(){
        return new User("Elder", "elder@eldermoraes.com");
    }
}
```

4. Then, create the Controller:

```
@Controller
@Path("userController")
public class UserController {
    @Inject
    Models models;
    @Inject
    UserBean userBean;
    @GET
    public String user(){
        models.put("user", userBean.getUser());
        return "/user.jsp";
    }
}
```

5. And finally, create the web page (the View):

```
<head>
    <meta http-equiv="Content-Type" content="text/html;
    charset=UTF-8">
    <title>User MVC</title>
</head>
<body>
    <h1>${user.name}/${user.email}</h1>
</body>
```

6. Run it on a Jakarta EE 8 server and access this URL:

```
http://localhost:8080/ch01-mvc/webresources/userController
```

How it works...

The main actor in this whole scenario is the `Models` class injected into the Controller, shown as follows:

```
@Inject
Models models;
```

It's a class from MVC 1.0 API that has the responsibility, in this recipe, of letting the `User` object to be available for the View layer. It's injected (using CDI) and uses another injected bean, `userBean`, to do it:

```
models.put("user", userBean.getUser());
```

So, the View can easily access the values from the `User` object using expression language as follows:

```
<h1>${user.name}/${user.email}</h1>
```

See also

- You can stay tuned with everything related to the MVC specification at `https://github.com/mvc-spec`.
- The source code of this recipe is at `https://github.com/eldermoraes/javaee8-cookbook/tree/master/chapter01/ch01-mvc`.

2
Server-Side Development

Jakarta EE is typically used for **server-side development**. Most of its APIs are powerful and used for server-side processing and management.

This chapter will provide you with some common and useful scenarios that you may face as a Jakarta EE developer and will show you how to deal with them.

In this chapter, we will cover the following recipes:

- Using Jakarta CDI to inject context and dependencies
- Using Jakarta Bean Validation for data validation
- Using Jakarta Servlet for request and response management
- Using Server Push to make objects available beforehand
- Using EJB and JTA for transaction management
- Using EJB to deal with concurrency
- Using JPA for smart data persistence
- Using EJB and JPA for data caching
- Using Jakarta Batch processing

Let's get started!

Using Jakarta CDI to inject context and dependencies

Jakarta **Contexts and Dependency Injection** (CDI) is one of the most important APIs under the Jakarta EE umbrella. Introduced in Java EE 6, it now has a big influence over many other APIs.

In the recipe, you will learn how to use Jakarta CDI in a couple of different ways and situations.

Getting ready

First, let's add the required dependency:

```
<dependency>
 <groupId>javax</groupId>
 <artifactId>javaee-api</artifactId>
 <version>8.0</version>
 <scope>provided</scope>
</dependency>
```

How to do it...

You need to perform the following steps to complete this recipe:

1. We are going to build a JAX-RS-based application, so we will start by preparing the application:

```
@ApplicationPath("webresources")
public class Application extends javax.ws.rs.core.Application {
}
```

2. Then, we will create a User class as our main object:

```
public class User implements Serializable {

    private String name;
    private String email;

    //DO NOT FORGET TO ADD THE GETTERS AND SETTERS
}
```

3. Our User class doesn't have a default constructor, so Jakarta CDI doesn't know how to construct the class when it tries to inject it. Therefore, we need to create a factory class and use the @Produces annotation over its methods:

```
public class UserFactory implements Serializable{

    @Produces
    public User getUser() {
        return new User("Elder Moraes", "elder@eldermoraes.com");
    }

}
```

4. Let's create an enumeration so that we can list our profile types:

```
public enum ProfileType {
    ADMIN, OPERATOR;
}
```

5. Next, we will create a custom annotation:

```
@Qualifier
@Retention(RetentionPolicy.RUNTIME)
@Target({ElementType.TYPE, ElementType.FIELD, ElementType.METHOD,
ElementType.PARAMETER})
public @interface Profile {
    ProfileType value();
}
```

6. Add this to an interface in order to prototype the user profile behavior:

```
public interface UserProfile {
    ProfileType type();
}
```

7. Now that we have defined the profile list and its behavior with respect to the user, we can give it a proper implementation for an admin profile:

```
@Profile(ProfileType.ADMIN)
public class ImplAdmin implements UserProfile{

    @Override
    public ProfileType type() {
        System.out.println("User is admin");
        return ProfileType.ADMIN;
    }
}
```

8. The same can be done for an operator profile:

```
@Profile(ProfileType.OPERATOR)
@Default
public class ImplOperator implements UserProfile{

    @Override
    public ProfileType type() {
        System.out.println("User is operator");
        return ProfileType.OPERATOR;
    }
}
```

9. Then, we need to create a REST endpoint by injecting all the objects that we are going to use into it:

```
@Path("userservice/")
@RequestScoped
public class UserService {
    @Inject
    private User user;
    @Inject
    @Profile(ProfileType.ADMIN)
    private UserProfile userProfileAdmin;
    @Inject
    @Profile(ProfileType.OPERATOR)
    private UserProfile userProfileOperator;
    @Inject
    private UserProfile userProfileDefault;
    @Inject
    private Event<User> userEvent;


    ...
```

10. This method injects the user through Jakarta CDI and sends them to the result page:

```
@GET
@Path("getUser")
public Response getUser(@Context HttpServletRequest  request,
        @Context HttpServletResponse response)
        throws ServletException, IOException{
    request.setAttribute("result", user);
    request.getRequestDispatcher("/result.jsp")
    .forward(request, response);
    return Response.ok().build();
}
```

11. The following code does the same but with an admin profile:

```
@GET
@Path("getProfileAdmin")
public Response getProfileAdmin(@Context HttpServletRequest request,
        @Context HttpServletResponse response)
        throws ServletException, IOException{
    request.setAttribute("result",
    fireUserEvents(userProfileAdmin.type())));
    request.getRequestDispatcher("/result.jsp")
    .forward(request, response);
    return Response.ok().build();
}
```

12. The following code does the same but with an operator profile:

```
@GET
@Path("getProfileOperator")
public Response getProfileOperator(@Context HttpServletRequest request,
        @Context HttpServletResponse response)
        throws ServletException, IOException{
    request.setAttribute("result",
    fireUserEvents(userProfileOperator.type()));
    request.getRequestDispatcher("/result.jsp")
    .forward(request, response);
    return Response.ok().build();
}
```

13. Finally, we send the default profile to the result page:

```
@GET
@Path("getProfileDefault")
public Response getProfileDefault(@Context HttpServletRequest request,
        @Context HttpServletResponse response)
        throws ServletException, IOException{
    request.setAttribute("result",
     fireUserEvents(userProfileDefault.type()));
    request.getRequestDispatcher("/result.jsp")
     .forward(request, response);
    return Response.ok().build();
}
```

14. We use the `fireUserEvents` method to fire an event and async events over a previously injected `User` object:

```
private ProfileType fireUserEvents(ProfileType type){
    userEvent.fire(user);
    userEvent.fireAsync(user);
    return type;
}
public void sendUserNotification(@Observes User user){
    System.out.println("sendUserNotification: " + user);
}
public void sendUserNotificationAsync(@ObservesAsync User user){
    System.out.println("sendUserNotificationAsync: " + user);
}
```

15. Now, we need to build a page to call each endpoint method:

```
<body>
 <a href="http://localhost:8080/ch02-
 cdi/webresources/userservice/getUser">getUser</a>
```

```
<br>
<a href="http://localhost:8080/ch02-
cdi/webresources/userservice/getProfileAdmin">getProfileAdmin</a>
<br>
<a href="http://localhost:8080/ch02-
cdi/webresources/userservice/getProfileOperator">getProfileOperator
</a>
<br>
<a href="http://localhost:8080/ch02-
cdi/webresources/userservice/getProfileDefault">getProfileDefault</
a>
</body>
```

16. Finally, we use an expression language to print the result on the result page:

```
<body>
    <h1>${result}</h1>
    <a href="javascript:window.history.back();">Back</a>
</body>
```

How it works...

Well, there's a lot happening here! First, we should have a look at the @Produces annotation. This is a Jakarta CDI annotation that says to the server, *Hey! This method knows how to construct a User object.*

Since we didn't create a default constructor for the User class, the getUser method from our factory will be injected into our context as one.

The second annotation is our custom @Profile annotation, which has our ProfileType enumeration as a parameter. It is the qualifier for our UserProfile objects.

Now, let's have a look at these declarations:

```
@Profile(ProfileType.ADMIN)
public class ImplAdmin implements UserProfile{
    ...
}

@Profile(ProfileType.OPERATOR)
@Default
public class ImplOperator implements UserProfile{
    ...
}
```

This code will *teach* Jakarta CDI how to inject a UserProfile object:

- If the object is annotated as `@Profile(ProfileType.ADMIN)`, use `ImplAdmin`.
- If the object is annotated as `@Profile(ProfileType.OPERATOR)`, use `ImplOperator`.
- If the object is not annotated, use `ImplOperator`, as it has the `@Default` annotation.

We can see these in action in our endpoint declaration:

```
@Inject
@Profile(ProfileType.ADMIN)
private UserProfile userProfileAdmin;
@Inject
@Profile(ProfileType.OPERATOR)
private UserProfile userProfileOperator;
@Inject
private UserProfile userProfileDefault;
```

So, Jakarta CDI is helping us use the context to inject the right implementation of the `UserProfile` interface.

By taking a look at the endpoint methods, we will see the following:

```
@GET
@Path("getUser")
public Response getUser(@Context HttpServletRequest request,
        @Context HttpServletResponse response)
        throws ServletException, IOException{
    request.setAttribute("result", user);
    request.getRequestDispatcher("/result.jsp")
    .forward(request, response);
    return Response.ok().build();
}
```

Note that we included `HttpServletRequest` and `HttpServletResponse` as parameters for our method, but annotated them as `@Context`. So, even though this is not a servlet context (when we have easy access to request and response references), we can ask Jakarta CDI to give us a proper reference to them.

Finally, we have our user event engine, as follows:

```
@Inject
private Event<User> userEvent;

    ...

private ProfileType fireUserEvents(ProfileType type){
    userEvent.fire(user);
    userEvent.fireAsync(user);
    return type;
}
public void sendUserNotification(@Observes User user){
    System.out.println("sendUserNotification: " + user);
}
public void sendUserNotificationAsync(@ObservesAsync User user){
    System.out.println("sendUserNotificationAsync: " + user);
}
```

So, we are using the `@Observes` and `@ObserversAsync` annotations to say to Jakarta CDI, *Hey CDI! Watch over the User object... when somebody fires an event over it, I want you to do something.*

And for *something*, Jakarta CDI understands this as calling the `sendUserNotification` and `sendUserNotificationAsync` methods. Try it for yourself!

Obviously, `@Observers` will be executed synchronously, while `@ObservesAsync` will be executed asynchronously.

There's more...

We used Eclipse GlassFish to run this recipe. You can do this with whatever Jakarta EE 8-compatible server you want, and you can even use Jakarta CDI with Java SE without any server. Take a look at the *Running your first Jakarta CDI 2.0 code* recipe from `Chapter 1`, *New Features and Improvements*, for more information.

See also

You can view the full source code for this recipe at `https://github.com/eldermoraes/javaee8-cookbook/tree/master/chapter02/ch02-cdi`.

Using Jakarta Bean Validation for data validation

You can use Bean Validation to constrain your data in many different ways. In this recipe, we are going to use it to validate a JSF form so that we can validate it as soon as the user tries to submit it and avoid any invalid data right away.

Getting ready

First, we need to add our dependencies:

```
<dependency>
    <groupId>javax</groupId>
    <artifactId>javaee-api</artifactId>
    <version>8.0</version>
    <scope>provided</scope>
</dependency>
```

How to do it...

You need to perform the following steps to complete this recipe:

1. Let's create a User object that will be attached to our JSF page:

```
@Named
@RequestScoped
public class User {
    @NotBlank (message = "Name should not be blank")
    @Size (min = 4, max = 10, message = "Name should be between
    4 and 10 characters")
    private String name;
    @Email (message = "Invalid e-mail format")
    @NotBlank (message = "E-mail should not be blank")
    private String email;
    @PastOrPresent (message = "Created date should be
    past or present")
    @NotNull (message = "Create date should not be null")
    private LocalDate created;
    @Future (message = "Expires should be a future date")
    @NotNull (message = "Expires should not be null")
    private LocalDate expires;
```

```
//DO NOT FORGET TO IMPLEMENT THE GETTERS AND SETTERS

...
```

2. Now, we need to define the method that will be fired once all the data is valid:

```
public void valid(){
    FacesContext
            .getCurrentInstance()
            .addMessage(
                null,
                new FacesMessage(FacesMessage.SEVERITY_INFO,
                "Your data is valid", ""));
}
```

3. Now, our JSF page references each `User` class field that's been declared, as follows:

```
<h:body>
 <h:form>
 <h:outputLabel for="name" value="Name" />
 <h:inputText id="name" value="#{user.name}" />
 <br/>
 <h:outputLabel for="email" value="E-mail" />
 <h:inputText id="email" value="#{user.email}" />
 <br/>
 <h:outputLabel for="created" value="Created" />
 <h:inputText id="created" value="#{user.created}">
     <f:convertDateTime type="localDate" pattern="dd/MM/uuuu" />
 </h:inputText>
 <br/>
 <h:outputLabel for="expire" value="Expire" />
 <h:inputText id="expire" value="#{user.expires}">
     <f:convertDateTime type="localDate" pattern="dd/MM/uuuu" />
 </h:inputText>
 <br/>
 <h:commandButton value="submit" type="submit"
 action="#{user.valid()}" />
 </h:form>
</h:body>
```

If you run this code, all the fields will be validated once you click the **Submit** button. Try it for yourself!

How it works...

Let's check each declared constraint:

```
@NotBlank (message = "Name should not be blank")
@Size (min = 4, max = 10,message = "Name should be between
        4 and 10 characters")
private String name;
```

The `@NotBlank` annotation will deny not only null values, but also whitespace values, and `@Size` speaks for itself:

```
@Email (message = "Invalid e-mail format")
@NotBlank (message = "E-mail shoud not be blank")
private String email;
```

The `@Email` constraint will check the email string format:

```
@PastOrPresent (message = "Created date should be past or present")
@NotNull (message = "Create date should not be null")
private LocalDate created;
```

`@PastOrPresent` will constrain `LocalDate` to be in the past or until the present date. It can't be in the future.

Here, we can't use `@NotBlank` as there is no blank date, only null, so we avoid this by using `@NotNull`:

```
@Future (message = "Expires should be a future date")
@NotNull (message = "Expires should not be null")
private LocalDate expires;
```

This is the same as the preceding constraint, but constraints for a future date.

In our UI, there are two places we should take a careful look at:

```
<h:inputText id="created" value="#{user.created}">
    <f:convertDateTime type="localDate" pattern="dd/MM/uuuu" />
</h:inputText>

. . .

<h:inputText id="expire" value="#{user.expires}">
    <f:convertDateTime type="localDate" pattern="dd/MM/uuuu" />
</h:inputText>
```

Here, we are using `convertDateTime` to automatically convert the data that's inputted into `inputText` according to the `dd/MM/uuuu` pattern.

See also

You can view the full source code for this recipe at `https://github.com/eldermoraes/javaee8-cookbook/tree/master/chapter02/ch02-beanvalidation`.

Using Jakarta Servlet for request and response management

Jakarta Servlet was created even before Jakarta EE existed – actually, before J2EE existed! It became part of EE in J2EE 1.2 (Servlet 2.2) in 1999.

This is a powerful tool that's used to deal with request/response contexts. This recipe will show you an example of how to do this.

Getting ready

Let's add our dependencies:

```
<dependency>
    <groupId>javax</groupId>
    <artifactId>javaee-api</artifactId>
    <version>8.0</version>
    <scope>provided</scope>
</dependency>
```

How to do it...

You need to perform the following steps to complete this recipe:

1. Let's create a `User` class for our recipe:

```
public class User {

    private String name;
    private String email;
```

```
//DO NOT FORGET TO IMPLEMENT THE GETTERS AND SETTERS

}
```

2. Now, let's add our servlet:

```
@WebServlet(name = "UserServlet", urlPatterns = {"/UserServlet"})
public class UserServlet extends HttpServlet {
    private User user;
    @PostConstruct
    public void instantiateUser(){
        user = new User("Elder Moraes", "elder@eldermoraes.com");
    }

    . . .
```

 We used the `@PostConstruct` annotation over the `instantiateUser()` method here. It says to the server that whenever this servlet is constructed (a new instance is up and running), it can run this method.

3. We also need to implement the `init()` and `destroy()` super methods:

```
@Override
public void init() throws ServletException {
    System.out.println("Servlet " + this.getServletName() +
                    " has started");
}

@Override
public void destroy() {
    System.out.println("Servlet " + this.getServletName() +
                    " has destroyed");
}
```

4. We also need to implement `doGet()` and `doPost()`:

```
@Override
protected void doGet(HttpServletRequest request,
HttpServletResponse response)
        throws ServletException, IOException {
    doRequest(request, response);
}

@Override
protected void doPost(HttpServletRequest request,
HttpServletResponse response)
        throws ServletException, IOException {
```

```
        doRequest(request, response);
    }
```

5. Both `doGet()` and `doPost()` will call our custom method, that is, `doRequest()`:

```
protected void doRequest(HttpServletRequest request,
HttpServletResponse response)
        throws ServletException, IOException {
    response.setContentType("text/html;charset=UTF-8");
    try (PrintWriter out = response.getWriter()) {
        out.println("<html>");
        out.println("<head>");
        out.println("<title>Servlet UserServlet</title>");
        out.println("</head>");
        out.println("<body>");
        out.println("<h2>Servlet UserServlet at " +
                    request.getContextPath() + "</h2>");
        out.println("<h2>Now: " + new Date() + "</h2>");
        out.println("<h2>User: " + user.getName() + "/" +
                    user.getEmail() + "</h2>");
        out.println("</body>");
        out.println("</html>");
    }
}
```

6. Finally, we have a web page so that we can call our servlet:

```
<body>
    <a href="<%=request.getContextPath()%>/UserServlet">
    <%=request.getContextPath() %>/UserServlet</a>
</body>
```

How it works...

The Jakarta EE server itself will call the `doGet()` or `doPost()` methods, depending on the HTTP method used by the caller. In our recipe, we are redirecting them both to the same `doRequest()` method.

The `init()` method belongs to the servlet life cycle that's managed by the server and is executed as a first method after the servlet's instantiation.

The `destroy()` method also belongs to the servlet life cycle and is executed as the last method before the instance's deallocation.

There's more...

The `init()` behavior seems similar to `@PostConstruct`, but this last one is executed before `init()`, so keep this in mind when using both.

`@PostConstruct` is executed right after the default constructor.

Be careful when using the `destroy()` method and avoid holding a memory reference; otherwise, you can mess up the servlet life cycle and run into memory leaks.

See also

You can view the full source code for this recipe at `https://github.com/eldermoraes/javaee8-cookbook/tree/master/chapter02/ch02-servlet`.

Using Server Push to make objects available beforehand

One of the most important new features of Jakarta Servlet 4 is its HTTP/2.0 support. It brings another cool and reliable feature – Server Push.

This recipe will show you how to use Server Push in a filter and push the resources needed in every request that we want.

Getting ready

First, we need to add the required dependencies:

```xml
<dependency>
    <groupId>javax</groupId>
    <artifactId>javaee-api</artifactId>
    <version>8.0</version>
    <scope>provided</scope>
</dependency>
```

How to do it...

To complete this recipe, please perform the following steps:

1. First, we need to create `UserServlet`, which will call `user.jsp`:

```
@WebServlet(name = "UserServlet", urlPatterns = {"/UserServlet"})
public class UserServlet extends HttpServlet {

    protected void doRequest(HttpServletRequest request,
                             HttpServletResponse response)
        throws ServletException, IOException {
      request.getRequestDispatcher("/user.jsp").forward(request,
response);
        System.out.println("Redirected to user.jsp");
    }

    @Override
    protected void doGet(HttpServletRequest request,
                         HttpServletResponse response)
        throws ServletException, IOException {
      doRequest(request, response);
    }

    @Override
    protected void doPost(HttpServletRequest request,
                          HttpServletResponse response)
        throws ServletException, IOException {
      doRequest(request, response);
    }
}
```

2. We need to do the same with `ProfileServlet`, but call `profile.jsp`:

```
@WebServlet(name = "ProfileServlet", urlPatterns =
{"/ProfileServlet"})
public class ProfileServlet extends HttpServlet {

    protected void doRequest(HttpServletRequest request,
                             HttpServletResponse response)
        throws ServletException, IOException {
      request.getRequestDispatcher("/profile.jsp").
      forward(request, response);
      System.out.println("Redirected to profile.jsp");
    }

    @Override
    protected void doGet(HttpServletRequest request,
```

```
                            HttpServletResponse response)
            throws ServletException, IOException {
        doRequest(request, response);
    }

    @Override
    protected void doPost(HttpServletRequest request,
                            HttpServletResponse response)
            throws ServletException, IOException {
        doRequest(request, response);
    }
}
```

3. Now, we need to create a filter that will be executed on every request (`urlPatterns = {"/*"}`):

```
@WebFilter(filterName = "PushFilter", urlPatterns = {"/*"})
public class PushFilter implements Filter {
    @Override
    public void doFilter(ServletRequest request,
    ServletResponse response,
            FilterChain chain)
            throws IOException, ServletException {
        HttpServletRequest httpReq = (HttpServletRequest)request;
        PushBuilder builder = httpReq.newPushBuilder();
        if (builder != null){
            builder
                .path("resources/javaee-logo.png")
                .path("resources/style.css")
                .path("resources/functions.js")
                .push();
            System.out.println("Resources pushed");
        }

        chain.doFilter(request, response);
    }
}
```

4. Next, we need to create a page so that we can call our servlets:

```
<body>
 <a href="UserServlet">User</a>
 <br/>
 <a href="ProfileServlet">Profile</a>
</body>
```

5. Here are the pages that will be called by the servlets. First, there's the `user.jsp` page:

```html
<head>
    <meta http-equiv="Content-Type" content="text/html;
     charset=UTF-8">
    <link rel="stylesheet" type="text/css"
     href="resources/style.css">
    <script src="resources/functions.js"></script>
    <title>User Push</title>
</head>

<body>
    <h1>User styled</h1>
    <img src="resources/javaee-logo.png">
    <br />
    <button onclick="message()">Message</button>
    <br />
    <a href="javascript:window.history.back();">Back</a>
</body>
```

6. Second, the `profile.jsp` page is called:

```html
<head>
    <meta http-equiv="Content-Type" content="text/html; charset=UTF-8">
    <link rel="stylesheet" type="text/css" href="resources/style.css">
    <script src="resources/functions.js"></script>
    <title>User Push</title>
</head>

<body>
    <h1>Profile styled</h1>
    <img src="resources/javaee-logo.png">
    <br />
    <button onclick="message()">Message</button>
    <br />
    <a href="javascript:window.history.back();">Back</a>
</body>
```

When you run the preceding code, make sure to use the HTTPS port as it only works under this protocol; for example, `https://localhost:4848/ch02-serverpush-1.0`.

How it works...

A web application running under HTTP/1.0 sends a request to the server when it finds references for an image file, CSS file, and any other resources needed to render a web page.

With HTTP/2.0, you still can do this, but now, you can do this a lot better – the server can now push the resources beforehand, avoiding unnecessary new requests, decreasing the server load, and improving performance.

In this recipe, our resources are represented by the following code:

```
meta http-equiv="Content-Type" content="text/html; charset=UTF-8">
link rel="stylesheet" type="text/css" href="resources/style.css">
script src="resources/functions.js"></script>
```

The push happens at this part of our filter:

```
HttpServletRequest httpReq = (HttpServletRequest)request;
PushBuilder builder = httpReq.newPushBuilder();
if (builder != null){
        builder
            .path("resources/javaee-logo.png")
            .path("resources/style.css")
            .path("resources/functions.js")
            .push();
        System.out.println("Resources pushed");
    }
```

So, when the browser needs those resources to render the web page, they are already available.

There's more...

Note that your browser needs to support the Server Push feature; otherwise, your page will work as usual. So, make sure you check that `PushBuilder` is null before using it and ensure all users will have the working application.

JSF 2.3 is built on top of the Server Push feature, so if you just migrate your JSF application to a Jakarta EE 8-compatible server, you get its performance boost for free!

Finally, Server Push only works under a **Secure Sockets Layer** (**SSL**) protocol, so pay attention to it.

See also

You can view the full source code for this recipe at `https://github.com/eldermoraes/` `javaee8-cookbook/tree/master/chapter02/ch02-serverpush`.

Using EJB and JTA for transaction management

Jakarta Transaction (formerly **JTA**) is an API that enables distributed transactions over the Jakarta EE environment. It is most powerful when you delegate transaction management to the server.

This recipe will show you how to do this!

Getting ready

First, add the required dependencies:

```xml
<dependency>
    <groupId>org.hibernate</groupId>
    <artifactId>hibernate-entitymanager</artifactId>
    <version>4.3.1.Final</version>
</dependency>
<dependency>
    <groupId>junit</groupId>
    <artifactId>junit</artifactId>
    <version>4.12</version>
    <scope>test</scope>
</dependency>
<dependency>
    <groupId>org.hamcrest</groupId>
    <artifactId>hamcrest-core</artifactId>
    <version>1.3</version>
    <scope>test</scope>
</dependency>
<dependency>
    <groupId>javax</groupId>
    <artifactId>javaee-api</artifactId>
    <version>8.0</version>
    <scope>provided</scope>
</dependency>
<dependency>
```

```
        <groupId>org.apache.openejb</groupId>
        <artifactId>openejb-core</artifactId>
        <version>4.7.4</version>
        <scope>test</scope>
    </dependency>
```

How to do it...

You need to perform the following steps to complete this recipe:

1. First, we need to create our persistence unit (at `persistence.xml`):

```
<persistence-unit name="ch02-jta-pu" transaction-type="JTA">
    <provider>org.hibernate.ejb.HibernatePersistence</provider>
    <jta-data-source>userDb</jta-data-source>
    <non-jta-data-source>userDbNonJta</non-jta-data-source>
    <exclude-unlisted-classes>false</exclude-unlisted-classes>

    <properties>
        <property name="javax.persistence.schema-
          generation.database.action"
          value="create"/>
    </properties>
</persistence-unit>
```

2. Then, we need to create a `User` class as an entity (`@Entity`):

```
@Entity
public class User implements Serializable {

    private static final long serialVersionUID = 1L;

    @Id
    @GeneratedValue(strategy = GenerationType.AUTO)
    private Long id;
    private String name;
    private String email;

    protected User() {
    }
    public User(Long id, String name, String email) {
        this.id = id;
        this.name = name;
        this.email = email;
    }
```

```
                //DO NOT FORGET TO IMPLEMENT THE GETTERS AND SETTERS
    }
```

3. We also need a Jakarta **Enterprise Bean** (formerly **EJB**) to perform the operations over the User entity:

```
@Stateful
public class UserBean {

    @PersistenceContext(unitName = "ch02-jta-pu",
    type = PersistenceContextType.EXTENDED)
    private EntityManager em;
    public void add(User user){
        em.persist(user);
    }
    public void update(User user){
        em.merge(user);
    }
    public void remove(User user){
        em.remove(user);
    }
    public User findById(Long id){
        return em.find(User.class, id);
    }
}
```

4. Then, we need to create our unit test:

```
public class Ch02JtaTest {
    private EJBContainer ejbContainer;
    @EJB
    private UserBean userBean;
    public Ch02JtaTest() {
    }
    @Before
    public void setUp() throws NamingException {
        Properties p = new Properties();
        p.put("userDb", "new://Resource?type=DataSource");
        p.put("userDb.JdbcDriver", "org.hsqldb.jdbcDriver");
        p.put("userDb.JdbcUrl", "jdbc:hsqldb:mem:userdatabase");

        ejbContainer = EJBContainer.createEJBContainer(p);
        ejbContainer.getContext().bind("inject", this);
    }
    @After
    public void tearDown() {
        ejbContainer.close();
    }
```

```
@Test
public void validTransaction() throws Exception{
    User user = new User(null, "Elder Moraes",
                         "elder@eldermoraes.com");
    userBean.add(user);
    user.setName("John Doe");
    userBean.update(user);
    User userDb = userBean.findById(1L);
    assertEquals(userDb.getName(), "John Doe");
    }
}
```

How it works...

The key code line in this recipe for JTA is as follows:

```
<persistence-unit name="ch02-jta-pu" transaction-type="JTA">
```

When you use `transaction-type='JTA'`, you are saying to the server that it should take care of all transactions made under this context. If you use RESOURCE-LOCAL instead, you are saying that you are taking care of the transactions:

```
@Test
public void validTransaction() throws Exception{
    User user = new User(null, "Elder Moraes",
    "elder@eldermoraes.com");
    userBean.add(user);
    user.setName("John Doe");
    userBean.update(user);
    User userDb = userBean.findById(1L);
    assertEquals(userDb.getName(), "John Doe");
}
```

Each called method of `UserBean` starts a transaction to be completed and will run into a rollback if there's an issue while the transaction is alive. This would be committed to the end of it.

There's more...

Another important piece of code is the following one:

```
@Stateful
public class UserBean {
```

```
        @PersistenceContext(unitName = "ch02-jta-pu",
                            type = PersistenceContextType.EXTENDED)
        private EntityManager em;


        ...

    }
```

Here, we are defining `PersistenceContext` as `EXTENDED`. This means that this persistence context is bound to the `@Stateful` bean until it is removed from the container.

The other option is `TRANSACTION`, which means the persistence context will only live for the duration of the transaction.

See also

You can view the full source code for this recipe at `https://github.com/eldermoraes/javaee8-cookbook/tree/master/chapter02/ch02-jta`.

Using EJB to deal with concurrency

Concurrency management is one of the biggest advantages supplied by a Jakarta EE server. You can rely on a ready environment to deal with this tricky topic.

This recipe will show you how to set up your own **Jakarta Enterprise Beans** (formerly **EJBs**) to use it!

Getting ready

To get ready, you simply need to add a Jakarta EE dependency to your project:

```
<dependency>
    <groupId>javax</groupId>
    <artifactId>javaee-api</artifactId>
    <version>8.0</version>
    <scope>provided</scope>
</dependency>
```

How to do it...

This recipe will take you through three scenarios. Let's get started:

1. In the first scenario, `LockType` is defined at the class level:

```
@Singleton
@ConcurrencyManagement(ConcurrencyManagementType.CONTAINER)
@Lock(LockType.READ)
@AccessTimeout(value = 10000)
public class UserClassLevelBean {

    private int userCount;

    public int getUserCount() {
        return userCount;
    }
    public void addUser(){
        userCount++;
    }

}
```

2. In the second scenario, `LockType` is defined at the method level:

```
@Singleton
@ConcurrencyManagement(ConcurrencyManagementType.CONTAINER)
@AccessTimeout(value = 10000)
public class UserMethodLevelBean {

    private int userCount;
    @Lock(LockType.READ)
    public int getUserCount(){
        return userCount;
    }
    @Lock(LockType.WRITE)
    public void addUser(){
        userCount++;
    }
}
```

3. The third scenario is a self-managed bean:

```
@Singleton
@ConcurrencyManagement(ConcurrencyManagementType.BEAN)
public class UserSelfManagedBean {

    private int userCount;
```

```
        public int getUserCount() {
            return userCount;
        }
        public synchronized void addUser(){
            userCount++;
        }
    }
```

Now, let's see how this recipe works.

How it works...

The first thing to have a look at is the following:

```
@ConcurrencyManagement(ConcurrencyManagementType.CONTAINER)
```

This is completely redundant! Singleton beans are container-managed by default, so you don't need to specify them.

Singletons are designed for concurrent access, so they are the perfect use case for this recipe.

Now, let's check the LockType defined at the class level:

```
@Lock(LockType.READ)
@AccessTimeout(value = 10000)
public class UserClassLevelBean {
    ...
}
```

When we use the @Lock annotation at the class level, the informed LockType will be used for all class methods.

In this case, LockType.READ means that many clients can access a resource at the same time. This is usually used for reading data.

In the case of some kind of locking, LockType will use the @AccessTimeout annotation time defined to run into a timeout or not.

Now, let's check the LockType defined at the method level:

```
@Lock(LockType.READ)
public int getUserCount(){
    return userCount;
}
@Lock(LockType.WRITE)
```

```
public void addUser(){
    userCount++;
}
```

Here, we are basically saying that `getUserCount()` can be accessed by many users at once (`LockType.READ`), but `addUser()` will be accessed just by one user at a time (`LockType.WRITE`).

The last case is the self-managed bean:

```
@ConcurrencyManagement(ConcurrencyManagementType.BEAN)
public class UserSelfManagedBean{

    ...

    public synchronized void addUser(){
        userCount++;
    }

    ...

}
```

In this case, you have to manage all the concurrency issues for your bean in your code. We used the *synchronized* qualifier as an example.

There's more...

Unless you really *really* need to, don't use self-managed beans. The Jakarta EE container has been (well) designed to do this in a very efficient and elegant way.

See also

You can view the full source code for this recipe at `https://github.com/eldermoraes/javaee8-cookbook/tree/master/chapter02/ch02-ejb-concurrency`.

Using JPA for smart data persistence

Jakarta Persistence (formerly **JPA**) is a specification that describes an interface for managing relational databases using Jakarta EE.

It eases data manipulation and reduces a lot of the code written for it, especially if you are used to the SQL **American National Standards Institute** (**ANSI**).

This recipe will show you how to use it to persist your data.

Getting ready

First, let's add the required dependencies:

```xml
<dependency>
    <groupId>org.hibernate</groupId>
    <artifactId>hibernate-entitymanager</artifactId>
    <version>4.3.1.Final</version>
</dependency>
<dependency>
    <groupId>junit</groupId>
    <artifactId>junit</artifactId>
    <version>4.12</version>
    <scope>test</scope>
</dependency>
<dependency>
    <groupId>org.hamcrest</groupId>
    <artifactId>hamcrest-core</artifactId>
    <version>1.3</version>
    <scope>test</scope>
</dependency>
<dependency>
    <groupId>javax</groupId>
    <artifactId>javaee-api</artifactId>
    <version>8.0</version>
    <scope>provided</scope>
</dependency>
<dependency>
    <groupId>org.apache.openejb</groupId>
    <artifactId>openejb-core</artifactId>
    <version>4.7.4</version>
    <scope>test</scope>
</dependency>
```

How to do it...

To complete this recipe, we need to perform the following steps:

1. Let's begin by creating an entity (you can view it as a table):

```
@Entity
public class User implements Serializable {

    private static final long serialVersionUID = 1L;

    @Id
    @GeneratedValue(strategy = GenerationType.AUTO)
    private Long id;
    private String name;
    private String email;

    protected User() {
    }
    public User(Long id, String name, String email) {
        this.id = id;
        this.name = name;
        this.email = email;
    }

    //DO NOT FORGET TO IMPLEMENT THE GETTERS AND SETTERS
}
```

2. Here, we will declare our persistence unit (at `persistence.xml`):

```
<persistence-unit name="ch02-jpa-pu" transaction-type="JTA">
    <provider>org.hibernate.ejb.HibernatePersistence</provider>
    <jta-data-source>userDb</jta-data-source>
    <exclude-unlisted-classes>false</exclude-unlisted-classes>

    <properties>
        <property name="javax.persistence.schema-
          generation.database.action"
          value="create"/>
    </properties>
</persistence-unit>
```

3. Now, we need to create a session bean to manage our data:

```
@Stateless
public class UserBean {

    @PersistenceContext(unitName = "ch02-jpa-pu",
```

```
        type = PersistenceContextType.TRANSACTION)
    private EntityManager em;
    public void add(User user){
        em.persist(user);
    }
    public void update(User user){
        em.merge(user);
    }
    public void remove(User user){
        em.remove(user);
    }
    public User findById(Long id){
        return em.find(User.class, id);
    }
}
```

4. Here, we're using a unit test to try it out:

```
public class Ch02JpaTest {
    private EJBContainer ejbContainer;
    @EJB
    private UserBean userBean;
    public Ch02JpaTest() {
    }
    @Before
    public void setUp() throws NamingException {
        Properties p = new Properties();
        p.put("userDb", "new://Resource?type=DataSource");
        p.put("userDb.JdbcDriver", "org.hsqldb.jdbcDriver");
        p.put("userDb.JdbcUrl", "jdbc:hsqldb:mem:userdatabase");

        ejbContainer = EJBContainer.createEJBContainer(p);
        ejbContainer.getContext().bind("inject", this);
    }
    @After
    public void tearDown() {
        ejbContainer.close();
    }
    @Test
    public void persistData() throws Exception{
        User user = new User(null, "Elder Moraes",
        "elder@eldermoraes.com");
        userBean.add(user);
        user.setName("John Doe");
        userBean.update(user);
        User userDb = userBean.findById(1L);
        assertEquals(userDb.getName(), "John Doe");
```

```
        }
    }
```

Now, let's see how this recipe works.

How it works...

Let's break down our **Persistence Unit (PU)**.

The following line defines the pu name and the transaction type used:

```
<persistence-unit name="ch02-jpa-pu" transaction-type="JTA">
```

The following line shows the provider the JPA implementation used:

```
<provider>org.hibernate.ejb.HibernatePersistence</provider>
```

This is the data source name that will be accessed through the **Java Naming and Directory Interface (JNDI)**:

```
<jta-data-source>userDb</jta-data-source>
```

The following line lets all your entities be available for this pu, so you don't need to declare each one:

```
<exclude-unlisted-classes>false</exclude-unlisted-classes>
```

The following code allows the database objects to be created if they don't exist:

```
<properties>
<property name="javax.persistence.schema-
generation.database.action"
            value="create"/>
</properties>
```

Now, let's have a look at UserBean:

```
@Stateless
public class UserBean {

    @PersistenceContext(unitName = "ch02-jpa-pu",
                        type = PersistenceContextType.TRANSACTION)
    private EntityManager em;

    ...

}
```

`EntityManager` is the object responsible for the interface between the bean and the data source. It's bound to the context by the `PersistenceContext` annotation.

Let's check the `EntityManager` operations, as follows:

```
public void add(User user){
em.persist(user);
}
```

The `persist()` method is used to add new data to the data source. At the end of its execution, the object is attached to the context:

```
public void update(User user){
em.merge(user);
}
```

The `merge()` method is used to update existing data on the data source. The object is first found at the context, then updated at the database and attached to the context with the new state:

```
public void remove(User user){
em.remove(user);
}
```

Now, let's look at the `remove()` method – guess what it is:

```
public User findById(Long id){
return em.find(User.class, id);
}
```

Finally, the `find()` method uses the `id` parameter to search for a database object with the same ID. That's why JPA demands that your entities have an ID declared with the `@Id` annotation.

See also

You can view the full source code for this recipe at `https://github.com/eldermoraes/javaee8-cookbook/tree/master/chapter02/ch02-jpa`.

Using EJB and JPA for data caching

Knowing how to build a simple and local cache for your application is an important skill. It may have a big impact on some data access performance and is quite easy to do.

This recipe will show you how to do this.

Getting ready

Simply add a Jakarta EE dependency to your project:

```
<dependency>
    <groupId>javax</groupId>
    <artifactId>javaee-api</artifactId>
    <version>8.0</version>
    <scope>provided</scope>
</dependency>
```

How to do it...

You need to perform the following steps to complete this recipe:

1. Let's create a `User` class. This will be our cached object:

```
public class User {
    private String name;
    private String email;
    //DO NOT FORGET TO IMPLEMENT THE GETTERS AND SETTERS
}
```

2. Next, create a singleton that will hold our user list cache:

```
@Singleton
@Startup
public class UserCacheBean {

    protected Queue<User> cache = null;
    @PersistenceContext
    private EntityManager em;

    public UserCacheBean() {
    }

    protected void loadCache() {
        List<User> list = em.createQuery("SELECT u FROM USER
                                    as u").getResultList();

        list.forEach((user) -> {
            cache.add(user);
        });
```

```
        }

        @Lock(LockType.READ)
        public List<User> get() {
            return cache.stream().collect(Collectors.toList());
        }

        @PostConstruct
        protected void init() {
            cache = new ConcurrentLinkedQueue<>();
            loadCache();
        }
    }
```

Now, let's see how this recipe works.

How it works...

First, let's understand our bean declaration:

```
@Singleton
@Startup
public class UserCacheBean {

    ...

    @PostConstruct
    protected void init() {
        cache = new ConcurrentLinkedQueue<>();
        loadCache();
    }
}
```

We are using a `Singleton` because it has one and only one instance in the application context. This is the way we want a data cache to be – we don't want different data being shared.

Also, note that we used the `@Startup` annotation. This tells the server that this bean should be *executed* once it is loaded and that the method annotated with `@PostConstruct` is used for it.

So, we use the startup time to load our cache:

```
protected void loadCache() {
    List<User> list = em.createQuery("SELECT u FROM USER
                                      as u").getResultList();
```

```
    list.forEach((user) -> {
            cache.add(user);
    });
}
```

Now, let's check the object holding our cache:

```
protected Queue<User> cache = null;

...

cache = new ConcurrentLinkedQueue<>();
```

`ConcurrentLinkedQueue` is a list that's built with one main purpose – to be accessed by multiple processes in a thread-safe environment. That's exactly what we need. This also offers great performance when we need to access its members.

Finally, let's check the access to our data cache:

```
Lock(LockType.READ)
public List<User> get() {
return cache.stream().collect(Collectors.toList());
}
```

We annotated the `get()` method with `LockType.READ`, which is telling the concurrency manager that it can be accessed by multiple processes at once in a thread-safe way.

There's more...

If you need big and complex caches in your application, you should use some enterprise cache solutions for better results.

See also

You can view the full source code for this recipe at `https://github.com/eldermoraes/javaee8-cookbook/tree/master/chapter02/ch02-datacache`.

Using Jakarta Batch processing

Running background tasks is a useful and important skill in an enterprise context.

You could use it to process data in bulk or just to separate it from the UI processes. This recipe will show you how to do this.

Getting ready

Let's add our dependencies:

```xml
<dependencies>
    <dependency>
        <groupId>org.hibernate</groupId>
        <artifactId>hibernate-entitymanager</artifactId>
        <version>5.2.10.Final</version>
        <scope>runtime</scope>
    </dependency>
    <dependency>
        <groupId>javax</groupId>
        <artifactId>javaee-api</artifactId>
        <version>8.0</version>
        <scope>provided</scope>
    </dependency>
</dependencies>
```

How to do it...

Perform the following steps to complete this recipe:

1. First, we need to define our persistence unit:

```xml
<persistence-unit name="ch02-batch-pu" >
  <provider>org.hibernate.jpa.HibernatePersistenceProvider</provider>
  <jta-data-source>java:app/userDb</jta-data-source>
  <exclude-unlisted-classes>false</exclude-unlisted-classes>
  <properties>
    <property name="javax.persistence.schema-
    generation.database.action"
    value="create"/>
    <property name="hibernate.transaction.jta.platform"
    value="org.hibernate.service.jta.platform
    .internal.SunOneJtaPlatform"/>
  </properties>
</persistence-unit>
```

2. Then, we need to declare a `User` entity:

```
@Entity
@Table(name = "UserTab")
public class User implements Serializable {

    private static final long serialVersionUID = 1L;

    @Id
    @NotNull
    private Integer id;

    private String name;

    private String email;

    public User() {
    }

    //DO NOT FORGET TO IMPLEMENT THE GETTERS AND SETTERS
}
```

3. Here, we're creating a job reader:

```
@Named
@Dependent
public class UserReader extends AbstractItemReader {

    private BufferedReader br;

    @Override
    public void open(Serializable checkpoint) throws Exception {
        br = new BufferedReader(
                new InputStreamReader(
                        Thread.currentThread()
                        .getContextClassLoader()
                        .getResourceAsStream
                        ("META-INF/user.txt")));
    }

    @Override
    public String readItem() {
        String line = null;

        try {
            line = br.readLine();
        } catch (IOException ex) {
            System.out.println(ex.getMessage());
```

```
            }

            return line;
        }
    }
```

4. Then, we need to create a job processor:

```
@Named
@Dependent
public class UserProcessor implements ItemProcessor {

    @Override
    public User processItem(Object line) {
        User user = new User();

        StringTokenizer tokens = new StringTokenizer((String)
        line, ",");
        user.setId(Integer.parseInt(tokens.nextToken()));
        user.setName(tokens.nextToken());
        user.setEmail(tokens.nextToken());
        return user;
    }
}
```

5. Here, we're creating a job writer:

```
@Named
@Dependent
public class UserWriter extends AbstractItemWriter {

    @PersistenceContext
    EntityManager entityManager;

    @Override
    @Transactional
    public void writeItems(List list) {
        for (User user : (List<User>) list) {
            entityManager.persist(user);
        }
    }
}
```

6. The processor, reader, and writer are referenced by the `acess-user.xml` file, which is located at `META-INF.batch-jobs`:

```xml
<?xml version="1.0" encoding="windows-1252"?>
<job id="userAccess"
     xmlns="http://xmlns.jcp.org/xml/ns/javaee"
     version="1.0">
    <step id="loadData">
        <chunk item-count="3">
            <reader ref="userReader"/>
            <processor ref="userProcessor"/>
            <writer ref="userWriter"/>
        </chunk>
    </step>
</job>
```

7. And finally, we create a bean to interact with the batch engine:

```java
@Named
@RequestScoped
public class UserBean {

    @PersistenceContext
    EntityManager entityManager;

    public void run() {
        try {
            JobOperator job = BatchRuntime.getJobOperator();
            long jobId = job.start("acess-user", new Properties());
            System.out.println("Job started: " + jobId);
        } catch (JobStartException ex) {
            System.out.println(ex.getMessage());
        }
    }

    public List<User> get() {
        return entityManager
                .createQuery("SELECT u FROM User as u", User.class)
                .getResultList();
    }
}
```

8. For the purpose of this example, we are going to use a JSF page to run the job and load the data:

```html
<h:body>
<h:form>
<h:outputLabel value="#{userBean.get()}" />
```

```
<br />
<h:commandButton value="Run" action="index"
actionListener="#{userBean.run()}"/>
<h:commandButton value="Reload" action="index"/>
</h:form>
</h:body>
```

Run it on a Jakarta EE server to load the web page. Click on the **Run** button and then the **Reload** button.

How it works...

UserReader extends the AbstractItemReader class, which has two key methods – open() and readItem(). In our case, the first one opens the META-INF/user.txt file, while the second one reads each line of the file.

After that, the UserProcessor class extends the ItemProcessor class, which has a processItem() method. It gets the item read by readItem() (from UserReader) to generate the User object that we want.

Once all the items have been processed and are available in a list (in memory), we use the UserWriter class. This extends the AbstractItemWriter class and contains the writeItems method. In our case, we use it to persist the data that we read from the user.txt file.

Now, we just need to use UserBean to run the job:

```
public void run() {
    try {
        JobOperator job = BatchRuntime.getJobOperator();
            long jobId = job.start("acess-user", new Properties());
        System.out.println("Job started: " + jobId);
        } catch (JobStartException ex) {
        System.out.println(ex.getMessage());
    }
}
```

The job.start() method is referencing the acess-user.xml file, thereby enabling our reader, processor, and writer to work together.

See also

You can view the full source code for this recipe at `https://github.com/eldermoraes/javaee8-cookbook/tree/master/chapter02/ch02-batch`.

Building Powerful Services with JSON and RESTful Features

3

Nowadays, using **Representational State Transfer (REST)** services with **JavaScript Object Notation (JSON)** is the most common method for data transfer between applications over the **HyperText Transfer Protocol (HTTP)** protocol and this is not a coincidence—this is fast and easy to do. It's easy to read, easy to parse, and, with **JSON with Padding (JSON-P)**, easy to code!

The following recipes will show you some such common scenarios and how to apply Jakarta EE to deal with them.

This chapter covers the following recipes:

- Building server-side events with JAX-RS
- Improving a service's capabilities with JAX-RS and Jakarta CDI
- Easing data and object representation with Jakarta JSON Binding
- Parsing, generating, transforming, and querying JSON objects using Jakarta JSON Processing

Building server-side events with JAX-RS

Usually, web applications rely on the events sent by the client side. So, basically, the server will only do something if it is asked to. But with the evolution of the technologies surrounding the internet (HTML5, mobile clients, smartphones, and so on), the server side has also had to evolve. So, that gave birth to server-side events, events fired by the server (as the name suggests).

With this recipe, you will learn how to use a server-side event to update a user view.

Getting ready

Start by adding the Jakarta EE dependency:

```
<dependencies>
    <dependency>
        <groupId>javax</groupId>
        <artifactId>javaee-api</artifactId>
        <version>8.0</version>
        <scope>provided</scope>
    </dependency>
</dependencies>
```

How to do it...

Perform the following steps to try this recipe:

1. First, we build a REST endpoint to manage the server events we are going to use, and to use REST, we should start by properly configuring it:

```
@ApplicationPath("webresources")
public class ApplicationConfig extends Application {

}
```

2. The following is quite a big chunk of code, but don't worry, we are going to split it up and understand each piece:

```
@Path("serverSentService")
@RequestScoped
public class ServerSentService {

    private static final Map<Long, UserEvent> POOL =
    new ConcurrentHashMap<>();

    @Resource(name = "LocalManagedExecutorService")
    private ManagedExecutorService executor;

    @Path("start")
    @POST
    public Response start(@Context Sse sse) {

        final UserEvent process = new UserEvent(sse);

        POOL.put(process.getId(), process);
        executor.submit(process);
```

```
                final URI uri =
UriBuilder.fromResource(ServerSentService.class).path
        ("register/{id}").build(process.getId());
        return Response.created(uri).build();
    }

    @Path("register/{id}")
    @Produces(MediaType.SERVER_SENT_EVENTS)
    @GET
    public void register(@PathParam("id") Long id,
            @Context SseEventSink sseEventSink) {
        final UserEvent process = POOL.get(id);

        if (process != null) {
            process.getSseBroadcaster().register(sseEventSink);
        } else {
            throw new NotFoundException();
        }
    }

    static class UserEvent implements Runnable {

        private final Long id;
        private final SseBroadcaster sseBroadcaster;
        private final Sse sse;

        UserEvent(Sse sse) {
            this.sse = sse;
            this.sseBroadcaster = sse.newBroadcaster();
            id = System.currentTimeMillis();
        }

        Long getId() {
            return id;
        }

        SseBroadcaster getSseBroadcaster() {
            return sseBroadcaster;
        }

        @Override
        public void run() {
            try {
                TimeUnit.SECONDS.sleep(5);
                sseBroadcaster.broadcast(sse.newEventBuilder().
                name("register").data(String.class, "Text from
event "
                                        + id).build());
```

```
                    sseBroadcaster.close();
            } catch (InterruptedException e) {
                System.out.println(e.getMessage());
            }
        }
    }
}
```

3. Here, we have a bean to manage the UI and help us with a better view of what is happening in the server:

```
@ViewScoped
@Named
public class SseBean implements Serializable {

    @NotNull
    @Positive
    private Integer countClient;
    private Client client;
    @PostConstruct
    public void init(){
        client = ClientBuilder.newClient();
    }
    @PreDestroy
    public void destroy(){
        client.close();
    }

    public void sendEvent() throws URISyntaxException,
InterruptedException {
        WebTarget target =
client.target(URI.create("http://localhost:8080/
                                                ch03-sse/"));
        Response response =
        target.path("webresources/serverSentService/start")
                .request()
                .post(Entity.json(""), Response.class);

        FacesContext.getCurrentInstance().addMessage(null,
                new FacesMessage("Sse Endpoint: " +
                response.getLocation())));

        final Map<Integer, String> messageMap = new
ConcurrentHashMap<>
            (countClient);
        final SseEventSource[] sources = new
        SseEventSource[countClient];
```

```
final String processUriString =
target.getUri().relativize(response.getLocation()).
toString();
final WebTarget sseTarget = target.path(processUriString);

for (int i = 0; i < countClient; i++) {
    final int id = i;
    sources[id] = SseEventSource.target(sseTarget).build();
    sources[id].register((event) -> {
        final String message =
event.readData(String.class);

            if (message.contains("Text")) {
                messageMap.put(id, message);
            }
    });
    sources[i].open();
}

TimeUnit.SECONDS.sleep(10);

for (SseEventSource source : sources) {
    source.close();
}

for (int i = 0; i < countClient; i++) {
    final String message = messageMap.get(i);

    FacesContext.getCurrentInstance().addMessage(null,
            new FacesMessage("Message sent to client " +
                            (i + 1) + ": " + message));
}
}

public Integer getCountClient() {
    return countClient;
}

public void setCountClient(Integer countClient) {
    this.countClient = countClient;
}

}
```

4. And finally, the UI is a code with a simple **JSF** (short for **JavaServer Faces**) page:

```
<h:body>
    <h:form>
```

```
            <h:outputLabel for="countClient" value="Number of Clients"
/>
            <h:inputText id="countClient"
value="#{sseBean.countClient}" />
            <br />
            <h:commandButton type="submit"
action="#{sseBean.sendEvent()}"
              value="Send Events" />
        </h:form>
    </h:body>
```

How it works...

We started with our SSE engine, the `ServerEvent` class, and a **JAX-RS** (short
for **JAVA API for RESTful Web Services**) endpoint—these hold all of the methods that we
need for this recipe.

Let's look at the first one:

```
@Path("start")
@POST
public Response start(@Context Sse sse) {

    final UserEvent process = new UserEvent(sse);

    POOL.put(process.getId(), process);
    executor.submit(process);

    final URI uri = UriBuilder.fromResource(ServerSentService.class).
    path("register/{id}").build(process.getId());
    return Response.created(uri).build();
}
```

Following are the main points:

1. This method will create and prepare an event to be sent by the server to the
   clients.
2. Then, the newly-created event is put in a HashMap called POOL.
3. Then, our event is attached to URI that represents another method in this same
   class (details are provided next).

Pay attention to this parameter:

```
@Context Sse sse
```

This brings the server-side events feature from the server context and lets you use it as you need and, of course, it is injected by Jakarta CDI (yes, **CDI**, short for **Contexts and Dependency Injection**, is everywhere!).

Now, we see our `register()` method:

```
@Path("register/{id}")
@Produces(MediaType.SERVER_SENT_EVENTS)
@GET
public void register(@PathParam("id") Long id,
        @Context SseEventSink sseEventSink) {
    final UserEvent event = POOL.get(id);

    if (event != null) {
        event.getSseBroadcaster().register(sseEventSink);
    } else {
        throw new NotFoundException();
    }
}
```

This is the very method that sends the events to your clients—check the `@Produces` annotation; it uses the new media type, `SERVER_SENT_EVENTS`.

The engine works, thanks to this small piece of code:

```
@Context SseEventSink sseEventSink

...

event.getSseBroadcaster().register(sseEventSink);
```

`SseEventSink` is a queue of events managed by the Jakarta EE server, and it is served to you by injection from the context.

Then, you get the process broadcaster and register it to this sink, which means that everything that this process broadcasts will be sent by the server from `SseEventSink`.

Now, we check our event setup:

```
static class UserEvent implements Runnable {

    ...

    UserEvent(Sse sse) {
        this.sse = sse;
        this.sseBroadcaster = sse.newBroadcaster();
        id = System.currentTimeMillis();
```

```
        }

        ...

        @Override
        public void run() {
            try {
                TimeUnit.SECONDS.sleep(5);
                sseBroadcaster.broadcast(sse.newEventBuilder().
                name("register").data(String.class, "Text from event "
                + id).build());
                sseBroadcaster.close();
            } catch (InterruptedException e) {
                System.out.println(e.getMessage());
            }
        }
    }
```

Now, pay attention to the following line:

```
this.sseBroadcaster = sse.newBroadcaster();
```

You'll remember that we've just used this broadcaster in the last class. Here, we see that this broadcaster is brought by the Sse object injected by the server.

This event implements the Runnable interface so we can use it with the executor (as explained before), so once it runs, you can broadcast to your clients:

```
sseBroadcaster.broadcast(sse.newEventBuilder().name("register").
data(String.class, "Text from event " + id).build());
```

This is the exact message that is sent to the client. This could be whatever message you need.

For this recipe, we used another class to interact with Sse. Let's highlight the most important parts:

```
        WebTarget target = client.target(URI.create
        ("http://localhost:8080/ch03-sse/"));
        Response response = target.path("webresources/serverSentService
                                    /start")
            .request()
            .post(Entity.json(""), Response.class);
```

This is a simple piece of code that you can use to call any JAX-RS endpoint.

And finally, the most important part of this mock client is as follows:

```
for (int i = 0; i < countClient; i++) {
    final int id = i;
    sources[id] = SseEventSource.target(sseTarget).build();
    sources[id].register((event) -> {
        final String message = event.readData(String.class);

        if (message.contains("Text")) {
            messageMap.put(id, message);
        }
    });
    sources[i].open();
}
```

Each message that is broadcast is read here:

```
final String message = messageMap.get(i);
```

It could be any client you want—another service, a web page, a mobile client, or anything.

Then, we check our UI:

```
<h:inputText id="countClient" value="#{sseBean.countClient}" />
...
<h:commandButton type="submit" action="#{sseBean.sendEvent()}"
value="Send Events" />
```

We are using the `countClient` field to fill the `countClient` value in the client, so you can play around with as many threads as you want.

There's more...

It's important to mention that **SSE (Server-Side Event)** is not supported in Microsoft Edge web browsers and that it is not as scalable as web sockets. In case you want to have full cross-browser support on the desktop side and/or better scalability (so, not only mobile apps but also web apps, which can open many more connections per instance), then WebSockets should be considered instead. Fortunately, standard Jakarta EE has supported WebSockets since Java EE 7.0.

See also

- The full source code of this recipe is available at `https://github.com/eldermoraes/javaee8-cookbook/tree/master/chapter03/ch03-sse`.

Improving service's capabilities with JAX-RS and Jakarta CDI

This recipe will show you how to take advantage of Jakarta CDI and JAX-RS features to reduce the effort and lower the complexity of writing powerful services.

Getting ready

Start by adding the Jakarta EE dependency:

```
<dependencies>
    <dependency>
        <groupId>javax</groupId>
        <artifactId>javaee-api</artifactId>
        <version>8.0</version>
        <scope>provided</scope>
    </dependency>
</dependencies>
```

How to do it...

To try this recipe, perform the following steps:

1. We first create a `User` class to be managed through our service:

```
public class User implements Serializable{

    private String name;
    private String email;

    public User(){
    }

    public User(String name, String email) {
        this.name = name;
```

```
        this.email = email;
    }

    //DO NOT FORGET TO IMPLEMENT THE GETTERS AND SETTERS

}
```

2. To have multiple sources of `User` objects, we create a `UserBean` class:

```java
@Stateless
public class UserBean {
    public User getUser(){
        long ts = System.currentTimeMillis();
        return new User("Bean" + ts, "user" + ts +
                        "@eldermoraes.com");
    }
}
```

3. And finally, we create our `UserService` endpoint:

```java
@Path("userservice")
public class UserService implements Serializable{
    @Inject
    private UserBean userBean;
    private User userLocal;
    @Inject
    private void setUserLocal(){
        long ts = System.currentTimeMillis();
        userLocal = new User("Local" + ts, "user" + ts +
                        "@eldermoraes.com");
    }
    @GET
    @Path("getUserFromBean")
    @Produces(MediaType.APPLICATION_JSON)
    public Response getUserFromBean(){
        return Response.ok(userBean.getUser()).build();
    }

    @GET
    @Path("getUserFromLocal")
    @Produces(MediaType.APPLICATION_JSON)
    public Response getUserFromLocal(){
        return Response.ok(userLocal).build();
    }
}
```

4. To load our UI, we have the `UserView` class, which will be like a controller between the UI and the service:

```
@ViewScoped
@Named
public class UserView implements Serializable {

    public void loadUsers() {
        Client client = ClientBuilder.newClient();
        WebTarget target = client.target(URI.create
        ("http://localhost:8080/ch03-rscdi/"));
        User response = target.path("webresources/userservice/
                                    getUserFromBean")
                .request()
                .accept(MediaType.APPLICATION_JSON)
                .get(User.class);

        FacesContext.getCurrentInstance()
                .addMessage(null,
                        new FacesMessage("userFromBean: " +
                                        response));

        response = target.path("webresources/userservice
                               /getUserFromLocal")
                .request()
                .accept(MediaType.APPLICATION_JSON)
                .get(User.class);

        FacesContext.getCurrentInstance()
                .addMessage(null,
                        new FacesMessage("userFromLocal:
                                " + response));
    client.close();
        }

}
```

5. And we add a simple JSF page just to show the results:

```
<h:body>
<h:form>
<h:commandButton type="submit"
action="#{userView.loadUsers()}"
value="Load Users" />
</h:form>
</h:body>
```

How it works...

We used two kinds of injections:

- From `UserBean`, when `UserService` is attached to the context
- From `UserService` itself

Injection from `UserBean` is the simplest possible to perform:

```
@Inject
private UserBean userBean;
```

Injection from `UserService` itself is also simple:

```
@Inject
private void setUserLocal(){
    long ts = System.currentTimeMillis();
    userLocal = new User("Local" + ts, "user" + ts +
                        "@eldermoraes.com");
}
```

Here, `@Inject` works like the `@PostConstruct` annotation, with the server context running the method. But the result is quite the same.

Everything is injected, so now it's just a matter of getting the results:

```
response = target.path("webresources/userservice/getUserFromBean")
                .request()
                .accept(MediaType.APPLICATION_JSON)
                .get(User.class);

...

response = target.path("webresources/userservice/getUserFromLocal")
                .request()
                .accept(MediaType.APPLICATION_JSON)
                .get(User.class);
```

There's more...

As you can see, JAX-RS eases a lot of object parsing and representation:

```
@GET
@Path("getUserFromBean")
@Produces(MediaType.APPLICATION_JSON)
public Response getUserFromBean(){
```

```
        userFromBean = userBean.getUser();
        return Response.ok(userFromBean).build();
    }

    @GET
    @Path("getUserFromLocal")
    @Produces(MediaType.APPLICATION_JSON)
    public Response getUserFromLocal(){
        return Response.ok(userLocal).build();
    }
```

By using a `Response` returning object and
`@Produces(MediaType.APPLICATION_JSON)`, you give the framework the hard job of
parsing your `user` object to a JSON representation. Lots of effort is saved in a few lines!

You could also inject the user using a producer (the `@Produces` annotation). Check the
Jakarta CDI recipe from `Chapter 1`, *New Features and Improvements,* for more details.

See also

- Check the full source code of this recipe at `https://github.com/eldermoraes/`
  `javaee8-cookbook/tree/master/chapter03/ch03-rscdi`.

Easing data and objects representation with Jakarta JSON Binding

This recipe will show you how you can use the power of the Jakarta JSON Binding API to
give some flexibility to your data representation and help to transform your objects into
JSON messages.

Getting ready

Start by adding the Jakarta EE dependency:

```
<dependency>
    <groupId>javax</groupId>
    <artifactId>javaee-api</artifactId>
    <version>8.0</version>
    <scope>provided</scope>
</dependency>
```

How to do it...

Perform the following steps to try this recipe:

1. We first create a `User` class with some customization (the details follow):

```
public class User {

    private Long id;
    @JsonbProperty("fullName")
    private String name;
    private String email;
    @JsonbTransient
    private Double privateNumber;
    @JsonbDateFormat(JsonbDateFormat.DEFAULT_LOCALE)
    private Date dateCreated;
    public User(Long id, String name, String email,
                Double privateNumber, Date dateCreated) {
        this.id = id;
        this.name = name;
        this.email = email;
        this.privateNumber = privateNumber;
        this.dateCreated = dateCreated;
    }

    private User(){
    }

    //DO NOT FORGET TO IMPLEMENT THE GETTERS AND SETTERS
}
```

2. Here, we use `UserView` to return the user JSON to the UI:

```
@ViewScoped
@Named
public class UserView implements Serializable{
    private String json;
    public void loadUser(){
        long now = System.currentTimeMillis();
        User user = new User(now,
                "User" + now,
                "user" + now + "@eldermoraes.com",
                Math.random(),
                new Date());
        Jsonb jb = JsonbBuilder.create();
        json = jb.toJson(user);
        try {
            jb.close();
```

```
                } catch (Exception ex) {
                    System.out.println(ex.getMessage());
                }
            }

        public String getJson() {
            return json;
        }

        public void setJson(String json) {
            this.json = json;
        }
    }
```

3. We add a JSF page just to show the results:

```
<h:body>
<h:form>
<h:commandButton type="submit" action="#{userView.loadUser()}"
 value="Load User" />

<br />

<h:outputLabel for="json" value="User JSON" />
<br />
<h:inputTextarea id="json" value="#{userView.json}"
 style="width: 300px; height: 300px;" />
</h:form>
</h:body>
```

How it works...

We are using some Jakarta JSON Binding annotations to customize our user data representation:

```
@JsonbProperty("fullName")
private String name;
```

@JsonbProperty is used to change the field name to some other value:

```
@JsonbTransient
private Double privateNumber;
```

Use `@JsonbTransient` when you want to prevent some property appearing at the JSON representation:

```
@JsonbDateFormat(JsonbDateFormat.DEFAULT_LOCALE)
private Date dateCreated;
```

With `@JsonbDateFormat`, you use the API to automatically format your dates.

And then we use our UI manager to update the view:

```
public void loadUser(){
    long now = System.currentTimeMillis();
    User user = new User(now,
            "User" + now,
            "user" + now + "@eldermoraes.com",
            Math.random(),
            new Date());
    Jsonb jb = JsonbBuilder.create();
    json = jb.toJson(user);
}
```

See also

* The full source code of this recipe is available at `https://github.com/eldermoraes/javaee8-cookbook/tree/master/chapter03/ch03-jsonb`.

Parsing, generating, transforming, and querying JSON objects using Jakarta JSON Processing

Dealing with JSON objects is an activity that you can't avoid anymore. So, if you can do it by relying on a powerful and easy-to-use framework—even better!

This recipe will show you how you can use Jakarta JSON processing to carry out some different operations by using or generating JSON objects.

Getting ready

Start by adding the Jakarta EE dependency:

```
<dependency>
    <groupId>javax</groupId>
    <artifactId>javaee-api</artifactId>
    <version>8.0</version>
    <scope>provided</scope>
</dependency>
```

How to do it...

You will need to perform the following steps to try this recipe:

1. Let's create a `User` class to support our operations:

```
public class User {

    private String name;
    private String email;
    private Integer[] profiles;
    public User(String name, String email, Integer[] profiles) {
        this.name = name;
        this.email = email;
        this.profiles = profiles;
    }

    //DO NOT FORGET TO IMPLEMENT THE GETTERS AND SETTERS
}
```

2. Then, let's create a `UserView` class to do all of the JSON operations:

```
@ViewScoped
@Named
public class UserView implements Serializable{
    private static final JsonBuilderFactory BUILDERFACTORY =
    Json.createBuilderFactory(null);
    private final Jsonb jsonbBuilder = JsonbBuilder.create();
    private String fromArray;
    private String fromStructure;
    private String fromUser;
    private String fromJpointer;
    public void loadUserJson(){
        loadFromArray();
        loadFromStructure();
```

```
            loadFromUser();
        }
        private void loadFromArray(){
            JsonArray array = BUILDERFACTORY.createArrayBuilder()
                    .add(BUILDERFACTORY.createObjectBuilder()
                            .add("name", "User1")
                            .add("email", "user1@eldermoraes.com"))
                    .add(BUILDERFACTORY.createObjectBuilder()
                            .add("name", "User2")
                            .add("email", "user2@eldermoraes.com"))
                    .add(BUILDERFACTORY.createObjectBuilder()
                            .add("name", "User3")
                            .add("email", "user3@eldermoraes.com"))
                    .build();
            fromArray = jsonbBuilder.toJson(array);
        }
        private void loadFromStructure(){
            JsonStructure structure =
            BUILDERFACTORY.createObjectBuilder()
                    .add("name", "User1")
                    .add("email", "user1@eldermoraes.com")
                    .add("profiles",
    BUILDERFACTORY.createArrayBuilder()
                            .add(BUILDERFACTORY.createObjectBuilder()
                                    .add("id", "1")
                                    .add("name", "Profile1"))
                            .add(BUILDERFACTORY.createObjectBuilder()
                                    .add("id", "2")
                                    .add("name", "Profile2")))
                    .build();
            fromStructure = jsonbBuilder.toJson(structure);

            JsonPointer pointer = Json.createPointer("/profiles");
            JsonValue value = pointer.getValue(structure);
            fromJpointer = value.toString();
        }
        private void loadFromUser(){
            User user = new User("Elder Moraes",
            "elder@eldermoraes.com",
            new Integer[]{1,2,3});
            fromUser = jsonbBuilder.toJson(user);
        }

        //DO NOT FORGET TO IMPLEMENT THE GETTERS AND SETTERS
    }
```

3. Then, we create a JSF page to show the results:

```
<h:body>
<h:form>
<h:commandButton type="submit" action="#{userView.loadUserJson()}"
value="Load JSONs" />

<br />

<h:outputLabel for="fromArray" value="From Array" />
<br />
<h:inputTextarea id="fromArray" value="#{userView.fromArray}"
style="width: 300px; height: 150px" />
<br />

<h:outputLabel for="fromStructure" value="From Structure" />
<br />
<h:inputTextarea id="fromStructure"
value="#{userView.fromStructure}"
style="width: 300px; height: 150px" />
<br />

<h:outputLabel for="fromUser" value="From User" />
<br />
<h:inputTextarea id="fromUser" value="#{userView.fromUser}"
style="width: 300px; height: 150px" />

<br />
<h:outputLabel for="fromJPointer" value="Query with JSON Pointer
(from JsonStructure Above)" />
<br />
<h:inputTextarea id="fromJPointer"
 value="#{userView.fromJpointer}"
 style="width: 300px; height: 100px" />
</h:form>
</h:body>
```

How it works...

First, refer to the `loadFromArray()` method:

```
private void loadFromArray(){
    JsonArray array = BUILDERFACTORY.createArrayBuilder()
            .add(BUILDERFACTORY.createObjectBuilder()
                    .add("name", "User1")
                    .add("email", "user1@eldermoraes.com"))
```

```
        .add(BUILDERFACTORY.createObjectBuilder()
                .add("name", "User2")
                .add("email", "user2@eldermoraes.com"))
        .add(BUILDERFACTORY.createObjectBuilder()
                .add("name", "User3")
                .add("email", "user3@eldermoraes.com"))
        .build();
    fromArray = jsonbBuilder.toJson(array);
}
```

It uses the `BUILDERFACTORY` and `createArrayBuilder` methods to easily build an array of JSONs objects (each call of `createObjectBuilder` creates another array member). At the end, we use the Jakarta JSON binding to convert it into a JSON string:

```
private void loadFromStructure(){
    JsonStructure structure = BUILDERFACTORY.createObjectBuilder()
        .add("name", "User1")
        .add("email", "user1@eldermoraes.com")
        .add("profiles", BUILDERFACTORY.createArrayBuilder()
                .add(BUILDERFACTORY.createObjectBuilder()
                        .add("id", "1")
                        .add("name", "Profile1"))
                .add(BUILDERFACTORY.createObjectBuilder()
                        .add("id", "2")
                        .add("name", "Profile2")))
        .build();
    fromStructure = jsonbBuilder.toJson(structure);

    JsonPointer pointer = new JsonPointerImpl("/profiles");
    JsonValue value = pointer.getValue(structure);
    fromJpointer = value.toString();
}
```

Here, instead of an array, we are building a single JSON structure. Again, we use Jakarta JSON Binding to convert `JsonStructure` into a JSON string.

We also took advantage of having this `JsonStructure` ready and used it to query the user profiles using the `JsonPointer` object:

```
private void loadFromUser(){
    User user = new User("Elder Moraes", "elder@eldermoraes.com",
            new Integer[]{1,2,3});
    fromUser = jsonbBuilder.toJson(user);
}
```

And here was the simplest— creating an object and asking Jakarta JSON Binding to convert it into a JSON string.

See also

- Check the full source code of this recipe at `https://github.com/eldermoraes/javaee8-cookbook/tree/master/chapter03/ch03-jsonp`.

4
Web and Client-Server Communication

Web development is one of the greatest ways to use Jakarta EE. Actually, since before J2EE, we could use **JSPs** (short for **Java Server Pages**) and servlets, and that is how web development using Java began.

This chapter will show some advanced features for web development that will make your application faster and better—for you and your customer!

This chapter covers the following recipes:

- Using servlets for request and response management
- Building a UI with template features using JSF
- Improving response performance with Server Push

Using servlets for request and response management

Servlets are the core place to deal with requests and responses using Jakarta EE. If you are still not familiar with it, consider this. A JSP is simply a way to build a servlet once the page is called. So, it is the place to deal with this request.

This recipe will show you three features to take advantage of when using servlets:

- Load on startup
- Parameterized servlets
- Asynchronous servlets

Getting ready

We will start the recipe by adding the dependency to your project:

```
<dependency>
    <groupId>javax</groupId>
    <artifactId>javaee-api</artifactId>
    <version>8.0</version>
    <scope>provided</scope>
</dependency>
```

How to do it...

Let's build the features on which this recipe is based:

1. Firstly, let's start with our servlet, which will load on server startup:

```
@WebServlet(name = "LoadOnStartupServlet", urlPatterns =
{"/LoadOnStartupServlet"},
loadOnStartup = 1)
public class LoadOnStartupServlet extends HttpServlet {

    @Override
    public void init() throws ServletException {
        System.out.println("*******SERVLET LOADED
                        WITH SERVER's STARTUP*******");
    }

}
```

2. Next, we add a servlet with some parameters for its own initialization:

```
@WebServlet(name = "InitConfigServlet", urlPatterns =
{"/InitConfigServlet"},
        initParams = {
                @WebInitParam(name = "key1", value = "value1"),
                @WebInitParam(name = "key2", value = "value2"),
                @WebInitParam(name = "key3", value = "value3"),
```

```
                    @WebInitParam(name = "key4", value = "value4"),
                    @WebInitParam(name = "key5", value = "value5")
        }
)
public class InitConfigServlet extends HttpServlet {

    Map<String, String> param = new HashMap<>();
    @Override
    protected void doPost(HttpServletRequest req,
    HttpServletResponse resp)
    throws ServletException, IOException {
        doProcess(req, resp);
    }

    @Override
    protected void doGet(HttpServletRequest req,
    HttpServletResponse resp)
    throws ServletException, IOException {
        doProcess(req, resp);
    }
    private void doProcess(HttpServletRequest req,
    HttpServletResponse resp)
    throws IOException{
        resp.setContentType("text/html");
        PrintWriter out = resp.getWriter();
        if (param.isEmpty()){
            out.println("No params to show");
        } else{
            param.forEach((k,v) -> out.println("param: " + k + ",
                                value: " + v + "<br />"));
        }
    }

    @Override
    public void init(ServletConfig config) throws ServletException
{
        System.out.println("init");
        List<String> list =
        Collections.list(config.getInitParameterNames());
        list.forEach((key) -> {
            param.put(key, config.getInitParameter(key));
        });
    }

}
```

3. Then, we implement our asynchronous servlet, as follows:

```java
@WebServlet(urlPatterns = "/AsyncServlet", asyncSupported = true)
public class AsyncServlet extends HttpServlet {

    private static final long serialVersionUID = 1L;

    @Override
    protected void doGet(HttpServletRequest request,
            HttpServletResponse response) throws ServletException,
            IOException {
        long startTime = System.currentTimeMillis();
        System.out.println("AsyncServlet Begin, Name="
                + Thread.currentThread().getName() + ", ID="
                + Thread.currentThread().getId());

        String time = request.getParameter("timestamp");
        AsyncContext asyncCtx = request.startAsync();

        asyncCtx.start(() -> {
            try {
                Thread.sleep(Long.valueOf(time));
                long endTime = System.currentTimeMillis();
                long timeElapsed = endTime - startTime;
                System.out.println("AsyncServlet Finish, Name="
                        + Thread.currentThread().getName() + ",
ID="
                        + Thread.currentThread().getId() + ",
Duration="
                        + timeElapsed + " milliseconds.");

                asyncCtx.getResponse().getWriter().write
                ("Async process time: " + timeElapsed + "
milliseconds");
                asyncCtx.complete();
            } catch (InterruptedException | IOException ex) {
                System.err.println(ex.getMessage());
            }
        });
    }
}
```

4. Finally, we need a simple web page to try all of these servlets:

```html
<body>
    <a href="${pageContext.request.contextPath}/InitConfigServlet">
    InitConfigServlet</a>
    <br />
```

```
<br />
<form action="${pageContext.request.contextPath}/AsyncServlet"
 method="GET">
    <h2>AsyncServlet</h2>
    Milliseconds
    <br />
    <input type="number" id="timestamp" name="timestamp"
    style="width: 200px" value="5000"/>
    <button type="submit">Submit</button>
</form>

</body>
```

After this point, you are ready to try it.

How it works...

We have three major things happening here. Let's see how this works.

The load-on-startup servlet

If you want your servlet to be initialized when the server starts, then this is what you need. Usually, you will use it to load some cache, start a background process, log some information, or whatever you require, when the server has just started and cannot wait until somebody calls the servlet.

The key points of this kind of servlet are as follows:

- The LoadOnStartup parameter: This accepts any number of servlets. This number defines the order used by the server to execute all of the servlets that will run during startup. So, if you have more than one servlet running this way, remember to define the right order (if there is any). If there is no number defined or a negative one, the server will choose the default order.
- The init method: Remember to override the init method with the operation you would like to do at startup time, otherwise, your servlet will do nothing.

A servlet with initParams

Sometimes, you will need to define some parameters for your servlet that go beyond local variables—initParams is the place to do it. Consider the following code:

```
@WebServlet(name = "InitConfigServlet", urlPatterns =
{"/InitConfigServlet"},
        initParams = {
                @WebInitParam(name = "key1", value = "value1"),
                @WebInitParam(name = "key2", value = "value2"),
                @WebInitParam(name = "key3", value = "value3"),
                @WebInitParam(name = "key4", value = "value4"),
                @WebInitParam(name = "key5", value = "value5")
        }
)
```

The @WebInitParam annotation will handle them for you and these parameters will be available for the server through the ServletConfig object.

The asynchronous servlet

To understand what the asynchronous servlet is, let's split our AsyncServlet class into pieces:

```
@WebServlet(urlPatterns = "/AsyncServlet", asyncSupported = true)
```

Here, we defined our servlet for accepting async behavior by using the asyncSupported param:

```
AsyncContext asyncCtx = request.startAsync();
```

We used the request being processed to start a new async context.

Then, we start our async process:

```
asyncCtx.start(() -> {...
```

Here, we print our output to see the response and finish the async process:

```
asyncCtx.getResponse().getWriter().write("Async
process time: "
+ timeElapsed + " milliseconds");
asyncCtx.complete();
```

See also

- To get the full source code of this recipe, check `https://github.com/eldermoraes/javaee8-cookbook/tree/master/chapter04/ch04-servlet`.

Building a UI with template features using JSF

Jakarta Server Faces (JSF) is a powerful Jakarta EE API for building outstanding UIs, using both client and server features.

It goes much further when you are using JSPs, as you are not only using Java code inside HTML code but also referencing code injected in the server context.

This recipe will show you how to use the *Facelet template* feature to get more flexibility and reusability from your layout template.

Getting ready

Start by adding the dependency to your project:

```
<dependency>
    <groupId>javax</groupId>
    <artifactId>javaee-api</artifactId>
    <version>8.0</version>
    <scope>provided</scope>
</dependency>
```

How to do it...

To try this recipe, perform the following steps:

1. Let's first create our page layout with a header, content section, and footer:

```
<h:body>
    <div id="layout">
        <div id="header">
            <ui:insert name="header" >
                <ui:include src="header.xhtml" />
```

```
                </ui:insert>
            </div>
            <div id="content">
                <ui:insert name="content" >
                    <ui:include src="content.xhtml" />
                </ui:insert>
            </div>
            <div id="footer">
                <ui:insert name="footer" >
                    <ui:include src="footer.xhtml" />
                </ui:insert>
            </div>
        </div>
    </h:body>
```

2. Then, let's define the default header section:

```
<body>
    <h1>Template header</h1>
</body>
```

3. Now, we create the default content section:

```
<body>
    <h1>Template content</h1>
</body>
```

4. Next, we create the default footer section:

```
<body>
    <h1>Template content</h1>
</body>
```

5. And then a simple page is created using our default template:

```
<h:body>
    <ui:composition template="WEB-INF/template/layout.xhtml">

    </ui:composition>
</h:body>
```

6. Now, let's create another page and override just the content section:

```
<h:body>
    <ui:composition template="/template/layout.xhtml">
        <ui:define name="content">
            <h1><p style="color:red">User content. Timestamp: #
            {userBean.timestamp}</p></h1>
        </ui:define>
```

```
        </ui:composition>
    </h:body>
```

7. As this code calls `UserBean`, let's define it:

```
@Named
@RequestScoped
public class UserBean implements Serializable{

    public Long getTimestamp(){
        return new Date().getTime();
    }
}
```

8. Also, don't forget to include the `beans.xml` file inside the `WEB-INF` folder; otherwise, this bean will not work as expected:

```
<?xml version="1.0" encoding="UTF-8"?>
<beans xmlns="http://xmlns.jcp.org/xml/ns/javaee"
        xmlns:xsi="http://www.w3.org/2001/XMLSchema-instance"
        xsi:schemaLocation="http://xmlns.jcp.org/xml/ns/javaee
        http://xmlns.jcp.org/xml/ns/javaee/beans_1_1.xsd"
        bean-discovery-mode="all">
</beans>
```

If you want to try this code, run it in a Jakarta EE-compatible server and access the following URLs:

- `http://localhost:8080/ch04-jsf/`
- `http://localhost:8080/ch04-jsf/user.xhtml`

How it works...

The explanation is as simple as possible—`layout.xhtml` is our template. As long as you name each section (in our case, its header, content, and footer), whatever JSF page uses it will inherit its layout.

Any page using this layout and wanting to customize some of those defined sections should just describe the desired section as we did in the `user.xhtml` file, as follows:

```
<ui:composition template="/template/layout.xhtml">
    <ui:define name="content">
        <h1><font color="red">User content. Timestamp: #
            {userBean.timestamp}
        </font></h1>
```

```
        </ui:define>
    </ui:composition>
```

See also

- To get the full source code of this recipe, check `https://github.com/eldermoraes/javaee8-cookbook/tree/master/chapter04/ch04-jsf`.

Improving response performance with Server Push

One of the main features of HTTP/2.0 is Server Push. Whenever it is available—by which I mean it gets the support of the protocol from the server and client browser—it lets the server send (`"push"`) data to the client before the client asks for it.

This is one of the most popular features in JSF 2.3 and probably the one that demands less effort to use if your application is based on JSF—just migrate to a Jakarta EE 8-compatible server and then you are done.

This recipe will show you how to use it in your application and will even let you compare performance between HTTP/1.0 and HTTP/2.0 in the same scenario.

Getting ready

Start by adding the dependency to your project:

```
<dependency>
    <groupId>javax</groupId>
    <artifactId>javaee-api</artifactId>
    <version>8.0</version>
    <scope>provided</scope>
</dependency>
```

How to do it...

The only step to be performed in this recipe is the following:

Add this single servlet:

```java
@WebServlet(name = "ServerPushServlet", urlPatterns =
{"/ServerPushServlet"})
public class ServerPushServlet extends HttpServlet {

    @Override
    protected void doGet(HttpServletRequest request,
    HttpServletResponse response)
            throws ServletException, IOException {
        doRequest(request, response);
    }

    private void doRequest(HttpServletRequest request,
    HttpServletResponse response) throws IOException{
        String usePush = request.getParameter("usePush");
        if ("true".equalsIgnoreCase(usePush)){
            PushBuilder pb = request.newPushBuilder();
            if (pb != null) {
                for(int row=0; row < 5; row++){
                    for(int col=0; col < 8; col++){
                        pb.path("image/keyboard_buttons/keyboard_buttons-"
                                + row + "-" + col + ".jpeg")
                        .addHeader("content-type", "image/jpeg")
                        .push();
                    }
                }
            }
        }

        try (PrintWriter writer = response.getWriter()) {
            StringBuilder html = new StringBuilder();
            html.append("<html>");
            html.append("<center>");
            html.append("<table cellspacing='0' cellpadding='0'
                        border='0'>");

            for(int row=0; row < 5; row++){
                html.append(" <tr>");
                for(int col=0; col < 8; col++){
                    html.append(" <td>");
                    html.append("<img
                    src='image/keyboard_buttons/keyboard_buttons-" +
                        row + "-" + col + ".jpeg' style='width:100px;
```

```
                        height:106.25px;'>");
                html.append(" </td>");
            }
            html.append(" </tr>");
        }
        html.append("</table>");
        html.append("<br>");
        if ("true".equalsIgnoreCase(usePush)){
            html.append("<h2>Image pushed by ServerPush</h2>");
        } else{
            html.append("<h2>Image loaded using HTTP/1.0</h2>");
        }
        html.append("</center>");
        html.append("</html>");
        writer.write(html.toString());
    }
}

}
```

We create a simple page to call both the `HTTP/1.0` and `HTTP/2.0` cases:

```
<body>
    <a href="ServerPushServlet?usePush=true">Use HTTP/2.0 (ServerPush)</a>
    <br />
    <a href="ServerPushServlet?usePush=false">Use HTTP/1.0</a>
</body>
```

And try it on a Jakarta EE 8-compatible server using this URL:

```
https://localhost:8181/ch04-serverpush
```

How it works...

The image loaded in this recipe was shared in 25 pieces. When there is no HTTP/2.0 available, the server will wait for 25 requests made by `img src` (from HTML) and then reply to each one of them with the proper image.

With HTTP/2.0, the server can push them all beforehand. The magic is done here:

```
PushBuilder pb = request.newPushBuilder();
        if (pb != null) {
            for(int row=0; row < 5; row++){
                for(int col=0; col < 8; col++){
                    pb.path("image/keyboard_buttons/keyboard_buttons-"
                            + row + "-" + col + ".jpeg")
```

```
                                .addHeader("content-type", "image/jpeg")
                                .push();
                    }
            }
        }
```

To check whether your images are loaded using Server Push or not, open the developer console of your browser, go to network monitoring, and then load the page. You should see information about who sent each image to the browser. If there is something like **Push** or **ServerPush**, you are using it!

There's more...

Server Push will only work under the Secure Sockets Layer (**SSL**). In other words, if you are using Eclipse GlassFish 5 and are trying to run this recipe, your URL should be something like this:

```
    https://localhost:8181/ch04-serverpush
```

If you miss it, the code will still work but using HTTP/1.0, which means that when the code asks for `newPushBuilder`, it will return `null` (not available):

```
    if (pb != null) {
        ...
    }
```

So, if you really mean to use Server Push, it would be a good idea to let all set (install an SSL certificate, for example) and maybe close the `8080` port (so you can guarantee that your Server Push code is used).

See also

- To get the full source code of this recipe, check `https://github.com/eldermoraes/javaee8-cookbook/tree/master/chapter04/ch04-serverpush`.

5
Security of the Enterprise Architecture

Security is one of the hottest topics of all time in the software industry, and there's no reason for that to change any time soon. Actually, it will probably become even hotter as time goes by.

With all your data being streamed through the cloud, passing through uncountable servers, links, databases, sessions, devices, and so on, what you would expect, at the very least, is for it to be well-protected and secure and its integrity to be kept intact.

Jakarta EE has its own Security API, with Soteria being one of its reference implementations.

Security is a subject worthy of dozens of books; that's a fact. However, this chapter will only cover some of the most common use cases you may come across in your daily projects.

This chapter covers the following recipes:

- Domain protection with authentication
- Granting rights through authorization
- Protecting data confidentiality and integrity with SSL/TLS
- Using declarative security
- Using programmatic security

Domain protection with authentication

Authentication is whatever process, task, and/or policy is used to define who can access your domain. It's like a badge that you use to access your office.

In applications, the most common use of authentication is to allow users who are already registered with your domain to access it.

This recipe will show you how to use some simple code and configuration to control who can and cannot access some of the resources of your application.

Getting ready

Let's start by adding our dependency:

```
<dependency>
    <groupId>javax</groupId>
    <artifactId>javaee-api</artifactId>
    <version>8.0</version>
    <scope>provided</scope>
</dependency>
```

How to do it...

Follow these steps to complete this recipe:

1. First, make some configuration changes in the `web.xml` file:

```
<security-constraint>
    <web-resource-collection>
        <web-resource-name>CH05-Authentication</web-resource-name>
        <url-pattern>/authServlet</url-pattern>
    </web-resource-collection>
    <auth-constraint>
        <role-name>role1</role-name>
    </auth-constraint>
</security-constraint>

<security-role>
    <role-name>role1</role-name>
</security-role>
```

2. Next, create a servlet that will deal with our user access:

```
@DeclareRoles({"role1", "role2", "role3"})
@WebServlet(name = "/UserAuthenticationServlet", urlPatterns =
{"/UserAuthenticationServlet"})
public class UserAuthenticationServlet extends HttpServlet {
```

```
private static final long serialVersionUID = 1L;

@Inject
private javax.security.enterprise.SecurityContext
securityContext;

@Override
public void doGet(HttpServletRequest request,
HttpServletResponse response) throws ServletException,
IOException {

    String name = request.getParameter("name");
    if (null != name || !"".equals(name)) {
        AuthenticationStatus status =
        securityContext.authenticate(
                request, response,
AuthenticationParameters.withParams().credential
                (new CallerOnlyCredential(name)));

        response.getWriter().write("Authentication status: "
        + status.name() + "\n");
    }

    String principal = null;
    if (request.getUserPrincipal() != null) {
        principal = request.getUserPrincipal().getName();
    }

    response.getWriter().write("User: " + principal + "\n");
    response.getWriter().write("Role \"role1\" access: " +
    request.isUserInRole("role1") + "\n");
    response.getWriter().write("Role \"role2\" access: " +
    request.isUserInRole("role2") + "\n");
    response.getWriter().write("Role \"role3\" access: " +
    request.isUserInRole("role3") + "\n");
    response.getWriter().write("Access to /authServlet? " +
    securityContext.hasAccessToWebResource("/authServlet") +
    "\n");
    }
}
```

3. Finally, we will create a class that will define our authentication policy:

```
@ApplicationScoped
public class AuthenticationMechanism implements
HttpAuthenticationMechanism {

    @Override
```

```
public AuthenticationStatus validateRequest(HttpServletRequest
request,
HttpServletResponse response, HttpMessageContext
httpMessageContext)
throws AuthenticationException {

    if (httpMessageContext.isAuthenticationRequest()) {

        Credential credential =
        httpMessageContext.getAuthParameters().getCredential();
        if (!(credential instanceof CallerOnlyCredential)) {
            throw new IllegalStateException("Invalid
            mechanism");
        }

        CallerOnlyCredential callerOnlyCredential =
        (CallerOnlyCredential) credential;

        if ("user".equals(callerOnlyCredential.getCaller())) {
            return
            httpMessageContext.notifyContainerAboutLogin
            (callerOnlyCredential.getCaller(), new HashSet<>
            (Arrays.asList("role1","role2")));
        } else{
            throw new AuthenticationException();
        }

    }

    return httpMessageContext.doNothing();
}

}
```

If you run this project in a Jakarta EE 8-compatible server, you should use the following URL (assuming that you are running locally; if not, make the appropriate changes):

```
http://localhost:8080/ch05-authentication/UserAuthenticationServlet
?name=user
```

4. This should result in a page that shows the following messages:

```
Authentication status: SUCCESS
User: user
Role "role1" access: true
Role "role2" access: true
Role "role3" access: false
Access to /authServlet? true
```

Try making a change to the `name` parameter, as follows:

```
http://localhost:8080/ch05-authentication/UserAuthenticationServlet
?name=anotheruser
```

5. The result will be as follows:

```
Authentication status: SEND_FAILURE
User: null
Role "role1" access: false
Role "role2" access: false
Role "role3" access: false
Access to /authServlet? false
```

Now, let's see how this works.

How it works...

Let's split up the code we've provided so that we can understand what's happening.

In the `web.xml` file, we are creating a security constraint:

```
<security-constraint>
    ...
</security-constraint>
```

We're defining a resource inside it:

```
<web-resource-collection>
    <web-resource-name>CH05-Authentication</web-resource-name>
    <url-pattern>/authServlet</url-pattern>
</web-resource-collection>
```

We're also defining an authorization policy. In this case, it's a role:

```
<auth-constraint>
    <role-name>role1</role-name>
</auth-constraint>
```

Now, we have `UserAuthenticationServlet`. We should pay attention to this annotation:

```
@DeclareRoles({"role1", "role2", "role3"})
```

This defines which roles are part of the context of this particular servlet.

Another important factor in this scene is the following one:

```
@Inject
private SecurityContext securityContext;
```

Here, we are asking the server to give us a security context so that we can use it. This will make sense in a minute.

Then, if the `name` parameter is filled, we reach the following line:

```
AuthenticationStatus status = securityContext.authenticate(
        request, response, withParams().credential(new
        CallerOnlyCredential(name)));
```

This will ask the Jakarta EE server to process authentication. But... based on what? That's where our `HttpAuthenticationMechanism` implementation comes in.

Since the preceding code created `CallerOnlyCredential`, our authentication mechanism will be based on it:

```
Credential credential = httpMessageContext.getAuthParameters()
.getCredential();
if (!(credential instanceof CallerOnlyCredential)) {
    throw new IllegalStateException("Invalid mechanism");
}

CallerOnlyCredential callerOnlyCredential =
(CallerOnlyCredential) credential;
```

Once we have a `credential` instance, we can check whether the user exists:

```
if ("user".equals(callerOnlyCredential.getCaller())) {
    ...
} else{
    throw new AuthenticationException();
}
```

In this example, we have just compared the names of the user, but in a real-life scenario, you could search your database, a **Lightweight Directory Access Protocol (LDAP)** server, and so on.

If the user exists, we proceed with the authentication process based on some rules:

```
return httpMessageContext.notifyContainerAboutLogin
(callerOnlyCredential.getCaller(), new HashSet<>(asList("role1","role2")));
```

In this case, we have said that the user has access to `"role1"` and `"role2"`.

Once authentication is complete, it goes back to the servlet and uses the result to finish the process:

```
response.getWriter().write("Role \"role1\" access: " +
request.isUserInRole("role1") + "\n");
response.getWriter().write("Role \"role2\" access: " +
request.isUserInRole("role2") + "\n");
response.getWriter().write("Role \"role3\" access: " +
request.isUserInRole("role3") + "\n");
response.getWriter().write("Access to /authServlet? " +
securityContext.hasAccessToWebResource("/authServlet") + "\n");
```

So, this code will print `true` for `"role1"` and `"role2"`, and `false` for `"role3"`. Because `"/authServlet"` is allowed for `"role1"`, the user will have access to it.

See also

- The full source code for this recipe can be found at `https://github.com/ eldermoraes/javaee8-cookbook/tree/master/chapter05/ch05- authentication`.

Granting rights through authorization

If authentication is the way you define who can access a particular resource, authorization is the way you define what a user can and cannot do once they have access to the domain.

It's like allowing someone to get into your house, but denying them access to the remote control for your TV (very important access, by the way), or allowing access to the remote control, but denying access to adult channels.

One way to do this is through profiles, and that's what we are going to do in this recipe.

Getting ready

Let's start by adding the dependency:

```
<dependency>
    <groupId>javax</groupId>
    <artifactId>javaee-api</artifactId>
    <version>8.0</version>
    <scope>provided</scope>
</dependency>
```

How to do it...

Follow these steps to complete this recipe:

1. First, we will define some roles in a separate class so that we can reuse it:

```
public class Roles {
    public static final String ROLE1 = "role1";
    public static final String ROLE2 = "role2";
    public static final String ROLE3 = "role3";
}
```

2. Then, we need to define some things that the application's users can do:

```
@Stateful
public class UserActivity {
    @RolesAllowed({Roles.ROLE1})
    public void role1Allowed(){
        System.out.println("role1Allowed executed");
    }
    @RolesAllowed({Roles.ROLE2})
    public void role2Allowed(){
        System.out.println("role2Allowed executed");
    }

    @RolesAllowed({Roles.ROLE3})
    public void role3Allowed(){
        System.out.println("role3Allowed executed");
    }

    @PermitAll
    public void anonymousAllowed(){
        System.out.println("anonymousAllowed executed");
    }
```

```
    @DenyAll
    public void noOneAllowed(){
        System.out.println("noOneAllowed executed");
    }
}
```

3. Let's create an interface for executable tasks:

```
public interface Executable {
    void execute() throws Exception;
}
```

4. Now, let's create another for the roles that will execute them:

```
public interface RoleExecutable {
    void run(Executable executable) throws Exception;
}
```

5. We need to create an executor for each role. An executor is like an environment that owns the rights of that role:

```
@Named
@RunAs(Roles.ROLE1)
public class Role1Executor implements RoleExecutable {

    @Override
    public void run(Executable executable) throws Exception {
        executable.execute();
    }

}
@Named
@RunAs(Roles.ROLE2)
public class Role2Executor implements RoleExecutable {

    @Override
    public void run(Executable executable) throws Exception {
        executable.execute();
    }

}
@Named
@RunAs(Roles.ROLE3)
public class Role3Executor implements RoleExecutable {

    @Override
    public void run(Executable executable) throws Exception {
        executable.execute();
    }

}
```

6. Then, we implement `HttpAuthenticationMechanism`:

```
@ApplicationScoped
public class AuthenticationMechanism implements
HttpAuthenticationMechanism {

    @Override
    public AuthenticationStatus validateRequest(HttpServletRequest
     request, HttpServletResponse response, HttpMessageContext
     httpMessageContext) throws AuthenticationException {

        if (httpMessageContext.isAuthenticationRequest()) {

            Credential credential =
            httpMessageContext.getAuthParameters()
            .getCredential();
            if (!(credential instanceof CallerOnlyCredential)) {
                throw new IllegalStateException("Invalid
                mechanism");
            }

            CallerOnlyCredential callerOnlyCredential =
            (CallerOnlyCredential) credential;

            if (null == callerOnlyCredential.getCaller()) {
                throw new AuthenticationException();
            } else switch (callerOnlyCredential.getCaller()) {
                case "user1":
                    return
                    httpMessageContext.
                    notifyContainerAboutLogin
                    (callerOnlyCredential.getCaller(),
                     new HashSet<>
                    (asList(Roles.ROLE1)));
                case "user2":
                    return
                    httpMessageContext.
                    notifyContainerAboutLogin
                    (callerOnlyCredential.getCaller(),
                     new HashSet<>
                    (asList(Roles.ROLE2)));
                case "user3":
                    return
                    httpMessageContext.
                    notifyContainerAboutLogin
                    (callerOnlyCredential.getCaller(),
                     new HashSet<>
                    (asList(Roles.ROLE3)));
```

```
                    default:
                        throw new AuthenticationException();
                }

            }

            return httpMessageContext.doNothing();
        }

    }
```

7. Finally, we create the servlet that will manage all these resources:

```
@DeclareRoles({Roles.ROLE1, Roles.ROLE2, Roles.ROLE3})
@WebServlet(name = "/UserAuthorizationServlet", urlPatterns =
{"/UserAuthorizationServlet"})
public class UserAuthorizationServlet extends HttpServlet {

    private static final long serialVersionUID = 1L;

    @Inject
    private SecurityContext securityContext;
    @Inject
    private Role1Executor role1Executor;
    @Inject
    private Role2Executor role2Executor;
    @Inject
    private Role3Executor role3Executor;
    @Inject
    private UserActivity userActivity;
    @Override
    public void doGet(HttpServletRequest request,
    HttpServletResponse
    response) throws ServletException, IOException {

        try {
            String name = request.getParameter("name");
            if (null != name || !"".equals(name)) {
                AuthenticationStatus status =
                securityContext.authenticate(
                        request, response, withParams().credential(
                        new CallerOnlyCredential(name)));

                response.getWriter().write("Authentication
                status: " + status.name() + "\n");
            }

            String principal = null;
```

```
if (request.getUserPrincipal() != null) {
    principal = request.getUserPrincipal().getName();
}

response.getWriter().write("User: " + principal +
"\n");
response.getWriter().write("Role \"role1\" access: " +
request.isUserInRole(Roles.ROLE1) + "\n");
response.getWriter().write("Role \"role2\" access: " +
request.isUserInRole(Roles.ROLE2) + "\n");
response.getWriter().write("Role \"role3\" access: " +
request.isUserInRole(Roles.ROLE3) + "\n");

RoleExecutable executable = null;

if (request.isUserInRole(Roles.ROLE1)) {
    executable = role1Executor;
} else if (request.isUserInRole(Roles.ROLE2)) {
    executable = role2Executor;
} else if (request.isUserInRole(Roles.ROLE3)) {
    executable = role3Executor;
}

if (executable != null) {
    executable.run(() -> {
        try {
            userActivity.role1Allowed();
            response.getWriter().write("role1Allowed
            executed: true\n");
        } catch (Exception e) {
            response.getWriter().write("role1Allowed
            executed: false\n");
        }

        try {
            userActivity.role2Allowed();
            response.getWriter().write("role2Allowed
            executed: true\n");
        } catch (Exception e) {
            response.getWriter().write("role2Allowed
            executed: false\n");
        }

        try {
            userActivity.role3Allowed();
            response.getWriter().write("role2Allowed
            executed: true\n");
        } catch (Exception e) {
```

```
                                    response.getWriter().write("role2Allowed
                                    executed: false\n");
                                }

                            });

                        }

                        try {
                            userActivity.anonymousAllowed();
                            response.getWriter().write("anonymousAllowed
                            executed: true\n");
                        } catch (Exception e) {
                            response.getWriter().write("anonymousAllowed
                            executed: false\n");
                        }
                        try {
                            userActivity.noOneAllowed();
                            response.getWriter().write("noOneAllowed
                            executed: true\n");
                        } catch (Exception e) {
                            response.getWriter().write("noOneAllowed
                            executed: false\n");
                        }

                    } catch (Exception ex) {
                        System.err.println(ex.getMessage());
                    }

                }
            }
```

To try this code out, run the following URLs:

- `http://localhost:8080/ch05-authorization/UserAuthorizationServlet?name=user1`
- `http://localhost:8080/ch05-authorization/UserAuthorizationServlet?name=user2`
- `http://localhost:8080/ch05-authorization/UserAuthorizationServlet?name=user3`

The result for `user1`, for example, will be as follows:

```
Authentication status: SUCCESS
User: user1
Role "role1" access: true
Role "role2" access: false
```

```
Role "role3" access: false
role1Allowed executed: true
role2Allowed executed: false
role2Allowed executed: false
anonymousAllowed executed: true
noOneAllowed executed: false
```

If you try this out with a user that doesn't exist, the result will be as follows:

```
Authentication status: SEND_FAILURE
User: null
Role "role1" access: false
Role "role2" access: false
Role "role3" access: false
anonymousAllowed executed: true
noOneAllowed executed: false
```

How it works...

Well, we have a lot of things happening here! Let's begin with the UserActivity class.

We used the @RolesAllowed annotation to define the role that can access each method of the class:

```
@RolesAllowed({Roles.ROLE1})
public void role1Allowed(){
    System.out.println("role1Allowed executed");
}
```

You can add more than one role inside the annotation (it's an array).

We also had two other interesting annotations, @PermitAll and @DenyAll:

- The @PermitAll annotation allows anyone to access the method, even without any authentication.
- The @DenyAll annotation denies everyone access to the method, even authenticated users with the highest privileges.

Then, we have what we called executors:

```
@Named
@RunAs(Roles.ROLE1)
public class Role1Executor implements RoleExecutable {

    @Override
    public void run(Executable executable) throws Exception {
```

```
            executable.execute();
    }
  }
```

We used the @RunAs annotation at the class level, which means that this class inherits all the privileges of the defined role (in this case, "role1"). This means that every single method of this class will have the "role1" privileges.

Now, if we look at the beginning of UserAuthorizationServlet, we'll see that we have an important object:

```
@Inject
private SecurityContext securityContext;
```

Here, we are asking the server to give us a security context instance so that we can use it for authentication purposes.

Then, if the name parameter is filled, we reach this line:

```
AuthenticationStatus status = securityContext.authenticate(
        request, response, withParams().credential(new
        CallerOnlyCredential(name)));
```

This will ask the Jakarta EE server to process authentication. That's where our HttpAuthenticationMechanism implementation comes in.

Since the preceding code created CallerOnlyCredential, our authentication mechanism will be based on it:

```
Credential credential = httpMessageContext.getAuthParameters().
getCredential();
if (!(credential instanceof CallerOnlyCredential)) {
    throw new IllegalStateException("Invalid mechanism");
}

CallerOnlyCredential callerOnlyCredential =
(CallerOnlyCredential) credential;
```

Once we have a credential instance, we can check whether the user exists:

```
if (null == callerOnlyCredential.getCaller()) {
    throw new AuthenticationException();
} else switch (callerOnlyCredential.getCaller()) {
    case "user1":
        return httpMessageContext.notifyContainerAboutLogin
        (callerOnlyCredential.getCaller(), new HashSet<>
        (asList(Roles.ROLE1)));
```

```
            case "user2":
                return httpMessageContext.notifyContainerAboutLogin
                (callerOnlyCredential.getCaller(), new HashSet<>
                (asList(Roles.ROLE2)));
            case "user3":
                return httpMessageContext.notifyContainerAboutLogin
                (callerOnlyCredential.getCaller(), new HashSet<>
                (asList(Roles.ROLE3)));
            default:
                throw new AuthenticationException();
    }
```

So, here, we are saying that `"user1"` has access to `"role1"`, `"user2"` has access to `"role2"`, and so on.

Once the user role has been defined, we are sent back to the servlet and can choose which environment (executor) will be used:

```
if (request.isUserInRole(Roles.ROLE1)) {
    executable = role1Executor;
} else if (request.isUserInRole(Roles.ROLE2)) {
    executable = role2Executor;
} else if (request.isUserInRole(Roles.ROLE3)) {
    executable = role3Executor;
}
```

Then, we can try all the methods of the `UserActivity` class. Only the methods that are allowed for that specific role will be executed; the others will fall into an exception, except for the `@PermitAll` method, which will run anyway, and `@DenyAll`, which won't run at all.

See also

- The full source code for this recipe can be found at `https://github.com/eldermoraes/javaee8-cookbook/tree/master/chapter05/ch05-authorization`.

Protecting data confidentiality and integrity with SSL/TLS

Security also means protecting your data when it's being transported. For this purpose, we can use a popular method called the **Secure Sockets Layer (SSL)**.

Transport Layer Security (TLS) is the newest version of SSL. SSL 3.0 and TLS 1.0 are the protocols supported by Eclipse GlassFish 5.

This recipe will show you how to enable Eclipse GlassFish so that it works properly with SSL. All Jakarta EE servers have their own way of doing this.

Getting ready

To enable SSL in GlassFish, you need to configure an HTTP listener for SSL. All you need to do is this:

1. Make sure GlassFish is up and running.
2. Use the `create-ssl` command to create your HTTP listener for SSL.
3. Restart the GlassFish server.

How to do it...

Follow these steps to complete this recipe:

1. To complete this task, you need to access the Eclipse GlassFish remote **command-line interface (CLI)**. You can do this by going to the following path:

   ```
   $GLASSFISH_HOME/bin
   ```

2. Once you are there, execute the following command:

   ```
   ./asadmin start-domain --verbose
   ```

3. Once the server is up and running, execute the following command:

   ```
   ./asadmin
   ```

4. When the prompt is ready, execute the following command:

   ```
   create-ssl --type http-listener --certname cookbookCert http-listener-1
   ```

5. Now, if you restart the server, your `http-listener-1` will work with SSL. If you want to drop SSL from the listener, just go back to the prompt and execute the following command:

   ```
   delete-ssl --type http-listener http-listener-1
   ```

How it works...

With SSL, both the client and the server encrypt data before sending it and decrypt data upon receiving it. When a browser opens a secured website (using HTTPS), something happens called a **handshake**.

In the handshake, the browser asks the server for a session; the server answers by sending a certificate and the public key. The browser validates the certificate and, if it is valid, generates a unique session key, encrypts it with the server public key, and sends it back to the server. Once the server receives the session key, it decrypts it with its private key.

Now, the client and the server have a copy of the session key and can ensure that the communication is secure.

There's more...

It's strongly recommended that you use a certificate from a **Certification Authority (CA)** instead of a self-created certificate, which is what we used in this recipe.

Check out `https://letsencrypt.org` to get your own free certificate.

The process of using it is the same; you just need to change the value in the `--certname` parameter.

See also

- For more information about all the security aspects and configuration for Eclipse GlassFish 5, check out `https://javaee.github.io/glassfish/doc/5.0/security-guide.pdf`. At the time of writing this book, no version of this documentation has been published under the EE4J project.

Using declarative security

When building your application's security features, you can use two approaches – programmatic security and declarative security:

- The programmatic approach is when you define the security policy of your application using code.
- The declarative approach is when you define the security policy by declaring the policies and then applying them accordingly.

This recipe will show you the declarative approach.

Getting ready

Let's start by adding the dependency:

```
<dependency>
    <groupId>javax</groupId>
    <artifactId>javaee-api</artifactId>
    <version>8.0</version>
    <scope>provided</scope>
</dependency>
```

How to do it...

Follow these steps to complete this recipe:

1. First, let's create a list of roles for our application:

```
public class Roles {
    public static final String ADMIN = "admin";
    public static final String USER = "user";
}
```

2. Now, we need to create a list of tasks that can be performed by only one of the roles – one task that everyone can do and another task that no one can do:

```
@Stateful
public class UserBean {
    @RolesAllowed({Roles.ADMIN})
    public void adminOperation(){
        System.out.println("adminOperation executed");
    }
```

```
@RolesAllowed({Roles.USER})
public void userOperation(){
    System.out.println("userOperation executed");
}

@PermitAll
public void everyoneCanDo(){
    System.out.println("everyoneCanDo executed");
}

@DenyAll
public void noneCanDo(){
    System.out.println("noneCanDo executed");
}
}
```

3. Now, we need to create an environment for both the USER and ADMIN roles so that they can carry out their tasks:

```
@Named
@RunAs(Roles.USER)
public class UserExecutor implements RoleExecutable {

    @Override
    public void run(Executable executable) throws Exception {
        executable.execute();
    }
}
@Named
@RunAs(Roles.ADMIN)
public class AdminExecutor implements RoleExecutable {

    @Override
    public void run(Executable executable) throws Exception {
        executable.execute();
    }
}
```

4. Then, we need to implement HttpAuthenticationMechanism:

```
@ApplicationScoped
public class AuthenticationMechanism implements
HttpAuthenticationMechanism {

    @Override
    public AuthenticationStatus validateRequest(HttpServletRequest
    request, HttpServletResponse response, HttpMessageContext
    httpMessageContext)
```

```
        throws AuthenticationException {

    if (httpMessageContext.isAuthenticationRequest()) {

        Credential credential =
        httpMessageContext.getAuthParameters().
        getCredential();
        if (!(credential instanceof CallerOnlyCredential)) {
            throw new IllegalStateException("Invalid
            mechanism");
        }

        CallerOnlyCredential callerOnlyCredential =
        (CallerOnlyCredential)
        credential;

        if (null == callerOnlyCredential.getCaller()) {
            throw new AuthenticationException();
        } else switch (callerOnlyCredential.getCaller()) {
            case Roles.ADMIN:
                return httpMessageContext
                .notifyContainerAboutLogin
                (callerOnlyCredential.getCaller(),
                 new HashSet<>
                (asList(Roles.ADMIN)));
            case Roles.USER:
                return httpMessageContext
                .notifyContainerAboutLogin
                (callerOnlyCredential.getCaller(),
                new HashSet<>
                (asList(Roles.USER)));
            default:
                throw new AuthenticationException();
        }

    }

    return httpMessageContext.doNothing();
    }

}
```

5. Finally, we need to create a servlet for each role (USER and ADMIN):

```
@DeclareRoles({Roles.ADMIN, Roles.USER})
@WebServlet(name = "/UserServlet", urlPatterns = {"/UserServlet"})
public class UserServlet extends HttpServlet {
```

```
private static final long serialVersionUID = 1L;

@Inject
private SecurityContext securityContext;

@Inject
private UserExecutor userExecutor;

@Inject
private UserBean userActivity;

@Override
public void doGet(HttpServletRequest request,
HttpServletResponse response) throws ServletException,
IOException {

    try {
        securityContext.authenticate(
                request, response, withParams().credential(new
                CallerOnlyCredential(Roles.USER)));

        response.getWriter().write("Role \"admin\" access: " +
        request.isUserInRole(Roles.ADMIN) + "\n");
        response.getWriter().write("Role \"user\" access: " +
        request.isUserInRole(Roles.USER) + "\n");

        userExecutor.run(() -> {
            try {
                userActivity.adminOperation();
                response.getWriter().write("adminOperation
                executed: true\n");
            } catch (Exception e) {
                response.getWriter().write("adminOperation
                executed: false\n");
            }

            try {
                userActivity.userOperation();
                response.getWriter().write("userOperation
                executed: true\n");
            } catch (Exception e) {
                response.getWriter().write("userOperation
                executed: false\n");
            }

        });

        try {
```

```
                userActivity.everyoneCanDo();
                response.getWriter().write("everyoneCanDo
                executed: true\n");
            } catch (Exception e) {
                response.getWriter().write("everyoneCanDo
                executed: false\n");
            }

            try {
                userActivity.noneCanDo();
                response.getWriter().write("noneCanDo
                executed: true\n");
            } catch (Exception e) {
                response.getWriter().write("noneCanDo
                executed: false\n");
            }

        } catch (Exception ex) {
            System.err.println(ex.getMessage());
        }


    }
}
@DeclareRoles({Roles.ADMIN, Roles.USER})
@WebServlet(name = "/AdminServlet", urlPatterns =
{"/AdminServlet"})
public class AdminServlet extends HttpServlet {

    private static final long serialVersionUID = 1L;

    @Inject
    private SecurityContext securityContext;

    @Inject
    private AdminExecutor adminExecutor;

    @Inject
    private UserBean userActivity;

    @Override
    public void doGet(HttpServletRequest request,
    HttpServletResponse
    response) throws ServletException, IOException {

        try {
            securityContext.authenticate(
                    request, response, withParams().credential(new
                    CallerOnlyCredential(Roles.ADMIN)));
```

```
            response.getWriter().write("Role \"admin\" access: " +
            request.isUserInRole(Roles.ADMIN) + "\n");
            response.getWriter().write("Role \"user\" access: " +
            request.isUserInRole(Roles.USER) + "\n");

            adminExecutor.run(() -> {
                try {
                    userActivity.adminOperation();
                    response.getWriter().write("adminOperation
                    executed: true\n");
                } catch (Exception e) {
                    response.getWriter().write("adminOperation
                    executed: false\n");
                }

                try {
                    userActivity.userOperation();
                    response.getWriter().write("userOperation
                    executed: true\n");
                } catch (Exception e) {
                    response.getWriter().write("userOperation
                    executed: false\n");
                }

            });

            try {
                userActivity.everyoneCanDo();
                response.getWriter().write("everyoneCanDo
                executed: true\n");
            } catch (Exception e) {
                response.getWriter().write("everyoneCanDo
                executed: false\n");
            }

            try {
                userActivity.noneCanDo();
                response.getWriter().write("noneCanDo
                executed: true\n");
            } catch (Exception e) {
                response.getWriter().write("noneCanDo
                executed: false\n");
            }

        } catch (Exception ex) {
            System.err.println(ex.getMessage());
        }
```

```
        }
    }
```

How it works...

By looking at `UserServlet` (which applies to the `USER` role), we can see the authentication step:

```
securityContext.authenticate(
        request, response, withParams().credential(new
        CallerOnlyCredential(Roles.ADMIN)));
```

For example, we've used the role name as a username because if we look at the `AuthenticationMechanism` class (which is implementing `HttpAuthenticationMechanism`), we can see it doing all the hard work of authenticating and assigning the right role to the user:

```
Credential credential =
httpMessageContext.getAuthParameters()
.getCredential();
if (!(credential instanceof CallerOnlyCredential)) {
    throw new IllegalStateException("Invalid mechanism");
}

CallerOnlyCredential callerOnlyCredential =
(CallerOnlyCredential)
credential;

if (null == callerOnlyCredential.getCaller()) {
    throw new AuthenticationException();
} else switch (callerOnlyCredential.getCaller()) {
    case Roles.ADMIN:
        return httpMessageContext.notifyContainerAboutLogin
        (callerOnlyCredential.getCaller(), new HashSet<>
        (asList(Roles.ADMIN)));
    case Roles.USER:
        return httpMessageContext.notifyContainerAboutLogin
        (callerOnlyCredential.getCaller(), new HashSet<>
        (asList(Roles.USER)));
    default:
        throw new AuthenticationException();
}
```

Let's go back to `UserServlet`. Now that the user has been assigned the correct role, it is just a matter of what they can and cannot do. This can be seen in the following code:

```
userExecutor.run(() -> {
    try {
        userActivity.adminOperation();
        response.getWriter().write("adminOperation
        executed: true\n");
    } catch (Exception e) {
        response.getWriter().write("adminOperation
        executed: false\n");
    }

    try {
        userActivity.userOperation();
        response.getWriter().write("userOperation
        executed: true\n");
    } catch (Exception e) {
        response.getWriter().write("userOperation
        executed:  false\n");
    }

});
```

We also need to try the tasks that everyone and no one can perform:

```
try {
    userActivity.everyoneCanDo();
    response.getWriter().write("everyoneCanDo
    executed: true\n");
} catch (Exception e) {
    response.getWriter().write("everyoneCanDo
    executed: false\n");
}

try {
    userActivity.noneCanDo();
    response.getWriter().write("noneCanDo
    executed: true\n");
} catch (Exception e) {
    response.getWriter().write("noneCanDo
    executed: false\n");
}
```

The `AdminServlet` class goes through exactly the same steps using an `AdminExecutor` environment, so we will omit it for the sake of space.

To try this code out for yourself, just run it on a Java EE 8-compatible server using the following URLs:

- `http://localhost:8080/ch05-declarative/AdminServlet`
- `http://localhost:8080/ch05-declarative/UserServlet`

The result for `AdminServlet` will be as follows:

```
Role "admin" access: true
Role "user" access: false
adminOperation executed: true
userOperation executed: false
everyoneCanDo executed: true
noneCanDo executed: false
```

See also

- The full source code for this recipe can be found at `https://github.com/eldermoraes/javaee8-cookbook/tree/master/chapter05/ch05-declarative`.

Using programmatic security

We've already looked at the declarative approach, so now, let's take a look at the programmatic approach. As we mentioned earlier, the programmatic approach is when you define the security policy of your application using code.

Getting ready

Let's start by adding the dependency:

```xml
<dependency>
    <groupId>javax</groupId>
    <artifactId>javaee-api</artifactId>
    <version>8.0</version>
    <scope>provided</scope>
</dependency>
```

How to do it...

Follow these steps to complete this recipe:

1. First, let's define our roles list:

```
public class Roles {
    public static final String ADMIN = "admin";
    public static final String USER = "user";
}
```

2. Now, let's define a list of tasks to be completed based on the role:

```
@Stateful
public class UserBean {
    @RolesAllowed({Roles.ADMIN})
    public void adminOperation(){
        System.out.println("adminOperation executed");
    }
    @RolesAllowed({Roles.USER})
    public void userOperation(){
        System.out.println("userOperation executed");
    }

    @PermitAll
    public void everyoneCanDo(){
        System.out.println("everyoneCanDo executed");
    }

}
```

3. Now, let's implement the `IndentityStore` interface. Here, we define our policy so that we can validate the user's identity:

```
@ApplicationScoped
public class UserIdentityStore implements IdentityStore {

    @Override
    public CredentialValidationResult validate(Credential
credential) {
        if (credential instanceof UsernamePasswordCredential) {
            return validate((UsernamePasswordCredential)
credential);
        }

        return CredentialValidationResult.NOT_VALIDATED_RESULT;
    }
```

```
    public CredentialValidationResult
validate(UsernamePasswordCredential
    usernamePasswordCredential) {

        if (usernamePasswordCredential.
        getCaller().equals(Roles.ADMIN)
            && usernamePasswordCredential.
            getPassword().compareTo("1234"))
        {

            return new CredentialValidationResult(
                new CallerPrincipal
                (usernamePasswordCredential.getCaller()),
                new HashSet<>(Arrays.asList(Roles.ADMIN)));
        } else if (usernamePasswordCredential.
          getCaller().equals(Roles.USER)
            && usernamePasswordCredential.
            getPassword().compareTo("1234"))
        {

            return new CredentialValidationResult(
                new CallerPrincipal
                (usernamePasswordCredential.getCaller()),
                new HashSet<>(Arrays.asList(Roles.USER)));
        }

        return CredentialValidationResult.INVALID_RESULT;
    }

}
```

4. Here, we need to implement the `HttpAuthenticationMethod` interface:

```
@ApplicationScoped
public class AuthenticationMechanism implements
HttpAuthenticationMechanism {

    @Inject
    private UserIdentityStore identityStore;
    @Override
    public AuthenticationStatus validateRequest(HttpServletRequest
    request,
    HttpServletResponse response, HttpMessageContext
    httpMessageContext)
    throws AuthenticationException {

        if (httpMessageContext.isAuthenticationRequest()) {
```

```
                    Credential credential =
                    httpMessageContext.getAuthParameters()
                    .getCredential();
                    if (!(credential instanceof
        UsernamePasswordCredential)) {
                        throw new IllegalStateException("Invalid
                        mechanism");
                    }

                    return httpMessageContext.notifyContainerAboutLogin
                    (identityStore.validate(credential));
                }

                return httpMessageContext.doNothing();
            }

        }
```

5. Finally, we need to create a servlet where the user will both authenticate and carry out their tasks:

```
@DeclareRoles({Roles.ADMIN, Roles.USER})
@WebServlet(name = "/OperationServlet", urlPatterns =
{"/OperationServlet"})
public class OperationServlet extends HttpServlet {

    private static final long serialVersionUID = 1L;

    @Inject
    private SecurityContext securityContext;

    @Inject
    private UserBean userActivity;

    @Override
    public void doGet(HttpServletRequest request,
    HttpServletResponse
    response) throws ServletException, IOException {

        String name = request.getParameter("name");
        String password = request.getParameter("password");

        Credential credential = new
    UsernamePasswordCredential(name,
        new Password(password));

        AuthenticationStatus status = securityContext.authenticate(
            request, response,
```

```
withParams().credential(credential));

response.getWriter().write("Role \"admin\" access: " +
request.isUserInRole(Roles.ADMIN) + "\n");
response.getWriter().write("Role \"user\" access: " +
request.isUserInRole(Roles.USER) + "\n");

if (status.equals(AuthenticationStatus.SUCCESS)) {

    if (request.isUserInRole(Roles.ADMIN)) {
        userActivity.adminOperation();
        response.getWriter().write("adminOperation
        executed: true\n");
    } else if (request.isUserInRole(Roles.USER)) {
        userActivity.userOperation();
        response.getWriter().write("userOperation
        executed: true\n");
    }

    userActivity.everyoneCanDo();
    response.getWriter().write("everyoneCanDo
    executed: true\n");

} else {
    response.getWriter().write("Authentication failed\n");
}

    }
}
```

To try out this code, run it in a Jakarta EE 8-compatible server using the following URLs:

- `http://localhost:8080/ch05-programmatic/OperationServlet?name=user&password=1234`

- `http://localhost:8080/ch05-programmatic/OperationServlet?name=admin&password=1234`

6. An example of the ADMIN role's result is as follows:

```
Role "admin" access: true
Role "user" access: false
adminOperation executed: true
everyoneCanDo executed: true
```

7. If you use a wrong username/password pair, you'll get the following result:

```
Role "admin" access: false
Role "user" access: false
Authentication failed
```

How it works...

Contrary to the declarative approach (see the preceding recipe), here, we are using code to validate the user. We did this by implementing the IdentityStore interface.

For example, even though we've hardcoded the password, we can use the same piece of code to validate the password against a database, LDAP, an external endpoint, and so on:

```
if (usernamePasswordCredential.getCaller().equals(Roles.ADMIN)
        &&
usernamePasswordCredential.getPassword().compareTo("1234"))
{

    return new CredentialValidationResult(
            new CallerPrincipal(usernamePasswordCredential
            .getCaller()),
            new HashSet<>(asList(Roles.ADMIN)));
} else if (usernamePasswordCredential.getCaller()
  .equals(Roles.USER)
        && usernamePasswordCredential.
        getPassword().compareTo("1234"))
{

    return new CredentialValidationResult(
            new CallerPrincipal(usernamePasswordCredential
            .getCaller()),
            new HashSet<>(asList(Roles.USER)));
}

return INVALID_RESULT;
```

Authenticating using IdentityStore means just delegating using HttpAuthenticationMethod:

```
Credential credential =
httpMessageContext.getAuthParameters().getCredential();
if (!(credential instanceof UsernamePasswordCredential)) {
    throw new IllegalStateException("Invalid mechanism");
}
```

```
return httpMessageContext.notifyContainerAboutLogin
(identityStore.validate(credential));
```

`OperationServlet` will try to perform authentication:

```
String name = request.getParameter("name");
String password = request.getParameter("password");

Credential credential = new UsernamePasswordCredential(name,
new Password(password));

AuthenticationStatus status = securityContext.authenticate(
        request, response,
    withParams().credential(credential));
```

Based on this, we can define the flow of what will happen next:

```
if (status.equals(AuthenticationStatus.SUCCESS)) {

    if (request.isUserInRole(Roles.ADMIN)) {
        userActivity.adminOperation();
        response.getWriter().write("adminOperation
        executed: true\n");
    } else if (request.isUserInRole(Roles.USER)) {
        userActivity.userOperation();
        response.getWriter().write("userOperation
        executed: true\n");
    }

    userActivity.everyoneCanDo();
    response.getWriter().write("everyoneCanDo executed:

true\n");

} else {
    response.getWriter().write("Authentication failed\n");
}
```

Pay attention! This is your code defining what each role will do.

See also

- The full source code for this recipe can be found at `https://github.com/ eldermoraes/javaee8-cookbook/tree/master/chapter05/ch05-programmatic`.

6
Reducing Coding Effort by Relying on Standards

One of the most important things that you need to know about Jakarta EE is that it is a standard, formerly managed by the **Java Community Process** (**JCP**) and now managed by the Eclipse Foundation.

A standard... for what? Well, for an application server! A Jakarta EE application server, for instance. This means that you can develop your Jakarta EE application knowing it will run in an environment that provides a bunch of resources that you can rely on. It also means you can easily move from one application server to another, as long as you stick to the Jakarta EE patterns instead of some vendor-specific feature (which is considered bad practice). Your application should have the same behavior no matter what Jakarta EE-compatible server you are using.

Beyond being a standard, Jakarta EE is also a certification. For a Jakarta EE server to be considered compatible, it has to pass a number of tests to guarantee that it implements every single point of the specification (**JSR** (short for **Java Specification Requests**)).

This amazing ecosystem means less coding of your application and gives you the chance to focus on what really matters to you or your client. Without a standard environment, you would need to implement your own code for request/response management, queues, connection pooling, and other stuff. You can definitely do that if you want, but you don't have to. Actually, you can even write your own Jakarta EE application server if you want to.

Having said that, let's move on with the chapter! In the following recipes, you are going to learn how to take advantage of some cool features already implemented on your favorite Jakarta EE application server.

Examples will be based on Eclipse GlassFish 5.1, but, as I mentioned before, they should have the same behavior for any other compatible implementation.

This chapter covers the following recipes:

- Preparing your application to use a connection pool
- Using messaging services for asynchronous communication
- Understanding a servlet's life cycle
- Transaction management

Preparing your application to use a connection pool

One of the first things we should learn in our lives, after feeding, is how to use a connection pool – especially when we are talking about databases. That's the case here.

Why? Because a connection opened with a database is costly in terms of the resources used for it. If we look closely at the process of opening a new connection, we see that it uses a lot of CPU resources, for example.

Maybe it won't make much of a difference if you have two users using a database with a couple of registers in a few tables. But it can start causing trouble if you have dozens of users, or if the database is large and gives you sleepless nights when you have hundreds of users using a huge database.

Actually, I myself saw in the early days of J2EE 1.3 (the year was 2002) a performance issue being solved by a connection pool in an application used by 20 people. There were a few users, but the database was really big and not so well designed (the same went for the application, I have to say).

But, you may say, why does a connection pool help us with this? Because once it is configured, the server will open all the connections you asked for when it starts up and will manage them for you.

The only thing you have to do is say, *"Hey, server! Could you lend me a database connection, please?"* and kindly give it back when you are done (which means as quickly as possible).

This recipe will show you how to do this.

Getting ready

First, add the right dependency to your project:

```
<dependency>
    <groupId>javax</groupId>
    <artifactId>javaee-api</artifactId>
    <version>8.0</version>
    <scope>provided</scope>
</dependency>
```

If you still haven't downloaded GlassFish 5 to your development environment, this is the right time to do it.

How to do it...

Please follow the steps given here to complete this recipe:

1. We will begin by configuring our connection pool in GlassFish 5. Once it is up and running, go to `http://localhost:8080`.

2. Now click on the **Go to the Administration Console** link, or, if you prefer, go straight to `http://localhost:4848/`.

3. Then, follow this path in the left menu: **Resources | JDBC | JDBC Connection Pools.**

4. Click on the **New** button. This will open the **New JDBC Connection Pool** page. Fill in the fields as described here:

- **Pool Name:** `MysqlPool`
- **Resource Type:** `javax.sql.DataSource`
- **Database Driver Vendor:** `MySql`

   Of course, you can make your own custom choices, but then we would be following different paths!

5. Click on the **Next** button. This will open the second step for our pool creation process.

   This new page has three sections: **General Settings**, **Pool Settings**, and **Transaction and Additional Properties**. For our recipe, we are only dealing with **General Settings** and **Additional Properties**.

6. In the **General Settings** section, make sure that **DataSource Classname** has this value selected:

```
com.mysql.jdbc.jdbc2.optional.MysqlDatasource
```

7. Now let's move to the **Additional Properties** section. There might be a bunch of properties listed, but we will just fill in a few of them:

- **DatabaseName**: `sys`
- **ServerName**: `localhost`
- **User**: `root`
- **Password**: `mysql`
- **PortNumber**: `3306`

8. Click on the **Finish** button and voilá! Your connection pool is ready...or almost ready.

   You can't access it until you do one more configuration. In the same menu, on the left, follow this path: **Resources | JDBC | JDBC Resources.**

9. Click on the **New** button and then fill in the fields like this:

- **JNDI Name**: `jdbc/MysqlPool`
- **Pool Name**: `MysqlPool`

Now you are good to go! Your connection pool is ready to be used.

Let's build a simple application to try it:

1. First, we create a class to get a connection from the pool:

```java
public class ConnectionPool {

    public static Connection getConnection() throws SQLException,
    NamingException {
        InitialContext ctx = new InitialContext();
        DataSource ds = (DataSource) ctx.lookup("jdbc/MysqlPool");

        return ds.getConnection();
    }
}
```

2. Then, we create a class that we will use as a representation of the `sys_config` table (MySQL's system table):

```
public class SysConfig {

    private final String variable;
    private final String value;

    public SysConfig(String variable, String value) {
        this.variable = variable;
        this.value = value;
    }

    public String getVariable() {
        return variable;
    }

    public String getValue() {
        return value;
    }
}
```

3. Here we create another class to create a list based on the data returned from the database:

```
@Stateless
public class SysConfigBean {

    public String getSysConfig() throws SQLException,
NamingException {
        String sql = "SELECT variable, value FROM sys_config";

        try (Connection conn = ConnectionPool.getConnection();
                PreparedStatement ps = conn.prepareStatement(sql);
                ResultSet rs = ps.executeQuery()
                Jsonb jsonb = JsonbBuilder.create()) {

            List<SysConfig> list = new ArrayList<>();
            while (rs.next()) {
                list.add(new SysConfig(rs.getString("variable"),
                rs.getString("value")));
            }

            Jsonb jsonb = JsonbBuilder.create();
            return jsonb.toJson(list);
        }
    }
}
```

4. Finally, we create a servlet that will try them all:

```
@WebServlet(name = "PoolTestServlet", urlPatterns =
{"/PoolTestServlet"})
public class PoolTestServlet extends HttpServlet {

    @EJB
    private SysConfigBean config;

    @Override
    protected void doGet(HttpServletRequest request,
    HttpServletResponse response)
            throws ServletException, IOException {

        try (PrintWriter writer = response.getWriter()) {
            config = new SysConfigBean();
            writer.write(config.getSysConfig());
        } catch (SQLException | NamingException ex) {
            System.err.println(ex.getMessage());
        }
    }
}
```

To try it, just open this URL in your browser:

```
http://localhost:8080/ch06-connectionpooling/PoolTestServlet
```

There's more...

Deciding how many connections your pool will hold, as well as all the other parameters, is an architectural decision made based on a number of factors, such as the type of data, database design, application and user behavior, and so on. We could write a whole book about it.

But if you are starting from scratch and/or still don't need much information, consider a number between 10% to 20% of your concurrent users. In other words, if your application has, for instance, 100 concurrent users, you should provide 10 to 20 connections to your pool.

You will know that your connections aren't enough if some methods are taking too much time to get a connection from the pool (it should take no time at all). That means that the server has no available connections at that moment.

So, you need to check whether there are some methods taking too long to complete, or even some part of your code that is not closing the connection (consider what gives the connection back to the server). Depending on the issue, it might not be a pooling problem but a design one.

Another important thing for dealing with connection pools is to use the *try-with-resources* statement as we did here:

```
try (Connection conn = ConnectionPool.getConnection();
        PreparedStatement ps = conn.prepareStatement(sql);
        ResultSet rs = ps.executeQuery()) {
```

This will guarantee that these resources will be properly closed once the method is done and also deals with their respective exceptions, helping you to write less code.

See also

- See this recipe's full source code at `https://github.com/eldermoraes/javaee8-cookbook/tree/master/chapter06/ch06-connectionpooling`.

Using messaging services for asynchronous communication

The message service, provided in Jakarta EE by the **Java Message Service** (**JMS**) API, is one of the most important and versatile features provided by Jakarta EE environments.

It uses the producer-consumer approach, where one peer (the producer) puts a message into a queue and another peer (the consumer) reads the message from there.

Both the producer and consumer can be different applications, even using different technologies.

This recipe will show you how to build a messaging service using Eclipse GlassFish 5.1. Each Jakarta EE server has its own way to set up the service, so if you are using some other implementations, you should take a look at its documentation.

On the other hand, the Jakarta EE code generated here will work on any Jakarta EE 8-compatible implementation. Standards for the win!

Getting ready

First, add the proper dependency to your project:

```
<dependency>
    <groupId>javax</groupId>
    <artifactId>javaee-api</artifactId>
    <version>8.0</version>
    <scope>provided</scope>
</dependency>
```

How to do it...

Please follow the steps given here to complete this recipe:

1. We will begin by configuring our messaging service in GlassFish 5. Once the server is up and running, go to `http://localhost:8080`.
2. Now click on the **Go to the Administration Console** link, or, if you prefer, go straight to `http://localhost:4848/`.

   Then, follow this path in the left menu:

   Resources | JMS Resources | Connection Factories

3. Click on the **New** button. When the page is open, fill in the **General Settings** section fields like this:

   - **JNDI Name**: `jms/JmsFactory`
   - **Resource Type**: `javax.jms.ConnectionFactory`

   We will not touch the **Pool Settings** section here, so just click on the **OK** button to register your new factory.

4. Now follow this path in the left menu:

   Resources | JMS Resources | Destination Resources

5. Click on the **New** button. When the page is open, fill in the section fields like this:

   - **JNDI Name**: `jms/JmsQueue`
   - **Physical Destination Name**: `JmsQueue`
   - **ResourceType**: `javax.jms.Queue`

Click on the **OK** button and you are ready! Now you have a connection factory to access your JMS server and a queue. So, let's build an application to use it:

1. First, we create a **Message Driven Bean** (**MDB**) as a listener for any message dropped into our queue. This is the consumer:

```
@MessageDriven(activationConfig = {
    @ActivationConfigProperty(propertyName = "destinationLookup",
    propertyValue = "jms/JmsQueue"),
    @ActivationConfigProperty(propertyName = "destinationType",
    propertyValue = "javax.jms.Queue")
})
public class QueueListener implements MessageListener {

    @Override
    public void onMessage(Message message) {
        TextMessage textMessage = (TextMessage) message;
        try {
            System.out.print("Got new message on queue: ");
            System.out.println(textMessage.getText());
            System.out.println();
        } catch (JMSException e) {
            System.err.println(e.getMessage());
        }
    }
}
```

2. Now we define the producer class:

```
@Stateless
public class QueueSender {

    @Resource(mappedName = "jms/JmsFactory")
    private ConnectionFactory jmsFactory;
    @Resource(mappedName = "jms/JmsQueue")
    private Queue jmsQueue;

    public void send() throws JMSException {
        MessageProducer producer;
        TextMessage message;

        try (Connection connection = jmsFactory.createConnection();
            Session session = connection.createSession(false,
            Session.AUTO_ACKNOWLEDGE)) {
            producer = session.createProducer(jmsQueue);
            message = session.createTextMessage();

            String msg = "Now it is " + new Date();
```

```
        message.setText(msg);
        System.out.println("Message sent to queue: " + msg);
        producer.send(message);

        producer.close();
    }
  }
}
```

3. We define a servlet to access the producer:

```
@WebServlet(name = "QueueSenderServlet", urlPatterns =
{"/QueueSenderServlet"})
public class QueueSenderServlet extends HttpServlet {
    @Inject
    private QueueSender sender;

    @Override
    protected void doGet(HttpServletRequest request,
    HttpServletResponse response)
            throws ServletException, IOException {
        try(PrintWriter writer = response.getWriter()){
            sender.send();
            writer.write("Message sent to queue.
            Check the log for details.");
        } catch (JMSException ex) {
            System.err.println(ex.getMessage());
        }
    }
}
```

4. Finally, we create a page just to call our servlet:

```
<html>
    <head>
        <title>JMS recipe</title>
        <meta http-equiv="Content-Type" content="text/html;
        charset=UTF-8">
    </head>
    <body>
        <p>
            <a href="QueueSenderServlet">Send Message to Queue</a>
        </p>
    </body>
</html>
```

Now just deploy and run it. Each time you call `QueueSenderServlet`, you should see something like this on your server log:

```
Info: Message sent to queue: Now it is Tue Dec 19 06:52:17 BRST 2017
Info: Got new message on queue: Now it is Tue Dec 19 06:52:17 BRST 2017
```

Let's see how the recipe works.

How it works...

Thanks to the standards implemented in the Jakarta EE 8 server, our MDB is 100% managed by the container. That's why we could just refer to the queue without looking back:

```
@MessageDriven(activationConfig = {
    @ActivationConfigProperty(propertyName = "destinationLookup",
    propertyValue = "jms/JmsQueue"),
    @ActivationConfigProperty(propertyName = "destinationType",
    propertyValue = "javax.jms.Queue")
})
```

We could have built a consumer with our own hands, but it would involve three times as many code lines and would be synchronous.

We get our container producer from a session provided by our factory and made for our queue:

```
try (Connection connection = jmsFactory.createConnection();
    Session session = connection.createSession(false,
    Session.AUTO_ACKNOWLEDGE)) {
    producer = session.createProducer(jmsQueue);
    ...
}
```

Then, all we have to do is to create and send the message:

```
message = session.createTextMessage();

String msg = "Now it is " + new Date();
message.setText(msg);
System.out.println("Message sent to queue: " + msg);
producer.send(message);
```

See also

- You can refer to the full source code for this recipe at `https://github.com/eldermoraes/javaee8-cookbook/tree/master/chapter06/ch06-jms`.

Understanding a servlet's life cycle

If you are used to creating web applications using Java EE, you probably will have already realized that most of the time, it is all about dealing with requests and responses, and the most popular way to do that is by using the Servlet API.

This recipe will show you how the server deals with its life cycles and what you should and should not be doing in your code.

Getting ready

First, add the proper dependency to your project:

```
<dependency>
    <groupId>javax</groupId>
    <artifactId>javaee-api</artifactId>
    <version>8.0</version>
    <scope>provided</scope>
</dependency>
```

How to do it...

To try this recipe, perform the following steps:

1. Write this simple servlet:

```
@WebServlet(name = "LifecycleServlet",
urlPatterns = {"/LifecycleServlet"})
public class LifecycleServlet extends HttpServlet {

    @Override
    protected void doGet(HttpServletRequest req,
    HttpServletResponse resp) throws ServletException, IOException {
        try(PrintWriter writer = resp.getWriter()){
            writer.write("doGet");
            System.out.println("doGet");
```

```
        }
    }
    @Override
    protected void doPost(HttpServletRequest req,
    HttpServletResponse resp) throws ServletException, IOException {
        try(PrintWriter writer = resp.getWriter()){
            writer.write("doPost");
            System.out.println("doPost");
        }
    }
    @Override
    protected void doDelete(HttpServletRequest req,
    HttpServletResponse resp) throws ServletException, IOException {
        try(PrintWriter writer = resp.getWriter()){
            writer.write("doDelete");
            System.out.println("doDelete");
        }
    }
    @Override
    protected void doPut(HttpServletRequest req,
    HttpServletResponse resp) throws ServletException, IOException {
        try(PrintWriter writer = resp.getWriter()){
            writer.write("doPut");
            System.out.println("doPut");
        }
    }
    @Override
    public void init() throws ServletException {
        System.out.println("init()");
    }

    @Override
    public void destroy() {
        System.out.println("destroy");
    }
}
```

Once it is deployed to your Jakarta EE server, I suggest you try it using a tool such as SoapUI or similar. It will allow you to send requests using GET, POST, PUT, and DELETE. The browser would only do GET.

2. If you do that, your system log will look just like this:

```
Info: init(ServletConfig config)
 Info: doGet
 Info: doPost
 Info: doPut
 Info: doDelete
```

3. If you undeploy your application, it will look as follows:

```
Info:    destroy
```

How it works...

If you pay attention, you will notice that the `init` log will show only after your servlet is called for the first time. That's when it is really loaded and it is the only time that this method will be called. So, if you have some one-shot code for this servlet, that's the place to do it.

Talking about the `doGet`, `doPost`, `doPut`, and `doDelete` methods, note that they were all automatically called by the server based on the request received. That's possible thanks to another method implemented by the server called `service`.

You could override the `service` method if you want, but it's bad practice and should be avoided. Do it only if you know exactly what you are doing; otherwise, you could give the wrong destination to some requests. This chapter is about relying on the standards, so why wouldn't you observe them?

Finally, we have the `destroy` method called when your application is undeployed. This is like the last breath of your servlet. It is also bad practice to add code here, as you could prevent some resource from being released, and/or run into some process errors.

See also

- You can refer to the full source code for this recipe at `https://github.com/eldermoraes/javaee8-cookbook/tree/master/chapter06/ch06-lifecycle`.

Transaction management

Transaction management is one of the trickier subjects in computer science. One single wrong line, one unpredicted situation, and your data and/or your user will suffer the consequences.

So, it would be nice if we could count on the server to do it for us. And most of the time we can, so let me show you how to do it.

Getting ready

First, add the proper dependency to your project:

```xml
<dependency>
    <groupId>javax</groupId>
    <artifactId>javaee-api</artifactId>
    <version>8.0</version>
    <scope>provided</scope>
</dependency>
```

How to do it...

There are three steps to completing this recipe. Let's perform them:

1. Let's build a bean that will perform all the transactions we need:

```java
@Stateful
@TransactionManagement
public class UserBean {
    private ArrayList<Integer> actions;
    @PostConstruct
    public void init(){
        actions = new ArrayList<>();
        System.out.println("UserBean initialized");
    }
    public void add(Integer action){
        actions.add(action);
        System.out.println(action + " added");
    }
    public void remove(Integer action){
        actions.remove(action);
        System.out.println(action + " removed");
    }
    public List getActions(){
        return actions;
    }
    @PreDestroy
    public void destroy(){
        System.out.println("UserBean will be destroyed");
    }
    @Remove
    public void logout(){
        System.out.println("User logout. Resources will be
        released.");
    }
```

```
@AfterBegin
public void transactionStarted(){
    System.out.println("Transaction started");
}
@BeforeCompletion
public void willBeCommited(){
    System.out.println("Transaction will be commited");
}
@AfterCompletion
public void afterCommit(boolean commited){
    System.out.println("Transaction commited? " + commited);
}
```
}

2. Then, create a test class to try it:

```
public class UserTest {
    private EJBContainer ejbContainer;
    @EJB
    private UserBean userBean;
    public UserTest() {
    }
    @Before
    public void setUp() throws NamingException {
        ejbContainer = EJBContainer.createEJBContainer();
        ejbContainer.getContext().bind("inject", this);
    }
    @After
    public void tearDown() {
        ejbContainer.close();
    }
    @Test
    public void test(){
        userBean.add(1);
        userBean.add(2);
        userBean.add(3);
        userBean.remove(2);
        int size = userBean.getActions().size();
        userBean.logout();
        Assert.assertEquals(2, size);
    }
}
```

3. If you try this test, you should see this output (it will run automatically when you build the project):

```
UserBean initialized
Transaction started
1 added
Transaction will be commited
Transaction commited? true
Transaction started
2 added
Transaction will be commited
Transaction commited? true
Transaction started
3 added
Transaction will be commited
Transaction commited? true
Transaction started
2 removed
Transaction will be commited
Transaction commited? true
Transaction started
Transaction will be commited
Transaction commited? true
Transaction started
User logout. Resources will be released.
UserBean will be destroyed
Transaction will be commited
Transaction commited? true
```

How it works...

The first thing we did was mark our bean to hold states and have its transactions managed by the server. An example of this is shown here:

```
@Stateful
@TransactionManagement
public class UserBean {
    ...
}
```

What happens then? There's no method that deals with adding or removing stuff or do any transaction management. But they are still managed. See the following code:

```
Transaction started
1 added
Transaction will be commited
Transaction commited? true
```

So, you have all the transaction intelligence without writing a single line of transaction stuff.

It will transact even when the bean releases its resources:

```
Transaction started
User logout. Resources will be released.
UserBean will be destroyed
Transaction will be commited
Transaction commited? true
```

See also

- Refer to the full source code for this recipe at `https://github.com/eldermoraes/javaee8-cookbook/tree/master/chapter06/ch06-transaction`.

7
Deploying and Managing Applications on Major Jakarta EE Servers

One of the most important skills you should have as a Jakarta EE developer is knowing how to work with the most widely used Jakarta EE application servers on the market.

As we have stated in preceding chapters, the standards involved in the Jakarta EE ecosystem allow you to reuse most of the knowledge you already have, no matter which server you are using.

However, when we are talking about deployment and some administration tasks, things could be different (and usually are). The differences are not in the way they work, but in the way they are done.

This chapter covers the following recipes:

- Understanding Apache TomEE
- Eclipse GlassFish
- Red Hat WildFly

Understanding Apache TomEE

If you have already used Apache Tomcat, you can consider yourself ready to use Apache TomEE. It is based on the Tomcat's core and implements the Jakarta EE specs.

Getting ready

You need to download Apache TomEE to your environment. To download it, just visit `http://tomee.apache.org/downloads.html`. This recipe is based on TomEE 8.0.0-M2.

Wherever possible, we will focus on doing tasks using the configuration files.

How to do it...

Follow these steps:

1. Deploy EAR, WAR, and JAR files—for **EAR** (short for **Enterprise Application aRchive**) and **WAR** (short for **Web Application Resource**) files, the deployment folder is as follows:

    $TOMEE_HOME/webapps

2. For **JAR** (short for **Java ARchive**) files, the folder is as follows:

    $TOMEE_HOME/lib

3. Create a datasource and a connection pool. To create a datasource and a connection pool to help you use databases in your project, edit the `$TOMEE_HOME/conf/tomee.xml` file. Inside the `<tomee>` node, insert a child node like the following:

```
<Resource id="MyDataSouceDs" type="javax.sql.DataSource">
    jdbcDriver = org.postgresql.Driver
    jdbcUrl = jdbc:postgresql://[host]:[port]/[database]
    jtaManaged = true
    maxActive = 20
    maxIdle = 20
    minIdle = 0
    userName = user
    password = password
</Resource>
```

 The preceding example targets PostgreSQL, so you will need to make some changes if you are using another database. Of course, you will also need to change the other parameters according to your needs.

4. To configure the logging for Apache TomEE, edit the
   $TOMEE_HOME/conf/logging.properties file. The file works with handlers
   like this:

   ```
   1catalina.org.apache.juli.AsyncFileHandler.level = FINE
   1catalina.org.apache.juli.AsyncFileHandler.directory =
   ${catalina.base}/logs
   1catalina.org.apache.juli.AsyncFileHandler.prefix = catalina.
   ```

   This can help you define the logging level, directory, and prefix according to your
   needs.

5. If you need to configure log rotation, add the following lines to your handler:

   ```
   1catalina.org.apache.juli.AsyncFileHandler.limit = 1024
   1catalina.org.apache.juli.AsyncFileHandler.count = 10
   ```

   In this example, we are defining this file to rotate on every 1024 kilobytes (1 MB)
   and keep the last 10 files on our disk.

6. To start Apache TomEE, execute this script:

   $TOMEE_HOME/bin/startup.sh

7. To stop Apache TomEE, execute the following script:

   $TOMEE_HOME/bin/shutdown.sh

8. If you want to build a cluster using Apache TomEE nodes, you need to edit
   the $TOMEE_HOME/conf/server.xml file. Then, find this line:

   ```
   <Engine name="Catalina" defaultHost="localhost">
   ```

9. Insert a child node, like this:

   ```
   <Cluster
     className="org.apache.catalina.ha.tcp.SimpleTcpCluster"
               channelSendOptions="8">

           <Manager
           className="org.apache.catalina.ha.session
                   .DeltaManager"
                   expireSessionsOnShutdown="false"
                   notifyListenersOnReplication="true"/>

           <Channel
             className="org.apache.catalina.tribes.group
   ```

```
              .GroupChannel">
              <Membership
              className="org.apache.catalina
              .tribes.membership .McastService"
                        address="228.0.0.4"
                        port="45564"
                        frequency="500"
                        dropTime="3000"/>
              <Receiver className="org.apache.catalina.tribes
              .transport.nio.NioReceiver"
                        address="auto"
                        port="4000"
                        autoBind="100"
                        selectorTimeout="5000"
                        maxThreads="6"/>

              <Sender className="org.apache.catalina.tribes
              .transport.ReplicationTransmitter">
                <Transport className="org.apache.catalina.tribes
                .transport.nio.PooledParallelSender"/>
              </Sender>
              <Interceptor className="org.apache.catalina.tribes
              .group.interceptors.TcpFailureDetector"/>
              <Interceptor className="org.apache.catalina.tribes
              .group.interceptors.MessageDispatchInterceptor"/>
            </Channel>

            <Valve className="org.apache.catalina
            .ha.tcp.ReplicationValve"
                    filter=""/>
            <Valve className="org.apache.catalina
            .ha.session.JvmRouteBinderValve"/>

            <Deployer className="org.apache.catalina
            .ha.deploy.FarmWarDeployer"
                    tempDir="/tmp/war-temp/"
                    deployDir="/tmp/war-deploy/"
                    watchDir="/tmp/war-listen/"
                    watchEnabled="false"/>

            <ClusterListener className="org.apache.catalina
            .ha.session.ClusterSessionListener"/>
        </Cluster>
```

This block will set up your server to run in a dynamic discovery cluster. What this means is that every server that runs in the same network using this configuration will become a new member in the cluster and so will share the active sessions.

All these parameters are very important, so I really recommend you keep all of them unless you are absolutely sure of what you are doing.

There's more...

The best way to set up a Jakarta EE cluster today is by using containers (especially Docker containers). So, I'd recommend that you have a look at `Chapter 11`, *Rising to the Cloud – Java EE, Containers, and Cloud Computing*. If you mix the content of that chapter with the content of this one, you will have a powerful environment for your application.

To allow your application to share its session with all the nodes in the cluster, you need to edit the `web.xml` file, find the `web-app` node, and insert this:

```
<distributable/>
```

Without it, your session clustering will not work. You also need to keep all the objects that you are holding in the session as serializable.

See also

- For more information about Apache TomEE, visit `http://tomee.apache.org/`

Eclipse GlassFish

The great thing about Eclipse GlassFish is that it was the **Reference Implementation (RI)** for many years. So, whenever you had a new version of Java EE being developed, you already had the respective Eclipse GlassFish version to try it.

Getting ready

You need to download Eclipse GlassFish to your environment. To download it, just visit `https://projects.eclipse.org/projects/ee4j.glassfish/downloads`. This recipe is based on version 5.1 (Jakarta EE 8 compatible).

Wherever possible, we will focus on doing the tasks using the configuration files.

How to do it...

Follow these steps:

1. First, we are deploying EAR, WAR, and JAR files. For EAR and WAR files, the deployment folder is the following:

   `$GLASSFISH_HOME/glassfish/domains/[domain_name]/autodeploy`

   Usually `domain_name` is `domain1`, unless you've changed it in the installation process. For JAR files, the folder is `$GLASSFISH_HOME/glassfish/lib`.

2. To create a datasource and a connection pool to help you use databases in your project, edit the `$GLASSFISH_HOME/glassfish/domains/[domain_name]/config/domain.xml` file. Inside the `<resources>` node, insert a child node like this one:

```
<jdbc-connection-pool
  pool-resize-quantity="4"
  max-pool-size="64"
  max-wait-time-in-millis="120000"
  driver-classname="com.mysql.jdbc.Driver"
  datasource-classname="com.mysql.jdbc.jdbc2.optional
  .MysqlDataSource"
  steady-pool-size="16"
  name="MysqlPool"
  idle-timeout-in-seconds="600"
  res-type="javax.sql.DataSource">
      <property name="databaseName" value="database"></property>
      <property name="serverName" value="[host]"></property>
      <property name="user" value="user"></property>
      <property name="password" value="password"></property>
      <property name="portNumber" value="3306"></property>
</jdbc-connection-pool>
<jdbc-resource pool-name="MySqlDs" jndi-name="jdbc/MySqlDs">
</jdbc-resource>
```

3. Then, look for this node:

```
<server config-ref="server-config" name="server">
```

4. Add this child to it:

```
<resource-ref ref="jdbc/MySqlDs"></resource-ref>
```

The example targets MySQL, so you will need to make some changes if you are using another database. Of course, you will also need to change the other parameters according to your needs.

5. To configure logging for Eclipse GlassFish, edit the `$GLASSFISH_HOME/glassfish/domains/domain1/config/logging.properties` file. The file works with handlers like this:

```
handlers=java.util.logging.ConsoleHandler
handlerServices=com.sun.enterprise.server.logging.GFFileHandler
java.util.logging.ConsoleHandler.formatter=com.sun.enterprise.serve
r.logging.UniformLogFormatter
com.sun.enterprise.server.logging.GFFileHandler.formatter=com.sun.e
nterprise.server.logging.ODLLogFormatter
com.sun.enterprise.server.logging.GFFileHandler.file=${com.sun.aas.
instanceRoot}/logs/server.log
com.sun.enterprise.server.logging.GFFileHandler.rotationTimelimitIn
Minutes=0
com.sun.enterprise.server.logging.GFFileHandler.flushFrequency=1
java.util.logging.FileHandler.limit=50000
com.sun.enterprise.server.logging.GFFileHandler.logtoConsole=false
com.sun.enterprise.server.logging.GFFileHandler.rotationLimitInByte
s=2000000
com.sun.enterprise.server.logging.GFFileHandler.excludeFields=
com.sun.enterprise.server.logging.GFFileHandler.multiLineMode=true
com.sun.enterprise.server.logging.SyslogHandler.useSystemLogging=fa
lse
java.util.logging.FileHandler.count=1
com.sun.enterprise.server.logging.GFFileHandler.retainErrorsStastic
sForHours=0
log4j.logger.org.hibernate.validator.util.Version=warn
com.sun.enterprise.server.logging.GFFileHandler.maxHistoryFiles=0
com.sun.enterprise.server.logging.GFFileHandler.rotationOnDateChang
e=false
java.util.logging.FileHandler.pattern=%h/java%u.log
java.util.logging.FileHandler.formatter=java.util.logging.XMLFormat
ter
```

So, you can define the logging level, directory, format, and more according to your needs.

6. If you need to configure log rotation, you have to focus on these lines:

```
com.sun.enterprise.server.logging.GFFileHandler
.rotationTimelimitInMinutes=0
com.sun.enterprise.server.logging.GFFileHandler
.rotationLimitInBytes=2000000
com.sun.enterprise.server.logging.GFFileHandler
.maxHistoryFiles=0
com.sun.enterprise.server.logging.GFFileHandler
.rotationOnDateChange=false
```

In this example, we are defining this file to rotate on every 2,000 kilobytes (2 MB) and will not rotate on date change. There's no limit for history files.

7. To start Eclipse GlassFish, just execute this script:

```
$GLASSFISH_HOME/bin/asadmin start-domain --verbose
```

8. To stop it, execute the following script:

```
$GLASSFISH_HOME/bin/asadmin stop-domain
```

9. Building a cluster using GlassFish is a little tricky and involves using both the command line and the admin panel, but it is completely doable! Let's check it out:

    1. First, you need two or more instances (called **nodes**) up and running. You can do it in any way you like—each one running in a different machine, using virtual machines, or using containers (my favorite option). Whichever way you choose, the way of getting the cluster up is the same.

    2. Get your first node and open its admin panel at `https://[hostname]:4848`.

    3. Click on the **Clusters** option in the left menu and then click on the **New** button. Name the cluster `myCluster` and click on the **OK** button.

    4. Select your cluster from the list. On the opened page, select the **Instances** option in the tab and then click on **New**. Name the instance `node1` and click on **OK**.

    5. Now, go to the **General** tab and click on the **Start Cluster** button. Voilá! Your cluster is up and running with your first node.

    6. Now, go to the second machine (VM, container, other servers, or any server) with GlassFish already installed and run this command:

    ```
    $GLASSFISH_HOME/bin/asadmin --host [hostname_node1] --port
    4848 create-local-instance --cluster myCluster node2
    ```

This will set the second machine as a member of the cluster. If you refresh the **Cluster** page on the first machine, you will see the new member (node2).

7. You will notice that node2 has stopped. Click on it and on the new page, click on the **Node** link (it will usually show the hostname of node2).
8. On the opened page, change the **Type** value to SSH. Some new fields will show up in an SSH section.
9. Change **SSH User Authentication** to SSH Password and fill the **SSH User Password** field with the right password.
10. Click on the **Save** button. If you encounter an SSH error (usually connection refused), set the **Force** option to **Enabled**, and click on **Save** button again.
11. Go back to the command line on the machine hosting node2 and run this command:

```
$GLASSFISH_HOME/glassfish/lib/nadmin start-local-instance --node [node2_hostname] --sync normal node2
```

If everything went well, your node2 should be up and running and you should now have a real cluster. You can repeat these steps however many times you need to add new nodes to your cluster.

There's more...

A common issue for this clustering with Eclipse GlassFish arises when you don't have the SSH service running in your nodes; as there are tons of options of them for many operating systems, we won't cover each one of them here.

The best way to set up a Jakarta EE cluster today is using containers (specially Docker containers). So, I'd recommend that you have a look at Chapter 11, *Rising to the Cloud – Java EE, Containers, and Cloud Computing*. If you mix that content with this, you will have a powerful environment for your application.

To allow your application to share its session with all the nodes in the cluster, you need to edit the web.xml file, find the web-app node, and insert this:

```
<distributable/>
```

Without it, your session clustering will not work. You need also to keep all the objects that you are holding in the session as serializable.

Finally, there's a commercial version of Eclipse GlassFish, which is Payara Server. If you are looking for support and other commercial perks, you should take a look at it.

See also

- For more information about Eclipse GlassFish, visit `https://projects.eclipse.org/projects/ee4j.glassfish`.

Red Hat WildFly

Red Hat WildFly is another great Jakarta EE implementation. It was known as **JBoss AS**, but changed its name some years ago (although we still have the JBoss EAP as the *enterprise-production ready* version). As its administration and use are slightly different from Apache TomEE and Eclipse GlassFish, it's worth having a proper look at.

Getting ready

You need to download Red Hat WildFly to your environment. To download it, just visit `http://wildfly.org/downloads/`. This recipe is based on version 16.0.0.Final (Jakarta EE 8 Full and Web Distribution). Wherever possible, we will focus on doing the tasks using the configuration files.

How to do it...

Follow these steps:

1. To deploy EAR, WAR, and JAR files, the deployment folder is as follows:

   ```
   $WILDFLY_HOME/standalone/deployments
   ```

   For JAR files (such as **Java Database Connectivity** (**JDBC**) connections, for example), WildFly creates a flexible folder structure. So, the best way to distribute them is by using its UI, as we will show in the next step.

2. Follow these steps to create your datasources and connection pool:
    1. To create a datasource and a connection pool to help you use databases in your project, start WildFly and visit the following URL:

        ```
        http://localhost:9990/
        ```

    2. Click on **Deployments** and then click on the **Add** button. On the opened page, select **Upload a new deployment** and click on the **Next** button. On the opened page, select the right JDBC connector (we will use MySQL for this recipe) and click on **Next**.
    3. Verify the information on the opened page and click on **Finish**.
    4. Now that your JDBC connector is available in the server, you can go ahead and create your datasource. Go to **Home** in the administration panel and click on the **Configuration** option.
    5. On the opened page, follow this path—**Subsystems** | **Datasources** | **Non-XA** | **Datasource** | **Add**.
    6. In the opened window, select **MySQL Datasource** and click on **Next**. Then, fill in the fields like this:
        - **Name**: MySqlDS
        - **JNDI Name**: java:/MySqlDS

    7. Click on **Next**. On the next page, click on **Detected Driver**, select the right MySQL connector (the one you just uploaded), and click on **Next**.
    8. The last step is to fill the connection settings fields, like this:
        - **Connection URL**: jdbc:mysql://localhost:3306/sys
        - **Username**: root
        - **Password**: mysql

    9. Click on the **Next** button, review the information, and click on **Finish**. Your newly created connection will appear in the datasources list. You can click on the drop-down list and select **Test** to check whether everything is working well.

3. To configure the logging for WildFly, edit the $WILDFLY_HOME/standalone/configuration/standalone.xml file.

4. To customize the logging properties, find the `<profile>` node and then find `<subsystem xmlns='urn:jboss:domain:logging:3.0'>` inside it. It is based on handles like this:

```
<console-handler name="CONSOLE">
        <level name="INFO"/>
        <formatter>
            <named-formatter name="COLOR-PATTERN"/>
        </formatter>
</console-handler>
<periodic-rotating-file-handler name="FILE"
 autoflush="true">
        <formatter>
            <named-formatter name="PATTERN"/>
        </formatter>
        <file relative-to="jboss.server.log.dir"
         path="server.log"/>
        <suffix value=".yyyy-MM-dd"/>
        <append value="true"/>
</periodic-rotating-file-handler>
<logger category="com.arjuna">
        <level name="WARN"/>
</logger>
<logger category="org.jboss.as.config">
        <level name="DEBUG"/>
</logger>
<logger category="sun.rmi">
        <level name="WARN"/>
</logger>
<root-logger>
        <level name="INFO"/>
        <handlers>
            <handler name="CONSOLE"/>
            <handler name="FILE"/>
        </handlers>
</root-logger>
<formatter name="PATTERN">
        <pattern-formatter pattern=
        "%d{yyyy-MM-dd HH:mm:ss,SSS} %-5p [%c] (%t)
%s%e%n"/>
</formatter>
<formatter name="COLOR-PATTERN">
        <pattern-formatter pattern="%K{level}%d
        {HH:mm:ss,SSS} %-5p [%c] (%t) %s%e%n"/>
</formatter>
```

5. By default, it will rotate daily:

```
<periodic-rotating-file-handler name="FILE"
 autoflush="true">
    <formatter>
        <named-formatter name="PATTERN"/>
    </formatter>
    <file relative-to="jboss.server.log.dir"
     path="server.log"/>
    <suffix value=".yyyy-MM-dd"/>
    <append value="true"/>
</periodic-rotating-file-handler>
```

6. If you want it to rotate based on the size, you should remove the preceding handler and then insert this one:

```
<size-rotating-file-handler name="FILE" autoflush="true">
    <formatter>
        <pattern-formatter pattern="%d{yyyy-MM-dd
        HH:mm:ss,SSS} %-5p [%c] (%t) %s%e%n"/>
    </formatter>
    <file relative-to="jboss.server.log.dir"
    path="server.log"/>
    <rotate-size value="2m"/>
    <max-backup-index value="5"/>
    <append value="true"/>
</size-rotating-file-handler>
```

In this case, the log will rotate when the file reaches 2 MB and will keep a history of five files in the backup.

7. To start Wildfly, just execute this script:

   $WILDFLY_HOME/bin/standalone.sh

8. To stop it, execute this script:

   $WILDFLY_HOME/bin/jboss-cli.sh --connect command=:shutdown

9. If you go to the $WILDFLY_HOME/standalone/configuration folder, you will see these files:
   - standalone.xml
   - standalone-ha.xml
   - standalone-full.xml
   - standalone-full-ha.xml

`standalone.xml` is the default, with all default configuration. To build a cluster, we need to use the `standalone-ha.xml` file (ha comes from **high availability**), so rename it to `standalone.xml`.

10. Then, you can start the server. You should not do the following:

    $WILDFLY_HOME/bin/standalone.sh

11. Instead, you should do this:

    $WILDFLY_HOME/bin/standalone.sh -b 0.0.0.0 -bmanagement 0.0.0.0

    You should now do the same in whatever other nodes (machines, VMs, containers, and so on) that you want to get into the cluster. Of course, they need to be in the same network.

There's more...

The best way to set up a Jakarta EE cluster today is by using containers (specially Docker containers). So, I'd recommend that you have a look at Chapter 11, *Rising to the Cloud – Java EE, Containers, and Cloud Computing*. If you mix that content with this, you will have a powerful environment for your application.

To allow your application to share its session with all nodes in the cluster, you need to edit the `web.xml` file, find the `web-app` node, and insert this:

```
<distributable/>
```

Without it, your session clustering will not work.

See also

- For more information about Red Hat WildFly, visit `http://wildfly.org/`.

8
Building Lightweight Solutions Using Microservices

Microservices is one of the top buzzwords nowadays. It's easy to understand why— in the growing

software industry, where the amount of services, data, and users is increasing exponentially, we need a way to build and deliver faster, decoupled, and scalable solutions.

Why are microservices good? Why use them? With growing demand, the need to deal with each module separately has increased. For example, in your customer application, perhaps user information needs to be scaled differently from the address information.

In the monolith paradigm, you need to deal with it atomically—you build a cluster for the whole application or you scale your entire host up (or down). The problem with this approach is that you can't focus your effort and resources on a specific feature, module, or function— you are always guided by what is needed at that moment.

In the microservice approach, you do it separately. Then, you can not only scale (up or down) one single unit in your application, but you can also separate your data for each service (which you should do), separate technology (best tool for the best work), and more.

Other than scale technology, microservices are made to scale people. With a bigger application, bigger architecture, and bigger databases, also come bigger teams. And if you build your team like a monolith application, you are probably getting likely results.

So, as the application is split into a few (or a lot of) modules, you can also define cross-functional teams to take care of each module. This means that each team can have its own programmer, designer, database administrator, system administrator, network specialist, manager, and so on. Each team has responsibility for the module it is dealing with.

This brings agility to the process of thinking about and delivering software and then maintaining and evolving it.

In this chapter, there are some recipes to help you to get started with microservices or go deeper into your ongoing project.

This chapter covers the following recipes:

- Building microservices from a monolith
- Building decoupled services
- Building an automated pipeline for microservices
- Determining the state of a microservice by using the MicroProfile Health Check API
- Generating and/or monitoring metrics with the MicroProfile Metrics API
- Exposing API documentation using MicroProfile OpenAPI

Building microservices from a monolith

One common question that I have already heard dozens of times is, *how do I break down my monolith into microservices?* or, *how do I migrate from a monolith approach to microservices?*

Well, that's what this recipe is all about.

Getting ready

For both monolith and microservice projects, we will use the same dependency:

```
<dependency>
    <groupId>javax</groupId>
    <artifactId>javaee-api</artifactId>
    <version>8.0</version>
    <scope>provided</scope>
</dependency>
```

How to do it...

We will go about this in two parts. First, we will build a monolith, and then we will build microservices from that monolith. Let's begin by building a monolith.

Building a monolith

To build the monolith, we need to perform the following steps:

1. First, we need the entities that will represent the data kept by the application. Here is the `User` entity:

```
@Entity
public class User implements Serializable {

    private static final long serialVersionUID = 1L;

    @Id
    @GeneratedValue(strategy = GenerationType.AUTO)
    private Long id;
    @Column
    private String name;
    @Column
    private String email;

    public User(){
    }

    public User(String name, String email) {
        this.name = name;
        this.email = email;
    }

    public Long getId() {
        return id;
    }

    public void setId(Long id) {
        this.id = id;
    }
    public String getName() {
        return name;
    }

    public void setName(String name) {
        this.name = name;
    }

    public String getEmail() {
        return email;
    }

    public void setEmail(String email) {
```

```
                this.email = email;
        }
    }
```

2. Here is the `UserAddress` entity:

```java
@Entity
public class UserAddress implements Serializable {

    private static final long serialVersionUID = 1L;

    @Id
    @GeneratedValue(strategy = GenerationType.AUTO)
    private Long id;

    @Column
    @ManyToOne
    private User user;
    @Column
    private String street;
    @Column
    private String number;
    @Column
    private String city;
    @Column
    private String zip;
    public UserAddress(){
    }
    public UserAddress(User user, String street, String number,
                        String city, String zip) {
        this.user = user;
        this.street = street;
        this.number = number;
        this.city = city;
        this.zip = zip;
    }

    public Long getId() {
        return id;
    }

    public void setId(Long id) {
        this.id = id;
    }

    public User getUser() {
        return user;
    }
```

```
        public void setUser(User user) {
            this.user = user;
        }

        public String getStreet() {
            return street;
        }

        public void setStreet(String street) {
            this.street = street;
        }

        public String getNumber() {
            return number;
        }

        public void setNumber(String number) {
            this.number = number;
        }

        public String getCity() {
            return city;
        }

        public void setCity(String city) {
            this.city = city;
        }

        public String getZip() {
            return zip;
        }

        public void setZip(String zip) {
            this.zip = zip;
        }
    }
```

3. Now we define one bean to deal with the transaction over each entity. Here is the UserBean class:

```
    @Stateless
    public class UserBean {

        @PersistenceContext
        private EntityManager em;

        public void add(User user) {
            em.persist(user);
```

```
        }

        public void remove(User user) {
            em.remove(user);
        }

        public void update(User user) {
            em.merge(user);
        }

        public User findById(Long id) {
            return em.find(User.class, id);
        }

        public List<User> get() {
            CriteriaBuilder cb = em.getCriteriaBuilder();
            CriteriaQuery<User> cq = cb.createQuery(User.class);
            Root<User> pet = cq.from(User.class);
            cq.select(pet);
            TypedQuery<User> q = em.createQuery(cq);
            return q.getResultList();
        }
    }
```

4. Here is the `UserAddressBean` class:

```
@Stateless
public class UserAddressBean {

    @PersistenceContext
    private EntityManager em;
    public void add(UserAddress address){
        em.persist(address);
    }
    public void remove(UserAddress address){
        em.remove(address);
    }
    public void update(UserAddress address){
        em.merge(address);
    }
    public UserAddress findById(Long id){
        return em.find(UserAddress.class, id);
    }
    public List<UserAddress> get() {
        CriteriaBuilder cb = em.getCriteriaBuilder();
        CriteriaQuery<UserAddress> cq =
cb.createQuery(UserAddress.class);
        Root<UserAddress> pet = cq.from(UserAddress.class);
```

```
            cq.select(pet);
            TypedQuery<UserAddress> q = em.createQuery(cq);
            return q.getResultList();
        }
    }
```

5. Finally, we build two services to perform the communication between the client and the beans. Here is the `UserService` class:

```
@Path("userService")
public class UserService {
    @EJB
    private UserBean userBean;
    @GET
    @Path("findById/{id}")
    @Consumes(MediaType.APPLICATION_JSON)
    @Produces(MediaType.APPLICATION_JSON)
    public Response findById(@PathParam("id") Long id){
        return Response.ok(userBean.findById(id)).build();
    }
    @GET
    @Path("get")
    @Consumes(MediaType.APPLICATION_JSON)
    @Produces(MediaType.APPLICATION_JSON)
    public Response get(){
        return Response.ok(userBean.get()).build();
    }
    @POST
    @Path("add")
    @Consumes(MediaType.APPLICATION_JSON)
    @Produces(MediaType.APPLICATION_JSON)
    public Response add(User user){
        userBean.add(user);
        return Response.accepted().build();
    }
    @DELETE
    @Path("remove/{id}")
    @Consumes(MediaType.APPLICATION_JSON)
    @Produces(MediaType.APPLICATION_JSON)
    public Response remove(@PathParam("id") Long id){
        userBean.remove(userBean.findById(id));
        return Response.accepted().build();
    }
}
```

6. Here is the `UserAddressService` class:

```
@Path("userAddressService")
public class UserAddressService {
    @EJB
    private UserAddressBean userAddressBean;
    @GET
    @Path("findById/{id}")
    @Consumes(MediaType.APPLICATION_JSON)
    @Produces(MediaType.APPLICATION_JSON)
    public Response findById(@PathParam("id") Long id){
        return Response.ok(userAddressBean.findById(id)).build();
    }
    @GET
    @Path("get")
    @Consumes(MediaType.APPLICATION_JSON)
    @Produces(MediaType.APPLICATION_JSON)
    public Response get(){
        return Response.ok(userAddressBean.get()).build();
    }
    @POST
    @Path("add")
    @Consumes(MediaType.APPLICATION_JSON)
    @Produces(MediaType.APPLICATION_JSON)
    public Response add(UserAddress address){
        userAddressBean.add(address);
        return Response.accepted().build();
    }
    @DELETE
    @Path("remove/{id}")
    @Consumes(MediaType.APPLICATION_JSON)
    @Produces(MediaType.APPLICATION_JSON)
    public Response remove(@PathParam("id") Long id){
        userAddressBean.remove(userAddressBean.findById(id));
        return Response.accepted().build();
    }
}
```

Now let's break the monolith down!

Building microservices from the monolith

Our monolith deals with `User` and `UserAddress`. So, we will break it down into three microservices— a user microservice, a user address microservice, and a gateway microservice. Let's see how:

- **The user microservice**: The `User` entity, `UserBean`, and `UserService` will remain exactly as they are in the monolith. Only, now, they will be delivered as a separate unit of deployment.
- **The user address microservice**: The `UserAddress` classes will suffer just a single change from the monolith version, but keep their original APIs (that is great for the client).
  Here is the `UserAddress` entity:

```
@Entity
public class UserAddress implements Serializable {

    private static final long serialVersionUID = 1L;

    @Id
    @GeneratedValue(strategy = GenerationType.AUTO)
    private Long id;

    @Column
    private Long idUser;
    @Column
    private String street;
    @Column
    private String number;
    @Column
    private String city;
    @Column
    private String zip;
    public UserAddress(){
    }
    public UserAddress(Long user, String street, String number,
                       String city, String zip) {
        this.idUser = user;
        this.street = street;
        this.number = number;
        this.city = city;
        this.zip = zip;
    }

    public Long getId() {
```

```
            return id;
        }

    public void setId(Long id) {
        this.id = id;
    }

    public Long getIdUser() {
        return idUser;
    }

    public void setIdUser(Long user) {
        this.idUser = user;
    }

    public String getStreet() {
        return street;
    }

    public void setStreet(String street) {
        this.street = street;
    }

    public String getNumber() {
        return number;
    }

    public void setNumber(String number) {
        this.number = number;
    }

    public String getCity() {
        return city;
    }

    public void setCity(String city) {
        this.city = city;
    }

    public String getZip() {
        return zip;
    }

    public void setZip(String zip) {
        this.zip = zip;
    }
}
```

Note that `User` is no longer a property/field in the `UserAddress` entity, but only a number (`idUser`). We will get into more details about it in the following section.

- **The gateway microservice**: The gateway service is an API between the application client and the services. Using it allows you to simplify this communication, also giving you the freedom of doing whatever you like with your services without breaking the API contracts (or at least minimizing them).

1. First, we create a class that helps us to deal with the responses:

```java
public class GatewayResponse {

    private String response;
    private String from;

    public String getResponse() {
        return response;
    }

    public void setResponse(String response) {
        this.response = response;
    }

    public String getFrom() {
        return from;
    }

    public void setFrom(String from) {
        this.from = from;
    }
}
```

2. Then, we create our gateway service:

```java
@Consumes(MediaType.APPLICATION_JSON)
@Path("gatewayResource")
@RequestScoped
public class GatewayResource {

    private final String hostURI = "http://localhost:8080/";
    private Client client;
    private WebTarget targetUser;
    private WebTarget targetAddress;

    @PostConstruct
    public void init() {
```

```
            client = ClientBuilder.newClient();
            targetUser = client.target(hostURI +
            "ch08-micro_x_mono-micro-user/");
            targetAddress = client.target(hostURI +
            "ch08-micro_x_mono-micro-address/");
    }

    @PreDestroy
    public void destroy(){
            client.close();
    }

    @GET
    @Path("getUsers")
    @Produces(MediaType.APPLICATION_JSON)
    public Response getUsers() {
            WebTarget service =
            targetUser.path("webresources/userService/get");

            Response response;
            try {
                response = service.request().get();
            } catch (ProcessingException e) {
                return Response.status(408).build();
            }

            GatewayResponse gatewayResponse = new GatewayResponse();
gatewayResponse.setResponse(response.readEntity(String.class));
            gatewayResponse.setFrom(targetUser.getUri().toString());

            return Response.ok(gatewayResponse).build();
    }

    @POST
    @Path("addAddress")
    @Produces(MediaType.APPLICATION_JSON)
    public Response addAddress(UserAddress address) {
            WebTarget service =
            targetAddress.path("webresources/userAddressService/add");

            Response response;
            try {
                response =
service.request().post(Entity.json(address));
            } catch (ProcessingException e) {
                return Response.status(408).build();
            }
```

```
            return Response.fromResponse(response).build();
        }

    }
```

As we receive the `UserAddress` entity in the gateway, we have to have a version of it in the gateway project too. For brevity, we will omit the code, as it is the same as in the `UserAddress` project.

How it works...

Let's understand how things work for each stage of the process.

The monolith application couldn't be simpler—it's just a project with two services using two beans to manage two entities. If you want to understand what is happening there regarding JAX-RS, Jakarta CDI, and/or Jakarta Persistence (formerly, JPA), check the relevant recipes earlier in this book.

So, we split the monolith into three projects (microservices)—the user service, the user address service, and the gateway service.

The user service classes remained unchanged after the migration from the monolith version. So, there's nothing to comment on.

The `UserAddress` class had to be changed to become a microservice. The first change was made on the entity.

Here is the monolith version:

```
@Entity
public class UserAddress implements Serializable {
    ...
    @Column
    @ManyToOne
    private User user;

    public UserAddress(User user, String street, String number,
                        String city, String zip) {
        this.user = user;
        ...
    }
    ...
}
```

Here is the microservice version:

```
@Entity
public class UserAddress implements Serializable {
    ...
    @Column
    private Long idUser;
    public UserAddress(Long user, String street, String number,
                       String city, String zip) {
        this.idUser = user;
        ...
    }
    ...
}
```

Note that, in the monolith version, user was an instance of the User entity:

```
private User user;
```

In the microservice version, it became a number:

```
private Long idUser;
```

This happened for two main reasons:

- In the monolith, we have the two tables in the same database (User and UserAddress), and they both have physical and logical relationships (foreign key). So, it makes sense to also keep the relationship between both the objects.
- The microservice should have its database, completely independent of the other services. So, we choose to keep only the user ID, as it is enough to load the address properly anytime the client needs it.

This change also resulted in a change in the constructor.

Here is the monolith version:

```
public UserAddress(User user, String street, String number,
                   String city, String zip)
```

Here is the microservice version:

```
public UserAddress(Long user, String street, String number,
                   String city, String zip)
```

This could have lead to a change of contract with the client regarding the change of the constructor signature. But thanks to the way it was built, it wasn't necessary.

Here is the monolith version:

```
public Response add(UserAddress address)
```

Here is the microservice version:

```
public Response add(UserAddress address)
```

Even if the method is changed, it could easily be solved with @Path annotation, or if we really need to change the client, it would be only the method name and not the parameters (which used to be more painful).

Finally, we have the gateway service, which is our implementation of the API gateway design pattern. Basically, it is the one single point to access the other services.

The nice thing about it is that your client doesn't need to care about whether the other services changed the URL or the signature or even whether they are available. The gateway will take care of them.

The bad part is that it is also on a single point of failure. Or, in other words, without the gateway, all services are unreachable. But you can deal with it by using a cluster, for example.

There's more...

Though Jakarta EE is perfect for microservices, other options use the same bases and may be a little lighter in some scenarios.

The clearer (and my favorite) way of doing it is by using Eclipse MicroProfile (http://microprofile.io/). It has defined the path and the standards for microservices in the Enterprise Java ecosystem.

As a standard, it has some implementations. Please refer to some of them here:

- **KumuluzEE** (https://ee.kumuluz.com/): It's based on Jakarta EE and has many microservice *must-have* features, such as service discovery. It won a Duke Choice Awards prize, which is huge!
- **Payara Micro** (https://www.payara.fish/payara_micro): Payara is the company that owns a commercial implementation of Eclipse GlassFish, the Payara Server, and from this, the company created the Payara Micro. The cool thing about it is that it is just a 60 MB JAR file that you start using the command line and boom! Your microservice is running.

- **Helidon** (`https://helidon.io`): It's a collection of Java libraries for writing microservices that run on top of Netty. It comes in two flavors— Helidon SE (a microframework) and Helidon MP (MicroProfile implementation).
- **Thoairntl** (`https://thorntail.io`): This was created by Red Hat and derived from Wildfly Swarm.

 One last note about the code covered in this recipe— it would be nice in a real-world solution to use a **Data Transfer Object** (**DTO**) to separate the database representation from the service one.

See also

The full source code of this recipe can be found in the following repositories:

- **Monolith**: `https://github.com/eldermoraes/javaee8-cookbook/tree/master/chapter08/ch08-micro_x_mono-mono`
- **User microservice**: `https://github.com/eldermoraes/javaee8-cookbook/tree/master/chapter08/ch08-micro_x_mono-micro-user`
- **UserAddress microservice**: `https://github.com/eldermoraes/javaee8-cookbook/tree/master/chapter08/ch08-micro_x_mono-micro-address`
- **Gateway microservice**: `https://github.com/eldermoraes/javaee8-cookbook/tree/master/chapter08/ch08-micro_x_mono-micro-gateway`

Building decoupled services

Maybe you have at least heard something about building decoupled things in the software world— decoupled classes, decoupled modules, and decoupled services.

But what does it mean for a software unit being decoupled from another?

Practically, two things are coupled when any changes made to one of them requires you to also change the other one. For example, if you have a method that returns a string and changes it to return a double, all of the methods calling that method are required to be changed.

There are levels of coupling. For example, you could have all of your classes and methods very well designed for loose coupling, but they are all written in Java. If you change one of them to .NET and would like to keep all of them together (in the same deployment package), you need to change all of the other ones into the new language.

Another thing to mention about coupling is how much one unit knows about the other. They are tightly coupled when they know a lot about each other; and they are the opposite, meaning loosely coupled, if they know a little or almost nothing about each other. This point of view is related mostly to the behavior of two (or more) parts.

The last way to look at coupling is in terms of a contract. If changing the contract breaks the clients, they are tightly coupled. If not, they are loosely coupled. That's why the best way to promote loose coupling is by using interfaces. As they create contracts for its implementers, using them for communication between classes promotes loose coupling.

Well...what about services? In our case, microservices.

When one service is loosely coupled from another, changing one does not require changing the other. You can think about both in terms of behavior or contract.

This is especially important when talking about microservices because you can have dozens, hundreds, or even thousands of them in your application and if changing one of them requires you to change the others, you could just ruin your entire application.

This recipe will show you how to avoid tight coupling in your microservices, from the first line of code, so you can avoid refactoring in the future (at least for this reason).

Getting ready

Let's start by adding our Jakarta EE 8 dependency:

```
<dependency>
    <groupId>javax</groupId>
    <artifactId>javaee-api</artifactId>
    <version>8.0</version>
    <scope>provided</scope>
</dependency>
```

How to do it...

There are three steps to accomplish this recipe.

1. First, we create a `User` POJO:

```
public class User implements Serializable{

    private String name;
    private String email;
```

```
                public String getName() {
                    return name;
                }

                public void setName(String name) {
                    this.name = name;
                }

                public String getEmail() {
                    return email;
                }

                public void setEmail(String email) {
                    this.email = email;
                }
            }
```

2. Then, we create a class with two methods (endpoints) for returning `User`:

```
@Path("userService")
public class UserService {
    @GET
    @Path("getUserCoupled/{name}/{email}")
    @Produces(MediaType.APPLICATION_JSON)
    public Response getUserCoupled(
            @PathParam("name") String name,
            @PathParam("email") String email){
        //GET USER CODE
        return Response.ok().build();
    }
    @GET
    @Path("getUserDecoupled")
    @Produces(MediaType.APPLICATION_JSON)
    public Response getUserDecoupled(@HeaderParam("User")
    User user){
        //GET USER CODE
        return Response.ok().build();
    }
}
```

3. Finally, we create another service (another project) to consume `UserService`:

```
@Path("doSomethingService")
public class DoSomethingService {
    private final String hostURI = "http://localhost:8080/";
    private Client client;
    private WebTarget target;
```

```
    @PostConstruct
    public void init() {
        client = ClientBuilder.newClient();
        target = client.target(hostURI + "ch08-decoupled-user/");
    }
    @Path("doSomethingCoupled")
    @Produces(MediaType.APPLICATION_JSON)
    public Response doSomethingCoupled(String name, String email){
        WebTarget service =
        target.path("webresources/userService/getUserCoupled");
        service.queryParam("name", name);
        service.queryParam("email", email);

        Response response;
        try {
            response = service.request().get();
        } catch (ProcessingException e) {
            return Response.status(408).build();
        }

        return
        Response.ok(response.readEntity(String.class)).build();
    }
    @Path("doSomethingDecoupled")
    @Produces(MediaType.APPLICATION_JSON)
    public Response doSomethingDecoupled(User user){
        WebTarget service =
        target.path("webresources/userService/getUserDecoupled");

        Response response;
        try {
            response = service.request().header("User",
            Entity.json(user)).get();
        } catch (ProcessingException e) {
            return Response.status(408).build();
        }

        return
Response.ok(response.readEntity(String.class)).build();
    }
}
```

How it works...

As you may have already noticed, we created two situations in the code of the preceding section— one coupled (`getUserCoupled`) and another decoupled (`getUserDecoupled`):

```
public Response getUserCoupled(
        @PathParam("name") String name,
        @PathParam("email") String email)
```

Why is this a coupled method and hence a coupled service? That's because it is highly attached to the method signature. Imagine it is a search service and `"name"` and `"email"` are filters. Now imagine that sometime in the future, you need to add another filter—one more parameter in the signature.

OK, you could keep the two methods available at the same time, so that you will not break the client contract and have to change all clients available. But maybe you have a lot of them— mobile, services, web pages, and many more. All of these need to be changed to support the new feature anyway. Wouldn't it be better to reduce the friction in this process?

Now, look at this:

```
public Response getUserDecoupled(@HeaderParam("User") User user)
```

In this `User` search method, what if you need to add a new parameter to the filter? Then, go ahead and add it! There are no changes in the contract, and all clients are happy.

If your `User` POJO starts with only two properties and ends with a hundred after a year, no problem. Your service contract is left untouched and even your clients, who are not using the new fields, are still working. Sweet!

The result of coupled/decoupled services can be seen in the calling service:

```
public Response doSomethingCoupled(String name, String email){
    WebTarget service =
    target.path("webresources/userService/getUserCoupled");
    service.queryParam("name", name);
    service.queryParam("email", email);

    ...
}
```

The calling service is coupled to the called one: it has to know the called service properties' names and needs to add/update each time it changes.

Now, look at this:

```
public Response doSomethingDecoupled(User user){
    WebTarget service =
    target.path("webresources/userService/getUserDecoupled");

    Response response;
    try {
        response = service.request().header("User",
        Entity.json(user)).get();
        ...
    }
}
```

In this case, you only need to refer to the one and only service parameter ("User") and it will never change, no matter how the User POJO is changed.

See also

See the full source code at the following links:

- **UserService**: https://github.com/eldermoraes/javaee8-cookbook/tree/master/chapter08/ch08-decoupled-user
- **DoSomethingService**: https://github.com/eldermoraes/javaee8-cookbook/tree/master/chapter08/ch08-decoupled-dosomethingwithuser

Building an automated pipeline for microservices

Maybe you are wondering, *why is there an automation recipe in a Jakarta EE 8 book?* or even, *is there any specification under Jakarta EE 8 that defines pipeline automation?*

The answer to the second question is *no*. At least no at this very moment. The answer to the first one I'll explain here.

Many times at conferences I am asked the question, *how do I migrate my monolith to microservices?* It comes in some variations, but at the end of the day, the question is the same.

People want to do it for different reasons:

- They want to keep up with the trend.
- They want to scale an application.
- They want to be able to use different stacks under the same solution.
- They want to look cool.

Any of these reasons are OK, and you can justify your migration to microservices with any of them if you want although I would question the real motivation of some of them.

Instead of giving them advice, tips, guidelines, or any other tech talk, I usually ask a simple question—*do you already have an automated pipeline for your monolith?*

Many times the answer is a disappointed *no*, followed by a curious, *why?*

Well, the answer is simple— if you don't automate the pipeline for a single monolith, which is one single file, and sometimes you have problems in building, testing, and/or deploying it, then what makes you think that it will be easier when you have dozens, hundreds, or even thousands of deployment files?

Let me be more specific:

- Do you build your deployment artifact manually, using an IDE or something?
- Do you deploy it manually?
- Have you ever had problems with the deployment for any reason such as errors, missing artifacts, or anything else?
- Have you ever had problems due to the lack of tests?

If you answered *yes* to at least one of these questions and don't have an automated pipeline, imagine these problems multiplied by, again, dozens, hundreds, or thousands.

Some people don't even write unit tests. Imagine those hidden errors going to production in a countless number of artifacts called **microservices**. Your microservices project will probably fail even before going live.

So, yes, you need to automate as many things as possible in your pipeline before even thinking of microservices. This is the only way to prevent problems from spreading out.

There are three maturity stages for an automation pipeline:

- **Continuous Integration** (**CI**): Basically, this ensures that your new code will be merged into the main branch (for example, the `master` branch) as soon as possible. It is based on the fact that the less code you merge, the fewer errors you add to it. It is reached mostly by running unit tests during build time.
- **Continuous delivery**: This is one step further from CI, where you guarantee your artifact will be ready to be deployed just by a click of a button. This usually requires an artifact repository for your binaries and a tool to manage it. When using continuous delivery, you decide when you will do the deployment, but the best practice is to do it as soon as possible to avoid adding a lot of new code in production in just one shot.
- **Continuous Deployment** (**CD**): This is the last, *state-of-the-art* part of automation. In CD, there is no human interaction since the code is committed until it is deployed in production. The only thing that would prevent an artifact from being deployed is an error in any of the pipeline stages. All of the major success cases of microservices worldwide use CD in their projects, doing hundreds or even thousands of deployments daily.

This recipe will show you how you can go from zero (no automation at all) to three (CD) in any Jakarta EE project. It's a bit of a conceptual recipe, but also with some code.

Going microservices is a huge thing and means lots of things both in your application and organization. Some people even say that microservices are all about scaling people and not technology.

Here we will, of course, keep on the tech side of things.

Getting ready

Being a lot of things, microservices will also bring a lot of tools with them. This recipe doesn't intend to go deep into the setup of each tool but shows you how it will work in a microservices-automated pipeline.

The tools chosen here are not the only option for the roles they perform. They are only my favorites for those roles.

To prepare your application—your microservices—for automation, you will need the following:

- **Apache Maven**: This is mainly used to build the stage and it will help you with many activities surrounding it. It manages the dependencies, runs unit tests, and much more.
- **JUnit**: This is used to write unit tests that will be executed at the build stage.
- **Git**: For the sake of the most sacred things you can imagine, use some version control for your source code. Here, I'll base it on GitHub.

To prepare the environment of your pipeline, you will need the following:

- **Sonatype Nexus**: This is a binary repository. In other words, when you build your artifact, it will be stored in Nexus and ready to be deployed wherever you need/want.
- **Jenkins**: I used to say that Jenkins is an automator for everything. In fact, I've worked in a project where we used it to build an automated pipeline (continuous delivery) for about 70 applications, with completely different technologies (languages, databases, operationig systems, and so on). You will use it basically for building and deploying.

How to do it...

In this section, you will be guided to reach each one of the three automation maturity stages—continuous integration, continuous delivery, and continuous deployment.

Continuous integration

Here, you need to make your new code go to the main branch as soon as possible. This will guarantee that your code is building properly and that the tests are planned and executed successfully. You will achieve it by using Git, Maven, and JUnit:

- **Git**: I'll not get too deeply into how to use Git and its commands, as it's not the focus of this book. If you are completely new to the Git world, get started by looking at this cheat sheet: `https://education.github.com/git-cheat-sheet-education.pdf`.
- **Maven**: Maven is one of the most powerful tools I've ever seen and hence has a bunch of features embedded. If you are new to it, check out this reference: `https://maven.apache.org/guides/MavenQuickReferenceCard.pdf`.

Let's try this out:

1. The most important file in a Maven-based project is `pom.xml` (**POM** or **Project Object Model**).

2. For example, when you create a new Java EE 8 project, it should look like this:

```xml
<?xml version="1.0" encoding="UTF-8"?>
<project xmlns="http://maven.apache.org/POM/4.0.0"
xmlns:xsi="http://www.w3.org/2001/XMLSchema-instance"
xsi:schemaLocation="http://maven.apache.org/POM/4.0.0
http://maven.apache.org/xsd/maven-4.0.0.xsd">
    <modelVersion>4.0.0</modelVersion>

    <groupId>com.eldermoraes</groupId>
    <artifactId>jakartaee8-project-template</artifactId>
    <version>1.0</version>
    <packaging>war</packaging>

    <name>jakartaee8-project-template</name>

    <properties>
<endorsed.dir>${project.build.directory}/endorsed</endorsed.dir>
    <project.build.sourceEncoding>UTF-8</project.build.sourceEncoding>
    </properties>
    <dependencies>
        <dependency>
            <groupId>javax</groupId>
            <artifactId>javaee-api</artifactId>
            <version>8.0</version>
            <scope>provided</scope>
        </dependency>
    </dependencies>

    <build>
        <plugins>
            <plugin>
                <groupId>org.apache.maven.plugins</groupId>
                <artifactId>maven-compiler-plugin</artifactId>
                <version>3.1</version>
                <configuration>
                    <source>1.8</source>
                    <target>1.8</target>
                    <compilerArguments>
<endorseddirs>${endorsed.dir}</endorseddirs>
                    </compilerArguments>
                </configuration>
            </plugin>
```

```
                        <plugin>
                            <groupId>org.apache.maven.plugins</groupId>
                            <artifactId>maven-war-plugin</artifactId>
                            <version>2.3</version>
                            <configuration>
        <failOnMissingWebXml>false</failOnMissingWebXml>
                            </configuration>
                        </plugin>
                    </plugins>
                </build>

        </project>
```

3. Then, your project is ready for building using Maven like this (running in the same folder where pom.xml is located):

   mvn

- **JUnit**: JUnit is used to run your unit tests. Let's check it:

1. Here is a class to be tested:

```
public class JUnitExample {
    @Size (min = 6, max = 10,message = "Name should be between 6
and 10
           characters")
    private String name;

    public String getName() {
        return name;
    }

    public void setName(String name) {
        this.name = name;
    }
}
```

2. Here is a testing class:

```
public class JUnitTest {
    private static Validator VALIDATOR;
    @BeforeClass
    public static void setUpClass() {
        VALIDATOR =
Validation.buildDefaultValidatorFactory().getValidator();
    }

    @Test
```

```
public void smallName(){
    JUnitExample junit = new JUnitExample();
    junit.setName("Name");
    Set<ConstraintViolation<JUnitExample>> cv =
    VALIDATOR.validate(junit);
    assertFalse(cv.isEmpty());
}
@Test
public void validName(){
    JUnitExample junit = new JUnitExample();
    junit.setName("Valid Name");
    Set<ConstraintViolation<JUnitExample>> cv =
    VALIDATOR.validate(junit);
    assertTrue(cv.isEmpty());
}

@Test
public void invalidName(){
    JUnitExample junit = new JUnitExample();
    junit.setName("Invalid Name");
    Set<ConstraintViolation<JUnitExample>> cv =
    VALIDATOR.validate(junit);
    assertFalse(cv.isEmpty());
}
}
```

3. Whenever you run the building process for this project, the preceding test will be executed and will ensure that those conditions are still valid.

Now, you are ready for continuous integration. Just make sure to merge your new and working code into the main branch as soon as possible. Now, let's move on to continuous delivery.

Continuous delivery

Now that you are a committer machine, let's go to the next level and make your application ready to deploy whenever you want.

You'll need your newly-built artifact to be available in a proper repository. This is when we use Sonatype Nexus.

I won't go into the setup details in this book. One easy way to do it is by using Docker containers. You can see more information about it at `https://hub.docker.com/r/sonatype/nexus/`. We can try these as follows:

1. Once your Nexus is available, you need to go to the `pom.xml` file and add this configuration:

```
<distributionManagement>
    <repository>
        <id>Releases</id>
        <name>Project</name>
        <url>[NEXUS_URL]/nexus/content/repositories/releases/</url>
    </repository>
</distributionManagement>
```

2. Now, instead of just building it, use the following:

```
mvn deploy
```

So, once your artifact is built, Maven will upload it to Sonatype Nexus. Now it is properly stored for future deployment.

Now you are almost ready to dance to the automation song. Let's bring Jenkins to the party.

As mentioned for Nexus, I will not get into the details about setting up Jenkins. I also recommend you do it using Docker. See the following link for details: `https://hub.docker.com/_/jenkins/`.

 If you have absolutely no idea on how to use Jenkins, please refer to this official guide: `https://jenkins.io/user-handbook.pdf`.

Once your Jenkins is up and running, you'll create two jobs:

- **Your-Project-Build**: This job will be used to build your project from the source code.
- **Your-Project-Deploy**: This job will be used to deploy your artifact after being built and stored in Nexus.

You will configure the first one to download the source code of your project and build it using Maven. The second will download it from Nexus and deploy it to the application server.

Remember that the deployment process involves some steps in most cases:

1. Stop the application server.
2. Remove the previous version.
3. Download the new version from Nexus.
4. Deploy the new version.
5. Start the application server.

So, you'd probably create a shell script to be executed by Jenkins. Remember, we are automating, so there are no manual processes.

Downloading the artifact can be a little tricky, so maybe you could use something like this in your shell script:

```
wget --user=username --password=password
"[NEXUS_URL]/nexus/service/local/artifact/maven/content?g=<group>&a=<artifa
ct>
&v=<version>&r=releases"
```

If everything goes fine until this point, then you'll have two buttons—one for building and another for deploying. You are ready and set to build with no need to use any IDE to deploy and no need to touch the application server.

Now you are sure that both processes (build and deploy) will be executed exactly the same way every time. You can now plan them to be executed in a shorter period of time.

Well, now, we will move to the next and best step—continuous deployment.

Continuous deployment

To move from delivery to deployment is a matter of maturity—you need a reliable process that ensures only the working code is going into production.

You already have your code running unit tests on every build. Actually, you didn't forget to write unit tests, right?

On every success, your built artifact is properly stored and you manage the right versioning for your application.

You have mastered the deployment process for your application, dealing properly with any condition that might occur. Your application server is never going down again without your knowledge and you achieved it with the help of just two buttons: build and deploy! You rock!

If you are at this point, your next move shouldn't be a big deal. You only need to automate the two jobs so you don't need to hit the button anymore.

In the build job, you'll set it to be executed whenever Jenkins finds any changes in the source code repository (check the documentation if you don't know how to do it).

Once it is done, there is just one last configuration—make the build step on the build job call another job, the deploy job. So any time the build is executed successfully, the deploy is also executed right away.

Cheers! You've made it.

There's more...

Of course, you will not only perform unit tests or API tests. You also need to test your UI, if you have one.

I'd recommend doing it using Selenium Webdriver. You can find more information here: `http://www.seleniumhq.org/docs/03_webdriver.jsp`.

In this case, you would probably want to deploy your application to a **Quality Assurance (QA)** environment, run the UI tests, and then go into production if everything is fine. So, it's just a matter of adding some new jobs to your pipeline, now that you know how to do it.

See also

The source code of the JUnit example can be found at `https://github.com/eldermoraes/javaee8-cookbook/tree/master/chapter08/ch08-automation`.

Determining the state of a microservice by using the MicroProfile Health Check API

According to the Eclipse MicroProfile Health Check specification, we have the following:

> *"...health checks are used to determine if a computing node needs to be discarded (terminated, shutdown) and eventually replaced by another (healthy) instance."*

So, when you think about the increasing granularity of distributed services in a microservice architecture, you really need to have (or should consider having) a way for your monitoring and management tools to deal with the health state of each service.

Here, in this recipe, you will learn how to use the Eclipse MicroProfile Health Check to provide endpoints that will expose the health check of your microservice in two ways: liveness and readiness.

Getting ready

The easiest way for you to create a Helidon MP project is by using a Maven archetype. Just execute this command:

```
mvn archetype:generate -DinteractiveMode=false \
  -DarchetypeGroupId=io.helidon.archetypes \
  -DarchetypeArtifactId=helidon-quickstart-mp \
  -DarchetypeVersion=1.4.1 \
  -DgroupId=com.eldermoraes.ch08 \
  -DartifactId=ch08-mphealthcheck \
  -Dpackage=com.eldermoraes.com.ch08.mphealthcheck
```

So, your starter project will be under the ch08-mphealthcheck folder:

```
cd ch08-mphealthcheck
```

Now, we are ready to go!

How to do it...

Your starter project will have some pre-built classes. We will create two other classes to provide the health check endpoints for your newly-created microservice:

1. First, we'll create a class named LivenessHealthCheck. It's pretty simple, so its full source code is here:

```
@Liveness
@ApplicationScoped
public class LivenessHealthCheck implements HealthCheck{
    @Override
    public HealthCheckResponse call() {
        return HealthCheckResponse.up("I'm up!");
    }
}
```

2. Then, let's build and run the project. Start by building and packaging it:

```
mvn package
```

3. Then, execute this command to run it:

```
java -jar target/ch08-mphealthcheck.jar
```

If everything went fine, you should see something like this in your Terminal:

```
2020.01.30 15:35:33 INFO org.jboss.weld.Version Thread[main,5,main]: WELD-000900: 3.1.1 (Final)
2020.01.30 15:35:33 INFO org.jboss.weld.Bootstrap Thread[main,5,main]: WELD-ENV-000020: Using jandex for bean discovery
2020.01.30 15:35:34 INFO org.jboss.weld.Bootstrap Thread[main,5,main]: WELD-000101: Transactional services not available. Injection of @Inject UserTransaction not available. Transactional
ed synchronously.
2020.01.30 15:35:34 INFO org.jboss.weld.Event Thread[main,5,main]: WELD-000411: Observer method [BackedAnnotatedMethod] public org.glassfish.jersey.ext.cdi1x.internal.ProcessAllAnnotatedT
e(@Observes ProcessAnnotatedType<?>, BeanManager) receives events for all annotated types. Consider restricting events using @WithAnnotations or a generic type with bounds.
2020.01.30 15:35:34 INFO org.jboss.weld.Event Thread[main,5,main]: WELD-000411: Observer method [BackedAnnotatedMethod] private io.helidon.microprofile.openapi.IndexBuilder.processAnnotat
AnnotatedType<X>) receives events for all annotated types. Consider restricting events using @WithAnnotations or a generic type with bounds.
2020.01.30 15:35:34 INFO org.jboss.weld.Bootstrap Thread[main,5,main]: WELD-ENV-002003: Weld SE container 7b348eda-da0e-4e2d-b90b-e2684a6557d0 initialized
2020.01.30 15:35:34 INFO io.helidon.microprofile.security.SecurityMpService Thread[main,5,main]: Security extension for microprofile is enabled, yet security configuration is missing from
ers configuration at key security.providers). Security will not have any valid provider.
2020.01.30 15:35:35 INFO io.smallrye.openapi.api.OpenApiDocument Thread[main,5,main]: OpenAPI document initialized: io.smallrye.openapi.api.models.OpenAPIImpl@74d3b638
2020.01.30 15:35:35 INFO io.helidon.webserver.NettyWebServer Thread[main,5,main]: Version: 1.4.1
2020.01.30 15:35:36 INFO io.helidon.webserver.NettyWebServer Thread[nioEventLoopGroup-2-1,10,main]: Channel '@default' started: [id: 0xd6339a97, L:/0:0:0:0:0:0:0:0:8080]
2020.01.30 15:35:36 INFO io.helidon.microprofile.server.ServerImpl Thread[nioEventLoopGroup-2-1,10,main]: Server initialized on http://localhost:8080 (and all other host addresses) in
http://localhost:8080/greet
```

4. Open a browser and navigate to this URL:

```
http://localhost:8080/health/live
```

If it's working, you will see something close to this:

```
{"outcome":"UP","status":"UP","checks":[{"name":"I'm live!","state":"UP","status":"UP"},{"name":"deadlock","state":"UP","status":"UP"},{"name":"diskSpace","state":
{"free":"169.61 GB","freeBytes":182114787328,"percentFree":"73.25%","total":"231.54 GB","totalBytes":248618848256}},{"name":"heapMemory","state":"UP","status":"UP",
MB","freeBytes":303366264,"max":"3.85 GB","maxBytes":4133486592,"percentFree":"98.99%","total":"329.00 MB","totalBytes":344981504}}]}
```

If this is the case, your liveness health check is working! Now, let's create the readiness one:

1. Create a class named `ReadinessHealthCheck` and code it like this:

```
@Readiness
@ApplicationScoped
public class ReadinessHealthCheck implements HealthCheck {
    @Override
    public HealthCheckResponse call() {
        if (isAcessible()){
            return HealthCheckResponse.up("I'm up and ready!");
        } else{
            return HealthCheckResponse.down("I'm up, but not
ready...");
        }
    }
    private boolean isAcessible(){
        return new Random().nextBoolean();
    }
}
```

2. Again, let's build and run it:

```
mvn package
java -jar target/ch08-mphealthcheck.jar
```

3. Now, you have a new URL to check another kind of health state:

```
http://localhost:8080/health/ready
```

If it's working, you will see something like this:

```
← → C ⌂   ⓘ localhost:8080/health/ready

{"outcome":"DOWN","status":"DOWN","checks":[{"name":"I'm live, but not ready...","state":"DOWN","status":"DOWN"}]}
```

Note that as it's just a simulation, your service will randomly return UP or DOWN each time that you call the URL:

```
← → C ⌂   ⓘ localhost:8080/health/ready

{"outcome":"UP","status":"UP","checks":[{"name":"I'm live and ready!","state":"UP","status":"UP"}]}
```

4. You can also just call the root health check endpoint:

```
http://localhost:8080/health
```

It will show you both endpoints (/ready and /live) in the same result:

```
← → C ⌂   ⓘ localhost:8080/health                                           ⊙ ☆ ƒ? ▢ ▢ ⊕ ▽

{"outcome":"DOWN","status":"DOWN","checks":[{"name":"I'm live!","state":"UP","status":"UP"},{"name":"I'm live, but not ready...","state":"DOWN","status
{"name":"deadlock","state":"UP","status":"UP"},{"name":"diskSpace","state":"UP","status":"UP","data":{"free":"169.61 GB","freeBytes":182115053568,"perc
GB","totalBytes":248618848256}},{"name":"heapMemory","state":"UP","status":"UP","data":{"free":"309.43 MB","freeBytes":324456200,"max":"3.85
GB","maxBytes":4133486592,"percentFree":"99.50%","total":"329.00 MB","totalBytes":344981504}}]}
```

If you got here successfully, congratulations! You are now able to manage the state of this microservice through the Eclipse MicroProfile Health Check API.

How it works...

The most important thing here is to understand the difference between liveness and readiness checkers:

- **Liveness**: It just shows whether your service is available or not.
- **Readiness**: It shows not only whether your service is available, but also whether it's ready to process requests.

Both situations have practical use cases.

You can use liveness just to monitor the health state of your single microservice. For example, if it is running under a Kubernetes cluster and it's liveness health check stops responding, Kubernetes can eliminate its pod and create another one.

On the other hand, you can use readiness to check some resources that your microservice need to respond to a request. It may needs to access a database, request a third-party service, or consume a message from a queue; if these resources are available, it will answer with *I'm up and ready!* but if they are not, it will return *I'm up, but not ready....*

There's more...

It's important to highlight something mentioned in the API specification—it's not intended (although it could be used) as a monitoring solution for human operators.

I would say—*do not use it as a solution for human operators! In fact, don't use human operators for this!*

Why am I saying this? Because of the increasing complexity of distributing your application, using a microservice approach will also increase the complexity of its monitoring and managing process. So, yes, use automated tools for that.

You can get more information about the Eclipse MicroProfile Health Check specification at `https://github.com/eclipse/microprofile-health`.

See also

Check the full source code of this recipe at `https://github.com/eldermoraes/javaee8-cookbook/tree/master/chapter08/ch08-mphealthcheck`.

Generating and/or monitoring metrics with the MicroProfile Metrics API

With the increase of the granularity of services (which came with the microservices approach), the complexity to manage all those little nodes of features (that is, microservices) also increases. So, being able to generate, store, and monitor its metrics has become the key to success, so you can have more data to help you to manage its complexity, even when it is growing.

In this recipe, you will learn how to do this using the Eclipse MicroProfile Metrics API. You will see the default metrics generated by the framework and how to generate metrics at the application level (metrics created by you), so you can monitor what makes sense for your business.

As MicroProfile is a specification and a standard, it has implementations. In this recipe, we will use Helidon MP (`https://helidon.io/`).

Getting ready

The easiest way for you to create a Helidon MP project is by using a Maven archetype. Just execute this command:

```
mvn archetype:generate -DinteractiveMode=false \
  -DarchetypeGroupId=io.helidon.archetypes \
  -DarchetypeArtifactId=helidon-quickstart-mp \
  -DarchetypeVersion=1.4.1 \
  -DgroupId=com.eldermoraes.ch08 \
  -DartifactId=ch08-mpmetrics \
  -Dpackage=com.eldermoraes.com.ch08.mpmetrics
```

So, your starter project will be under the `ch08-mpmetrics` folder:

```
cd ch08-mpmetrics
```

Now, we are ready to go!

How to do it...

Your starter project will have some pre-built classes. You can delete all of them, except for a class named `Main`:

1. Now create a class named `MpMetricsResource`. Set up its header like this:

```
@Path("/ch08mpmetrics")
@RequestScoped
public class MpMetricsResource {

    private static final JsonBuilderFactory JSON =
Json.createBuilderFactory(Collections.emptyMap());

}
```

2. Then, let's create a method that will perform some action so we can monitor its metrics. Inside the `MpMetricsResource` class, create this:

```
private String getResource() {
    Client client = null;
    String response;

    try {
        client = ClientBuilder.newClient();
        WebTarget target =
        client.target("https://eldermoraes.com/book");
        response = target.request()
                    .header("Content-Type", "application/json")
                    .get(String.class);
    } finally {
        if (client != null) {
            client.close();
        }
    }

    return response;
}
```

3. Now, we will create two methods that will generate metrics based on this preceding one. Remember, keep adding these methods to the `MpMetricsResource` class.

The first one will generate the `Timed` metrics, which are metrics based on the time that it takes the method to execute its tasks:

```
@Timed(name = "getResourceTimed")
@Path("/timed")
@GET
@Produces(MediaType.APPLICATION_JSON)
public JsonObject getResourceTimed() {
    String response = getResource();

    return JSON.createObjectBuilder()
            .add("message", response)
            .build();
}
```

4. The second one will generate the `Metered` metrics, which are metrics based on the frequency at which the method is called:

```
@Metered(name = "getResourceMetered")
@Path("/metered")
@GET
@Produces(MediaType.APPLICATION_JSON)
public JsonObject getResourceMetered() {
    String response = getResource();

    return JSON.createObjectBuilder()
            .add("message", response)
            .build();
}
```

Your `MpMetricsResource` is ready! You only need an `Application` class that will handle it for you. Just as a reminder, the `Application` class is a class specified by the JAX-RS specification to handle the REST endpoints inside your project.

5. Create a class named `MpMetricsApplication` and code it like this:

```
@ApplicationScoped
@ApplicationPath("/")
public class MpMetricsApplication extends Application {
    @Override
    public Set<Class<?>> getClasses() {
        return CollectionsHelper.setOf(MpMetricsResource.class);
    }
}
```

As an option, you can keep the original `Application` class created on your starter project and just change the parameter passed to the `.setOf(...)` method to receive the `MpMetricsResource` class.

So, you are ready to build and run your project to collect its metrics:

1. First, let's build it. Inside the project folder, execute this:

   ```
   mvn package
   ```

2. It will build your project and package it. Once it is done and if everything finished without any errors, execute this:

   ```
   java -jar target/ch08-mpmetrics.jar
   ```

   You should see something like this on your Terminal:

   ```
   2020.01.09 07:25:03 INFO org.jboss.weld.Version Thread[main,5,main]: WELD-000900: 3.1.1 (Final)
   2020.01.09 07:25:03 INFO org.jboss.weld.Bootstrap Thread[main,5,main]: WELD-ENV-000020: Using jandex for bean discovery
   2020.01.09 07:25:03 INFO org.jboss.weld.Bootstrap Thread[main,5,main]: WELD-000101: Transactional services not available. Injection of @Inject UserTransaction not available.
   ed synchronously.
   2020.01.09 07:25:03 INFO org.jboss.weld.Event Thread[main,5,main]: WELD-000411: Observer method [BackedAnnotatedMethod] public org.glassfish.jersey.ext.cdi1x.internal.ProcessAllA
   e(@Observes ProcessAnnotatedType<?>, BeanManager) receives events for all annotated types. Consider restricting events using @WithAnnotations or a generic type with bounds.
   2020.01.09 07:25:03 INFO org.jboss.weld.Event Thread[main,5,main]: WELD-000411: Observer method [BackedAnnotatedMethod] private io.helidon.microprofile.openapi.IndexBuilder.proce
   AnnotatedType<X>) receives events for all annotated types. Consider restricting events using @WithAnnotations or a generic type with bounds.
   2020.01.09 07:25:04 INFO org.jboss.weld.Bootstrap Thread[main,5,main]: WELD-ENV-002003: Weld SE container 9809a1b0-0dc9-4052-9479-7cdfd55ed438 initialized
   2020.01.09 07:25:04 INFO io.helidon.microprofile.security.SecurityMpService Thread[main,5,main]: Security extension for microprofile is enabled, yet security configuration is mis
   ers configuration at key security.providers). Security will not have any valid provider.
   2020.01.09 07:25:04 INFO io.smallrye.openapi.api.OpenApiDocument Thread[main,5,main]: OpenAPI document initialized: io.smallrye.openapi.api.models.OpenAPIImpl@6d3c232f
   2020.01.09 07:25:05 INFO io.helidon.webserver.NettyWebServer Thread[main,5,main]: Version: 1.4.1
   2020.01.09 07:25:05 INFO io.helidon.webserver.NettyWebServer Thread[nioEventLoopGroup-2-1,10,main]: Channel '@default' started: [id: 0x796b6d11, L:/0:0:0:0:0:0:0:0:8080]
   2020.01.09 07:25:05 INFO io.helidon.microprofile.server.ServerImpl Thread[nioEventLoopGroup-2-1,10,main]: Server initialized on http://localhost:8080 (and all other host addresse
   http://localhost:8080/ch08mpmetrics
   ```

3. Now your microservice is up and running, so you need to call the methods you've just created to be able to generate and check its metrics. Their URLs are as follows:

   ```
   http://localhost:8080/ch08mpmetrics/metered
   http://localhost:8080/ch08mpmetrics/timed
   ```

   Call each one of them a few times, so the metrics can be generated and checked. Fortunately, you don't have to do anything more for both cases!

4. These two metrics you've just created are automatically generated by the framework each time these methods are called. And for checking them, there is a default REST endpoint already available in your microservice (no, you didn't create it!). Just open this URL:

   ```
   http://localhost:8080/metrics/application
   ```

```
←  →  C  ⌂    ⓘ localhost:8080/metrics/application

# TYPE application_com_eldermoraes_com_ch08_mpmetrics_MpMetricsResource_getResourceMetered_total counter
# HELP application_com_eldermoraes_com_ch08_mpmetrics_MpMetricsResource_getResourceMetered_total
application_com_eldermoraes_com_ch08_mpmetrics_MpMetricsResource_getResourceMetered_total 4
# TYPE application_com_eldermoraes_com_ch08_mpmetrics_MpMetricsResource_getResourceMetered_rate_per_second gauge
application_com_eldermoraes_com_ch08_mpmetrics_MpMetricsResource_getResourceMetered_rate_per_second 8.496422698242626E-5
# TYPE application_com_eldermoraes_com_ch08_mpmetrics_MpMetricsResource_getResourceMetered_one_min_rate_per_second gauge
application_com_eldermoraes_com_ch08_mpmetrics_MpMetricsResource_getResourceMetered_one_min_rate_per_second 0.030856341651703634
# TYPE application_com_eldermoraes_com_ch08_mpmetrics_MpMetricsResource_getResourceMetered_five_min_rate_per_second gauge
application_com_eldermoraes_com_ch08_mpmetrics_MpMetricsResource_getResourceMetered_five_min_rate_per_second 0.009074772899633201
# TYPE application_com_eldermoraes_com_ch08_mpmetrics_MpMetricsResource_getResourceMetered_fifteen_min_rate_per_second gauge
application_com_eldermoraes_com_ch08_mpmetrics_MpMetricsResource_getResourceMetered_fifteen_min_rate_per_second 0.003227088757162994
# TYPE application_com_eldermoraes_com_ch08_mpmetrics_MpMetricsResource_getResourceTimed_rate_per_second gauge
application_com_eldermoraes_com_ch08_mpmetrics_MpMetricsResource_getResourceTimed_rate_per_second 8.496421811685727E-5
# TYPE application_com_eldermoraes_com_ch08_mpmetrics_MpMetricsResource_getResourceTimed_one_min_rate_per_second gauge
application_com_eldermoraes_com_ch08_mpmetrics_MpMetricsResource_getResourceTimed_one_min_rate_per_second 0.04423984338571901
# TYPE application_com_eldermoraes_com_ch08_mpmetrics_MpMetricsResource_getResourceTimed_five_min_rate_per_second gauge
application_com_eldermoraes_com_ch08_mpmetrics_MpMetricsResource_getResourceTimed_five_min_rate_per_second 0.009754115099857198
# TYPE application_com_eldermoraes_com_ch08_mpmetrics_MpMetricsResource_getResourceTimed_fifteen_min_rate_per_second gauge
application_com_eldermoraes_com_ch08_mpmetrics_MpMetricsResource_getResourceTimed_fifteen_min_rate_per_second 0.003305709235676515
# TYPE application_com_eldermoraes_com_ch08_mpmetrics_MpMetricsResource_getResourceTimed_mean_seconds gauge
application_com_eldermoraes_com_ch08_mpmetrics_MpMetricsResource_getResourceTimed_mean_seconds 2.1903487433781295
# TYPE application_com_eldermoraes_com_ch08_mpmetrics_MpMetricsResource_getResourceTimed_max_seconds gauge
application_com_eldermoraes_com_ch08_mpmetrics_MpMetricsResource_getResourceTimed_max_seconds 2.244906056
# TYPE application_com_eldermoraes_com_ch08_mpmetrics_MpMetricsResource_getResourceTimed_min_seconds gauge
application_com_eldermoraes_com_ch08_mpmetrics_MpMetricsResource_getResourceTimed_min_seconds 2.168440423
# TYPE application_com_eldermoraes_com_ch08_mpmetrics_MpMetricsResource_getResourceTimed_stddev_seconds gauge
application_com_eldermoraes_com_ch08_mpmetrics_MpMetricsResource_getResourceTimed_stddev_seconds 0.029908586123782437
# TYPE application_com_eldermoraes_com_ch08_mpmetrics_MpMetricsResource_getResourceTimed_seconds summary
# HELP application_com_eldermoraes_com_ch08_mpmetrics_MpMetricsResource_getResourceTimed_seconds
application_com_eldermoraes_com_ch08_mpmetrics_MpMetricsResource_getResourceTimed_seconds_count 4
application_com_eldermoraes_com_ch08_mpmetrics_MpMetricsResource_getResourceTimed_seconds{quantile="0.5"} 2.175777424
application_com_eldermoraes_com_ch08_mpmetrics_MpMetricsResource_getResourceTimed_seconds{quantile="0.75"} 2.179142523
application_com_eldermoraes_com_ch08_mpmetrics_MpMetricsResource_getResourceTimed_seconds{quantile="0.95"} 2.244906056
application_com_eldermoraes_com_ch08_mpmetrics_MpMetricsResource_getResourceTimed_seconds{quantile="0.98"} 2.244906056
application_com_eldermoraes_com_ch08_mpmetrics_MpMetricsResource_getResourceTimed_seconds{quantile="0.99"} 2.244906056
application_com_eldermoraes_com_ch08_mpmetrics_MpMetricsResource_getResourceTimed_seconds{quantile="0.999"} 2.244906056
```

If so, congratulations! You are collecting these metrics from your microservice.

How it works...

If you are familiar with annotations such as `@Path`, `@GET`, and `@Produces`, then the code of this recipe is not something new for you. So, how did we manage to get these metrics generated and checked?

We used two simple annotations— `@Timed` and `@Metered`:

```
@Timed(name = "getResourceTimed")
```

When we added this annotation to the `getResourceTimed` method, we were saying to the framework, *please, collect timed metrics for this method*:

```
@Metered(name = "getResourceMetered")
```

And there are also other metrics auto-generated by the framework. To check them, just open this URL:

```
http://localhost:8080/metrics
```

It will show you all of the metrics being collected so far (including yours).

There's more...

In this recipe, we covered two types of metrics supported by the Eclipse MicroProfile Metrics API— metered and timed. But there are others that you can also add to your application:

- Counted
- ConcurrentGauge
- Gauge

You can find more details about these metrics at `https://github.com/eclipse/microprofile-metrics/releases`.

See also

To see the full source code of this recipe, visit `https://github.com/eldermoraes/javaee8-cookbook/tree/master/chapter08/ch08-mpmetrics`.

Exposing API documentation using the MicroProfile OpenAPI

We know that a microservice is a self-contained component that performs some very specialized tasks with as much independence as possible.

But we also know that every component that we build has some kind of communication with other components (with rare exceptions). Usually, this communication happens through some kind of information sent and a response received. So, each service needs to know what should be sent to the other service and what kind of response is returned. Otherwise, this communication will have issues or even fail.

If you take care of both services or the people taking care of the other service are seated just behind you, fine. You just know it (or you just ask about it)! But things are completely different when you have dozens (hundreds or thousands) of microservices managed by teams distributed all over the world. Then, you'll need something more productive...

That's when API documentation comes to the rescue! And with Eclipse MicroProfile, this is pretty easy and is available right away through the implementation of OpenAPI, a well known open source project devoted to this matter. To get more details about it, visit https://www.openapis.org/.

This recipe will teach you how to document your service and how to see this documentation. I'll be able to provide useful information about your component in a way that anyone will be able to understand how it works.

Getting ready

The easiest way for you to create a Helidon MP project is by using a Maven archetype. Just execute this command:

```
mvn archetype:generate -DinteractiveMode=false \
  -DarchetypeGroupId=io.helidon.archetypes \
  -DarchetypeArtifactId=helidon-quickstart-mp \
  -DarchetypeVersion=1.4.1 \
  -DgroupId=com.eldermoraes.ch08 \
  -DartifactId=ch08-mpopenapi \
  -Dpackage=com.eldermoraes.com.ch08.mpopenapi
```

So, your starter project will be in the ch08-mpopenapi folder:

```
cd ch08-mpopenapi
```

Before continuing, edit the pom.xml of this project and add one dependency:

```
<dependency>
    <groupId>org.eclipse.microprofile.openapi</groupId>
    <artifactId>microprofile-openapi-api</artifactId>
</dependency>
```

Now, we are ready to go!

How to do it...

Your starter project will have some pre-built classes. You can delete all of them, except for a class named `Main`:

1. Now, create a class named `ContactResource`. Set up its header like this:

```
@Path("/")
@RequestScoped
@Tag(name = "Contact API service", description = "Methods for
Contact management")
public class ContactResource {


}
```

2. Then, let's create two methods so we can explore two ways of documenting our API. Create the first one like this:

```
@GET
@Path("/contacts")
@APIResponse(responseCode - "200",
        description = "Contact list response",
        name = "ContactListResponse"
)
public Response getContacts() {
    return Response.ok("This should be a contact list").build();
}
```

3. And the second one, we create like this:

```
@GET
@Path("/contact/{id}")
@APIResponse(responseCode = "200",
        description = "Single contact response",
        name = "SingleContactResponse"
)
@Parameter(name = "id",
        description = "Contact Id",
        required = true,
        allowEmptyValue = false
)
public Response getContactById(@PathParam("id") Long id) {
    return Response.ok("This is a single contact").build();
}
```

Your `ContactResource` is ready! You only need an `Application` class that will handle it for you. Just as a reminder, the `Application` class is a class specified by the JAX-RS specification to handle the REST endpoints inside your project.

4. Create a class named `ContactApplication` and code it like this:

```
@ApplicationScoped
@ApplicationPath("/ch08mpopenapi")
@OpenAPIDefinition(info = @Info(
        title = "Chapter 08 MicroProfile OpenAPI",
        version = "1.0.0",
        contact = @Contact(
                name = "Elder Moraes",
                email = "elder@eldermoraes.com",
                url = "https://eldermoraes.com")
),
        servers = {
            @Server(url = "/ch08mpopenapi", description =
"localhost")
        }
)
public class ContactApplication extends Application {

    @Override
    public Set<Class<?>> getClasses() {
        return CollectionsHelper.setOf(ContactResource.class);
    }
}
```

As an option, you can keep the original `*Application` class created on your starter project and just change the parameter passed to the `.setOf(...)` method to receive the `ContactResource` class.

So, you are ready to build and run your project:

1. First, let's build it. Inside the project folder, execute this:

    mvn package

2. It will build your project and package it. Once it is done and if everything finished without any errors, execute this:

    java -jar target/ch08-mpopenapi.jar

If everything went fine, your Terminal will show something like this:

```
File  Edit  View  Search  Terminal  Help
eldmorae@eldmorae-ThinkPad-T470:~/git/eldermoraes/javaee8-cookbook/chapter08/ch08-mpopenapi$ java -jar target/ch08-mpopenapi.jar
2020.01.29 18:20:04 INFO org.jboss.weld.Version Thread[main,5,main]: WELD-000900: 3.1.1 (Final)
2020.01.29 18:20:04 INFO org.jboss.weld.Bootstrap Thread[main,5,main]: WELD-ENV-000020: Using jandex for bean discovery
2020.01.29 18:20:04 INFO org.jboss.weld.Bootstrap Thread[main,5,main]: WELD-000101: Transactional services not available. Injection of @Inject UserTransaction not available. Transactional
ed synchronously.
2020.01.29 18:20:04 INFO org.jboss.weld.Event Thread[main,5,main]: WELD-000411: Observer method [BackedAnnotatedMethod] private io.helidon.microprofile.openapi.IndexBuilder.processAnnotat
AnnotatedType<X>) receives events for all annotated types. Consider restricting events using @WithAnnotations or a generic type with bounds.
2020.01.29 18:20:04 INFO org.jboss.weld.Event Thread[main,5,main]: WELD-000411: Observer method [BackedAnnotatedMethod] public org.glassfish.jersey.ext.cdi1x.internal.ProcessAllAnnotatedT
e(@Observes ProcessAnnotatedType<?>, BeanManager) receives events for all annotated types. Consider restricting events using @WithAnnotations or a generic type with bounds.
2020.01.29 18:20:05 INFO org.jboss.weld.Event Thread[main,5,main]: WELD-ENV-002003: Weld SE container 6eac48d6-5a3d-44ce-ad84-838427c53c20 initialized
2020.01.29 18:20:05 INFO io.helidon.microprofile.security.SecurityMpService Thread[main,5,main]: Security extension for microprofile is enabled, yet security configuration is missing from
ers configuration at key security.providers). Security will not have any valid provider.
2020.01.29 18:20:05 INFO io.smallrye.openapi.api.OpenApiDocument Thread[main,5,main]: OpenAPI document initialized: io.smallrye.openapi.api.models.OpenAPIImpl@3d5790ea
2020.01.29 18:20:06 INFO io.helidon.webserver.NettyWebServer Thread[main,5,main]: Version: 1.4.1
2020.01.29 18:20:06 INFO io.helidon.webserver.NettyWebServer Thread[nioEventLoopGroup-2-1,10,main]: Channel '@default' started: [id: 0x952f6b99, L:/0:0:0:0:0:0:0:0:8080]
2020.01.29 18:20:06 INFO io.helidon.microprofile.server.ServerImpl Thread[nioEventLoopGroup-2-1,10,main]: Server initialized on http://localhost:8080 (and all other host addresses) in
http://localhost:8080/ch08mpopenapi
```

3. Now, just open a browser and navigate to this URL:

```
http://localhost:8080/openapi
```

It will open a YAML file like this:

```
---
openapi: 3.0.1
info:
  title: Chapter 08 MicroProfile OpenAPI
  contact:
    name: Elder Moraes
    url: https://eldermoraes.com
    email: elder@eldermoraes.com
  version: 1.0.0
servers:
- url: /ch08mpopenapi
  description: localhost
tags:
- name: Contact API service
  description: Methods for Contact management
paths:
  /ch08mpopenapi/contact/{id}:
    get:
      tags:
      - Contact API service
      parameters:
      - name: id
        description: Contact Id
        required: true
        allowEmptyValue: false
      responses:
        "200":
          description: Single contact response
  /ch08mpopenapi/contacts:
    get:
      tags:
      - Contact API service
      responses:
        "200":
          description: Contact list response
```

That's it! Now, your API is documented and you can skip some phone calls to talk about it.

How it works...

It's all based on annotations. The main ones are those applied to the `ContactApplication` class because whatever is documented here will be the root of the API documentation. Let's check these annotations more closely:

```
@OpenAPIDefinition(info = @Info(
        title = "Chapter 08 MicroProfile OpenAPI",
        version = "1.0.0",
        contact = @Contact(
                name = "Elder Moraes",
                email = "elder@eldermoraes.com",
                url = "https://eldermoraes.com")
),
        servers = {
            @Server(url = "/ch08mpopenapi", description = "localhost")
        }
)
```

Note that we are just analyzing the `OpenAPI` annotations. These classes have other annotations, but they refer to other features.

The `@OpenAPIDefinition` annotation has under it all of the global information that you can provide about this API.

Now, let's check the documentation given to the `ContactResource` class:

```
@Tag(name = "Contact API service", description = "Methods for Contact
management")
```

The `@Tag` annotation will host general information about this service. Let's check the methods:

```
@APIResponse(responseCode = "200",
        description = "Contact list response",
        name = "ContactListResponse"
)
```

Here, the `@APIResponse` annotation gives information about the response given by the method.

If your method has some parameter, you just add something like this:

```
@Parameter(name = "id",
        description = "Contact Id",
        required = true,
        allowEmptyValue = false
)
```

So, no more guessing about how a service works: just inform it!

There's more...

The OpenAPI specification under Eclipse MicroProfile is a very rich and flexible feature, with a lot of different possibilities. To get more information, just check it out at `https://github.com/eclipse/microprofile-open-api/`.

See also

The full source code of this recipe is available at `https://github.com/eldermoraes/javaee8-cookbook/tree/master/chapter08/ch08-mpopenapi`.

9
Using Multithreading on Enterprise Context

Threading is a common issue in most software projects, no matter what language or technology is involved. With regard to enterprise applications, threading is even more important and, sometimes, harder.

A single mistake in a thread can affect the whole system, or even the whole infrastructure. Think about resources that are never released, memory consumption that never stops increasing, and so on.

The Jakarta EE environment has some great features for dealing with these and plenty of other challenges, and this chapter will show you some of them.

This chapter covers the following recipes:

- Building asynchronous tasks with returning results
- Using transactions with asynchronous tasks
- Checking the status of asynchronous tasks
- Building managed threads with returning results
- Scheduling asynchronous tasks with returning results
- Using injected proxies for asynchronous tasks

Building asynchronous tasks with returning results

One of the first challenges you will face if you have never worked with asynchronous tasks is how to return results from an asynchronous task if you don't know when the execution will end.

This recipe shows you how this is done. `AsyncResponse` for the win!

Getting ready

Let's first add our Jakarta EE 8 dependency:

```
<dependency>
    <groupId>javax</groupId>
    <artifactId>javaee-api</artifactId>
    <version>8.0</version>
    <scope>provided</scope>
</dependency>
```

How to do it...

Follow these five steps to complete this recipe:

1. First, create a `User` POJO:

```
package com.eldermoraes.ch09.async.result;

/**
 *
 * @author eldermoraes
 */
public class User {

    private Long id;
    private String name;

    public Long getId() {
        return id;
    }

    public void setId(Long id) {
        this.id = id;
```

```
        }

        public String getName() {
            return name;
        }

        public void setName(String name) {
            this.name = name;
        }
        public User(Long id, String name) {
            this.id = id;
            this.name = name;
        }
        @Override
        public String toString() {
            return "User{" + "id=" + id + ", name="
                        + name + '}';
        }

    }
```

2. Then, create `UserService` to emulate a remote slow endpoint:

```
@Stateless
@Path("userService")
public class UserService {
    @GET
    public Response userService(){
        try {
            TimeUnit.SECONDS.sleep(5);
            long id = new Date().getTime();
            return Response.ok(new User(id, "User " + id)).build();
        } catch (InterruptedException ex) {
            return
            Response.status(Response.Status.INTERNAL_SERVER_ERROR)
            .entity(ex).build();
        }
    }
}
```

3. Now, create an asynchronous client that reaches the endpoint and gets the result:

```
@Stateless
public class AsyncResultClient {

    private Client client;
    private WebTarget target;

    @PostConstruct
```

```
public void init() {
    client = ClientBuilder.newBuilder()
            .readTimeout(10, TimeUnit.SECONDS)
            .connectTimeout(10, TimeUnit.SECONDS)
            .build();
    target = client.target("http://localhost:8080/
            ch09-async-result/userService");
}

@PreDestroy
public void destroy(){
    client.close();
}
public CompletionStage<Response> getResult(){
    return
    target.request(MediaType.APPLICATION_JSON).rx().get();
}
}
```

4. Finally, create a service (endpoint) that uses the client to write the result in the response:

```
@Stateless
@Path("asyncService")
public class AsyncService {

    @Inject
    private AsyncResultClient client;

    @GET
    public void asyncService(@Suspended AsyncResponse response)
    {
        try{
            client.getResult().thenApply(this::readResponse)
            .thenAccept(response::resume);
        } catch(Exception e){
            response.resume(Response.status(Response.Status.
            INTERNAL_SERVER_ERROR).entity(e).build());
        }
    }

    private String readResponse(Response response) {
        return response.readEntity(String.class);
    }
}
```

5. To run this example, simply deploy it to Eclipse GlassFish 5.1 and open the following URL in your browser:

```
http://localhost:8080/ch09-async-result/asyncService
```

How it works...

Here, our remote endpoint creates `User` and converts it into a response entity:

```
return Response.ok(new User(id, "User " + id)).build();
```

So, with no effort at all, `User` is now a JSON object.

Now, let's take a look at the key method in `AsyncResultClient`:

```
public CompletionStage<Response> getResult(){
return target.request(MediaType.APPLICATION_JSON).rx().get();
}
```

The `rx()` method is part of the Reactive Client API introduced to Jakarta EE 8. We'll discuss Reactive in more detail in `Chapter 10`, *Using Event-Driven Programming to Build Reactive Applications*. It basically returns `CompletionStageInvoker`, which allows you to get `CompletionStage<Response>` (the returning value for this method).

In other words, this is an asynchronous/non-blocking code that gets results from the remote endpoint.

It should be noted that we use the `@Stateless` annotation with this client so that we can inject it into our main endpoint:

```
Inject
private AsyncResultClient client;
```

Here's our asynchronous method for writing a response:

```
GET
public void asyncService(@Suspended AsyncResponse response) {
        client.getResult().thenApply(this::readResponse)
    .thenAccept(response::resume);
}
```

Note that this is a `void` method; it doesn't return anything because it returns the result to a callback.

The `@Suspended` annotation, combined with `AsyncResponse`, resumes the response once the processing is complete as we use the following beautiful, one-line, Java 8-style code:

```
client.getResult().thenApply(this::readResponse)
.thenAccept(response::resume);
```

Before looking into the details, let's just clarify our local `readResponse` method:

```
private String readResponse(Response response) {
    return response.readEntity(String.class);
}
```

It just reads the `User` entity embedded in `Response` and transforms it into a `String` object (a JSON string).

Another way that this one-line code can be written is as follows:

```
client.getResult()
.thenApply(r -> readResponse(r))
.thenAccept(s -> response.resume(s));
```

However, the first way is more concise, less verbose, and more fun!

The key is the `resume` method from the `AsyncReponse` object. It writes the response to the callback and returns it to whoever asked for it.

See also

The full source code for this recipe can be found at `https://github.com/eldermoraes/javaee8-cookbook/tree/master/chapter09/ch09-async-result`.

Using transactions with asynchronous tasks

Using asynchronous tasks can already pose a challenge, but what if you want to add some spice and add a transaction to it?

Usually, a transaction refers to something such as code blocking. Isn't it awkward to combine two opposing concepts? Well, no! They can work together nicely, as this recipe shows.

Getting ready

Let's first add our Jakarta EE 8 dependency:

```
<dependency>
    <groupId>javax</groupId>
    <artifactId>javaee-api</artifactId>
    <version>8.0</version>
    <scope>provided</scope>
</dependency>
```

How to do it...

There are five steps to complete this recipe:

1. Let's first create a `User` POJO:

```
public class User {

    private Long id;
    private String name;

    public Long getId() {
        return id;
    }

    public void setId(Long id) {
        this.id = id;
    }

    public String getName() {
        return name;
    }

    public void setName(String name) {
        this.name = name;
    }
    public User(Long id, String name) {
        this.id = id;
        this.name = name;
```

```
        }
        @Override
        public String toString() {
            return "User{" + "id=" + id + ",
                        name=" + name + '}';
        }
    }
```

2. This is a slow bean that returns `User`:

```
@Stateless
public class UserBean {
    public User getUser(){
        try {
            TimeUnit.SECONDS.sleep(5);
            long id = new Date().getTime();
            return new User(id, "User " + id);
        } catch (InterruptedException ex) {
            System.err.println(ex.getMessage());
            long id = new Date().getTime();
            return new User(id, "Error " + id);
        }
    }
}
```

3. Now, we create a task that executes and returns `User`, using some transaction stuff:

```
public class AsyncTask implements Callable<User> {

    private UserTransaction userTransaction;
    private UserBean userBean;

    @Override
    public User call() throws Exception {
        performLookups();
        try {
            userTransaction.begin();
            User user = userBean.getUser();
            userTransaction.commit();
            return user;
        } catch (IllegalStateException | SecurityException |
            HeuristicMixedException | HeuristicRollbackException |
            NotSupportedException | RollbackException |
            SystemException e) {
            userTransaction.rollback();
            return null;
        }
```

```
    }

    private void performLookups() throws NamingException{
        userBean = CDI.current().select(UserBean.class).get();
        userTransaction = CDI.current()
        .select(UserTransaction.class).get();
    }
}
```

4. Finally, here is the service endpoint that uses the task to write the result to a response:

```
@Path("asyncService")
@RequestScoped
public class AsyncService {
    private AsyncTask asyncTask;
    @Resource(name = "LocalManagedExecutorService")
    private ManagedExecutorService executor;
    @PostConstruct
    public void init(){
        asyncTask = new AsyncTask();
    }
    @GET
    public void asyncService(@Suspended AsyncResponse response){
        Future<User> result = executor.submit(asyncTask);
        while(!result.isDone()){
            try {
                TimeUnit.SECONDS.sleep(1);
            } catch (InterruptedException ex) {
                System.err.println(ex.getMessage());
            }
        }
        try {
            response.resume(Response.ok(result.get()).build());
        } catch (InterruptedException | ExecutionException ex) {
            System.err.println(ex.getMessage());
            response.resume(Response.status(Response
            .Status.INTERNAL_SERVER_ERROR)
            .entity(ex.getMessage()).build());
        }
    }
}
```

5. To try this code, simply deploy it to Eclipse GlassFish 5.1 and open the following URL:

```
http://localhost:8080/ch09-async-transaction/asyncService
```

How it works...

The magic happens in the `AsyncTask` class, where we will first take a look at the `performLookups` method:

```
private void performLookups() throws NamingException{
    Context ctx = new InitialContext();
    userTransaction = (UserTransaction)
    ctx.lookup("java:comp/UserTransaction");
    userBean = (UserBean) ctx.lookup("java:global/
    ch09-async-transaction/UserBean");
}
```

This gives you the instances of both `UserTransaction` and `UserBean` from the application server. Then, you can relax and rely on what has already been instantiated.

As our task implements a `Callable<V>` object, it needs to implement the `call()` method, as follows:

```
@Override
public User call() throws Exception {
    performLookups();
    try {
        userTransaction.begin();
        User user = userBean.getUser();
        userTransaction.commit();
        return user;
    } catch (IllegalStateException | SecurityException |
            HeuristicMixedException | HeuristicRollbackException
            | NotSupportedException | RollbackException |
            SystemException e) {
        userTransaction.rollback();
        return null;
    }
}
```

You can see `Callable` as a `Runnable` interface that returns a result.

Our transaction code resides here:

```
userTransaction.begin();
User user = userBean.getUser();
userTransaction.commit();
```

If anything goes wrong, we have the following code:

```
} catch (IllegalStateException | SecurityException |
HeuristicMixedException | HeuristicRollbackException
          | NotSupportedException | RollbackException |
SystemException e) {
userTransaction.rollback();
          return null;
}
```

Now, we will look at `AsyncService`:

1. First, we have some declarations, as in the following code snippet:

```
private AsyncTask asyncTask;
@Resource(name = "LocalManagedExecutorService")
private ManagedExecutorService executor;
@PostConstruct
public void init(){
    asyncTask = new AsyncTask();
}
```

 We ask the container to give us an instance from `ManagedExecutorService`, which is responsible for executing the task in the enterprise context.

2. Then, we call an `init()` method and the bean is constructed (`@PostConstruct`). This instantiates the task.

    Now, we have our task execution:

```
@GET
public void asyncService(@Suspended AsyncResponse response){
    Future<User> result = executor.submit(asyncTask);
    while(!result.isDone()){
        try {
            TimeUnit.SECONDS.sleep(1);
        } catch (InterruptedException ex) {
            System.err.println(ex.getMessage());
        }
    }
    try {
        response.resume(Response.ok(result.get()).build());
    } catch (InterruptedException | ExecutionException ex) {
        System.err.println(ex.getMessage());
        response.resume(Response.status(Response.
```

```
                Status.INTERNAL_SERVER_ERROR)
                .entity(ex.getMessage()).build());
    }
 }
```

3. Note that the executor returns `Future<User>`:

```
Future<User> result = executor.submit(asyncTask);
```

This means this task is executed asynchronously.

4. Then, we can check its execution status until it's done, as follows:

```
while(!result.isDone()){
        try {
            TimeUnit.SECONDS.sleep(1);
        } catch (InterruptedException ex) {
            System.err.println(ex.getMessage());
        }
}
```

5. Once the task is done, we write it to the asynchronous response with the following code:

```
response.resume(Response.ok(result.get()).build());
```

See also

The full source code for this recipe can be found at `https://github.com/eldermoraes/ javaee8-cookbook/tree/master/chapter09/ch09-async-transaction`.

Checking the status of asynchronous tasks

Beyond executing asynchronous tasks, which opens up a lot of possibilities, it is sometimes useful and necessary to get the status of these tasks.

For example, you could use the status to check the time elapsed on each stage of a task. You should also think about logging and monitoring.

This recipe will show you an easy way of doing this.

Getting ready

Let's first add our Jakarta EE 8 dependency:

```
<dependency>
    <groupId>javax</groupId>
    <artifactId>javaee-api</artifactId>
    <version>8.0</version>
    <scope>provided</scope>
</dependency>
```

Refer to the *Using transactions with asynchronous tasks* recipe to see how `Callable` is used.

How to do it...

The following five steps are required to complete this recipe:

1. Let's first create a `User` POJO:

```
public class User {

    private Long id;
    private String name;

    public Long getId() {
        return id;
    }

    public void setId(Long id) {
        this.id = id;
    }

    public String getName() {
        return name;
    }

    public void setName(String name) {
        this.name = name;
    }
    public User(Long id, String name) {
        this.id = id;
        this.name = name;
    }
    @Override
    public String toString() {
        return "User{" + "id=" + id + ",
```

```
            name=" + name + '}';
    }
}
```

2. Then, create a slow bean to return `User`:

```java
public class UserBean {
    public User getUser(){
        try {
            TimeUnit.SECONDS.sleep(5);
            long id = new Date().getTime();
            return new User(id, "User " + id);
        } catch (InterruptedException ex) {
            long id = new Date().getTime();
            return new User(id, "Error " + id);
        }
    }
}
```

3. Now, create a `Managed` task so that we can monitor it:

```java
@Stateless
public class AsyncTask implements Callable<User>,
ManagedTaskListener {

    private final long instantiationMili = new Date().getTime();
    private static final Logger LOG = Logger.getAnonymousLogger();
    @Override
    public User call() throws Exception {
        return new UserBean().getUser();
    }

    @Override
    public void taskSubmitted(Future<?> future,
    ManagedExecutorService mes, Object o) {
        long mili = new Date().getTime();
        LOG.log(Level.INFO, "taskSubmitted: {0} -
        Miliseconds since instantiation: {1}",
        new Object[]{future, mili - instantiationMili});
    }

    @Override
    public void taskAborted(Future<?> future,
    ManagedExecutorService mes, Object o, Throwable thrwbl)
    {
        long mili = new Date().getTime();
        LOG.log(Level.INFO, "taskAborted: {0} -
        Miliseconds since instantiation: {1}",
```

```
        new Object[]{future, mili - instantiationMili});
    }

    @Override
    public void taskDone(Future<?> future,
    ManagedExecutorService mes, Object o,
    Throwable thrwbl) {
        long mili = new Date().getTime();
        LOG.log(Level.INFO, "taskDone: {0} -
        Miliseconds since instantiation: {1}",
        new Object[]{future, mili - instantiationMili});
    }

    @Override
    public void taskStarting(Future<?> future,
    ManagedExecutorService mes, Object o) {
        long mili = new Date().getTime();
        LOG.log(Level.INFO, "taskStarting: {0} -
        Miliseconds since instantiation: {1}",
        new Object[]{future, mili - instantiationMili});
    }

}
```

4. Finally, create a service endpoint to execute our task and return its results:

```
@Stateless
@Path("asyncService")
public class AsyncService {

    @Resource
    private ManagedExecutorService executor;

    @GET
    public void asyncService(@Suspended AsyncResponse response) {
        int i = 0;

        List<User> usersFound = new ArrayList<>();
        while (i < 4) {
            Future<User> result = executor.submit(new AsyncTask());

            while (!result.isDone()) {
                try {
                    TimeUnit.SECONDS.sleep(1);
                } catch (InterruptedException ex) {
                    System.err.println(ex.getMessage());
                }
            }
```

```
                    try {
                        usersFound.add(result.get());
                    } catch (InterruptedException | ExecutionException ex)
        {
                        System.err.println(ex.getMessage());
                    }

                    i++;
                }

            response.resume(Response.ok(usersFound).build());
        }

    }
```

5. To try this code, simply deploy it to Eclipse GlassFish 5 and open the following URL:

```
http://localhost:8080/ch09-task-status/asyncService
```

How it works...

If you followed the last recipe, you should already be familiar with the `Callable` task, so I won't go into detail about it here. Now, we implement our task using both the `Callable` and `ManagedTaskListener` interfaces. The latter interface provides us with all the methods for checking the task's status. Consider the following code block:

```
@Override
public void taskSubmitted(Future<?> future,
ManagedExecutorService mes, Object o) {
    long mili = new Date().getTime();
    LOG.log(Level.INFO, "taskSubmitted: {0} -
    Miliseconds since instantiation: {1}",
    new Object[]{future, mili - instantiationMili});
}

@Override
public void taskAborted(Future<?> future,
ManagedExecutorService mes, Object o, Throwable thrwbl) {
    long mili = new Date().getTime();
    LOG.log(Level.INFO, "taskAborted: {0} -
    Miliseconds since instantiation: {1}",
    new Object[]{future, mili - instantiationMili});
}

@Override
```

```
public void taskDone(Future<?> future,
ManagedExecutorService mes, Object o, Throwable thrwbl) {
    long mili = new Date().getTime();
    LOG.log(Level.INFO, "taskDone: {0} -
    Miliseconds since instantiation: {1}",
    new Object[]{future, mili - instantiationMili});
}

@Override
public void taskStarting(Future<?> future,
ManagedExecutorService mes, Object o) {
    long mili = new Date().getTime();
    LOG.log(Level.INFO, "taskStarting: {0} -
    Miliseconds since instantiation: {1}",
    new Object[]{future, mili - instantiationMili});
}
```

The best part is that you don't need to call any of these—ManagedExecutorService (explained next) does this for you.

Finally, we have AsyncService. The first declaration is for our executor:

```
@Resource
private ManagedExecutorService executor;
```

In the service itself, we get four users from our asynchronous task, as follows:

```
List<User> usersFound = new ArrayList<>();
    while (i < 4) {
    Future<User> result = executor.submit(new AsyncTask());

    while (!result.isDone()) {
    try {
        TimeUnit.SECONDS.sleep(1);
        } catch (InterruptedException ex) {
          System.err.println(ex.getMessage());
        }
    }

    try {
        usersFound.add(result.get());
        } catch (InterruptedException | ExecutionException ex) {
          System.err.println(ex.getMessage());
        }

    i++;
    }
```

Once done, it's written to the asynchronous response:

```
response.resume(Response.ok(usersFound).build());
```

Now, if you look at your server log output, there are messages from the `ManagedTaskListener` interface.

See also

- You can find the full source code for this recipe at `https://github.com/ eldermoraes/javaee8-cookbook/tree/master/chapter09/ch09-task-status`.

Building managed threads with returning results

Sometimes, you need to improve the way that you look at the threads you use—perhaps to improve your logging features or to manage their priorities. It would be nice if you could also get the results back from them. This recipe will show you how to do this.

Getting ready

Let's first add our Jakarta EE 8 dependency:

```
<dependency>
    <groupId>javax</groupId>
    <artifactId>javaee-api</artifactId>
    <version>8.0</version>
    <scope>provided</scope>
</dependency>
```

How to do it...

The following four steps are used to complete this recipe:

1. Let's first create a `User` POJO:

```java
public class User {

    private Long id;
    private String name;

    public Long getId() {
        return id;
    }

    public void setId(Long id) {
        this.id = id;
    }

    public String getName() {
        return name;
    }

    public void setName(String name) {
        this.name = name;
    }
    public User(Long id, String name) {
        this.id = id;
        this.name = name;
    }
    @Override
    public String toString() {
        return "User{" + "id=" + id + ",
        name=" + name + '}';
    }
}
```

2. Then, create a slow bean to return `User`:

```java
@Stateless
public class UserBean {
    @GET
    public User getUser(){
        try {
            TimeUnit.SECONDS.sleep(5);
            long id = new Date().getTime();
            return new User(id, "User " + id);
        } catch (InterruptedException ex) {
```

```
            long id = new Date().getTime();
            return new User(id, "Error " + id);
        }
    }
}
```

3. Finally, create an endpoint to get the result of the task:

```
@Stateless
@Path("asyncService")
public class AsyncService {

    @Inject
    private UserBean userBean;

    @Resource(name = "LocalManagedThreadFactory")
    private ManagedThreadFactory factory;

    @GET
    public void asyncService(@Suspended AsyncResponse
    response) {
        Thread thread = factory.newThread(() -> {
            response.resume(Response.ok(userBean
            .getUser()).build());
        });
        thread.setName("Managed Async Task");
        thread.setPriority(Thread.MIN_PRIORITY);
        thread.start();
    }

}
```

4. To try this code, simply deploy it to Eclipse GlassFish 5 and open the following URL:

```
http://localhost:8080/ch09-managed-thread/asyncService
```

How it works...

The only case where you should use threads in an enterprise context, if you really want to use them, is when the application server creates the thread. Here, we ask the container to do so using factory:

```
Resource(name = "LocalManagedThreadFactory")
private ManagedThreadFactory factory;
```

Using some functional-style code, we create our thread:

```
Thread thread = factory.newThread(() -> {
response.resume(Response.ok(userBean.getUser()).build());
 });
```

Now, moving on to the managed stuff, we can set the name and priority of the thread that we just created, as follows:

```
thread.setName("Managed Async Task");
thread.setPriority(Thread.MIN_PRIORITY);
```

Don't forget to ask the container to start the thread:

```
thread.start();
```

See also

You can find the full source code for this recipe at `https://github.com/eldermoraes/javaee8-cookbook/tree/master/chapter09/ch09-managed-thread`.

Scheduling asynchronous tasks with returning results

Using tasks also means being able to define when they should be executed. This recipe covers this, as well as getting the returning results whenever they return.

Getting ready

Let's first add our Jakarta EE 8 dependency:

```
<dependency>
    <groupId>javax</groupId>
    <artifactId>javaee-api</artifactId>
    <version>8.0</version>
    <scope>provided</scope>
</dependency>
```

How to do it...

The following five steps are used to complete this recipe:

1. Let's first create a `User` POJO:

```
public class User {

    private Long id;
    private String name;

    public Long getId() {
        return id;
    }

    public void setId(Long id) {
        this.id = id;
    }

    public String getName() {
        return name;
    }

    public void setName(String name) {
        this.name = name;
    }
    public User(Long id, String name) {
        this.id = id;
        this.name = name;
    }
    @Override
    public String toString() {
        return "User{" + "id=" + id + ",
        name=" + name + '}';
    }
}
```

2. Then, we create a slow bean to return `User`:

```
public class UserBean {
    public User getUser(){
        try {
            TimeUnit.SECONDS.sleep(5);
            long id = new Date().getTime();
            return new User(id, "User " + id);
        } catch (InterruptedException ex) {
            long id = new Date().getTime();
            return new User(id, "Error " + id);
```

```
            }
        }
    }
```

3. Now, we create a simple `Callable` task to communicate with the bean:

```java
public class AsyncTask implements Callable<User> {

    private final UserBean userBean =
    CDI.current().select(UserBean.class).get();

    @Override
    public User call() throws Exception {
        return userBean.getUser();
    }
}
```

4. Finally, we create a service to schedule and write the task's result in the response:

```java
@Stateless
@Path("asyncService")
public class AsyncService {

    @Resource(name = "LocalManagedScheduledExecutorService")
    private ManagedScheduledExecutorService executor;

    @GET
    public void asyncService(@Suspended AsyncResponse response) {

        ScheduledFuture<User> result = executor.schedule
        (new AsyncTask(), 5, TimeUnit.SECONDS);

        while (!result.isDone()) {
            try {
                TimeUnit.SECONDS.sleep(1);
            } catch (InterruptedException ex) {
                System.err.println(ex.getMessage());
            }
        }

        try {
            response.resume(Response.ok(result.get()).build());
        } catch (InterruptedException | ExecutionException ex) {
            System.err.println(ex.getMessage());
            response.resume(Response.status(Response.Status
            .INTERNAL_SERVER_ERROR).entity(ex.getMessage())
            .build());
        }
```

```
        }

    }
```

5. To try this code, simply deploy it to Eclipse GlassFish 5.1 and open the following URL:

```
http://localhost:8080/ch09-scheduled-task/asyncService
```

How it works...

All the magic of this recipe relies on the AsyncService class, so we will focus on that.

First, we ask the server for an instance of an executor:

```
Resource(name = "LocalManagedScheduledExecutorService")
private ManagedScheduledExecutorService executor;
```

However, we are not asking for just any executor—we want an executor that's specific to scheduling:

```
ScheduledFuture<User> result = executor.schedule(new AsyncTask(),
5, TimeUnit.SECONDS);
```

So, we schedule our task to be executed in 5 seconds. Note that we also don't use a regular Future instance, but rather ScheduledFuture:

```
while (!result.isDone()) {
  try {
      TimeUnit.SECONDS.sleep(1);
    } catch (InterruptedException ex) {
      System.err.println(ex.getMessage());
  }
}
```

The following code snippet shows you how we write the results to the response:

```
response.resume(Response.ok(result.get()).build());
```

See also

You can find the full source code for this recipe at https://github.com/eldermoraes/javaee8-cookbook/tree/master/chapter09/ch09-scheduled-task.

Using injected proxies for asynchronous tasks

When using tasks, you can also create your own executor. If you have very specific needs, an executor could really come in handy.

This recipe shows you how to create a proxy executor that can be injected and used in the whole context of your application.

Getting ready

Let's first add our Jakarta EE 8 dependency:

```
<dependency>
    <groupId>javax</groupId>
    <artifactId>javaee-api</artifactId>
    <version>8.0</version>
    <scope>provided</scope>
</dependency>
```

How to do it...

The following six steps are used to complete this recipe:

1. First, we create a User POJO:

```
public class User implements Serializable{

    private Long id;
    private String name;

    public Long getId() {
        return id;
    }

    public void setId(Long id) {
        this.id = id;
    }

    public String getName() {
        return name;
    }
```

```
        public void setName(String name) {
            this.name = name;
        }
        public User(Long id, String name) {
            this.id = id;
            this.name = name;
        }
        @Override
        public String toString() {
            return "User{" + "id=" + id + ",
            name=" + name + '}';
        }
    }
```

2. Then, we create a slow bean to return `User`:

```
public class UserBean {
    public User getUser(){
        try {
            TimeUnit.SECONDS.sleep(5);
            long id = new Date().getTime();
            return new User(id, "User " + id);
        } catch (InterruptedException ex) {
            long id = new Date().getTime();
            return new User(id, "Error " + id);
        }
    }
}
```

3. Now, we create a simple `Callable` task to communicate with the slow bean:

```
@Stateless
public class AsyncTask implements Callable<User>{

    @Override
    public User call() throws Exception {
        return new UserBean().getUser();
    }

}
```

4. Here, we call our proxy:

```
@Singleton
public class ExecutorProxy {

    @Resource(name = "LocalManagedThreadFactory")
    private ManagedThreadFactory factory;
```

```
@Resource(name = "LocalContextService")
private ContextService context;

private ExecutorService executor;

@PostConstruct
public void init(){
    executor = new ThreadPoolExecutor(1, 5, 10,
    TimeUnit.SECONDS, new ArrayBlockingQueue<>(5),
    factory);
}
public Future<User> submit(Callable<User> task){
    Callable<User> ctxProxy =
    context.createContextualProxy(task, Callable.class);
    return executor.submit(ctxProxy);
}

}
```

5. Finally, we create the endpoint that uses the proxy:

```
@Stateless
@Path("asyncService")
public class AsyncService {

    @Inject
    private ExecutorProxy executor;

    @GET
    public void asyncService(@Suspended AsyncResponse response)
    {
        Future<User> result = executor.submit(new AsyncTask());
        response.resume(Response.ok(result).build());
    }

}
```

6. To try this code, simply deploy it to Eclipse GlassFish 5.1 and open the following URL:

```
http://localhost:8080/ch09-proxy-task/asyncService
```

How it works...

The magic really happens in the `ExecutorProxy` task. First, note that we define it as
follows:

```
@Singleton
```

We need to make sure that we only have one instance of this task in the context.

Now, note that even though we create our own executor, we still rely on the application
server context for it:

```
Resource(name = "LocalManagedThreadFactory")
private ManagedThreadFactory factory;

Resource(name = "LocalContextService")
private ContextService context;
```

This guarantees that you don't violate any context rules and ruin your application
completely.

Then, we create a pool to execute the threads:

```
private ExecutorService executor;

PostConstruct
public void init(){
executor = new ThreadPoolExecutor(1, 5, 10,
TimeUnit.SECONDS, new ArrayBlockingQueue<>(5), factory);
}
```

Finally, we create a method to send tasks to the executing queue:

```
public Future<User> submit(Callable<User> task){
    Callable<User> ctxProxy = context.createContextualProxy(task,
    Callable.class);
    return executor.submit(ctxProxy);
}
```

Now, our proxy is ready to be injected:

```
Inject
private ExecutorProxy executor;
```

It is also ready to be called and to return results:

```
GET
public void asyncService(@Suspended AsyncResponse response) {
Future<User> result = executor.submit(new AsyncTask());
response.resume(Response.ok(result).build());
}
```

See also

- You can find the full source code for this recipe at `https://github.com/eldermoraes/javaee8-cookbook/tree/master/chapter09/ch09-proxy-task`.

10
Using Event-Driven Programming to Build Reactive Applications

Reactive development has become a trending topic in many developer conferences, meetups, blog posts, and countless other content sources (both online and offline).

But what is a reactive application? **The Reactive Manifesto** provides an official definition; you can find it at `https://www.reactivemanifesto.org` for more details.

In short, according to the manifesto, reactive systems are as follows:

- **Responsive**: The system responds promptly if possible.
- **Resilient**: The system stays responsive in the face of failure.
- **Elastic**: The system stays responsive under varying workloads.
- **Message-driven**: Reactive systems rely on asynchronous message-passing to establish a boundary between components, which ensures loose coupling, isolation, and location transparency.

This chapter shows you how to use the Jakarta EE 8 features to meet one or more of these reactive system requirements.

This chapter covers the following recipes:

- Building reactive applications using asynchronous servlets
- Building reactive applications using events and observers
- Building reactive applications using WebSocket
- Building reactive applications using message-driven beans
- Building reactive applications using Jakarta RESTful Web Services
- Building reactive applications using asynchronous session beans
- Using lambdas and `CompletableFuture` to improve reactive applications

Building reactive applications using asynchronous servlets

Servlets are probably one of the most (if not *the* most) well-known Jakarta EE technologies. Actually, servlets existed even before J2EE became a real specification.

This recipe shows you how to use servlets asynchronously.

Getting ready

Let's first add our Jakarta EE 8 dependency:

```
<dependency<
    <groupId<javax</groupId<
    <artifactId<javaee-api</artifactId<
    <version<8.0</version<
    <scope<provided</scope<
</dependency<
```

How to do it...

Perform the following steps to complete this recipe:

1. First, we create a `User` **Plain Old Java Object (POJO)**:

```
public class User implements Serializable{

    private Long id;
    private String name;
```

```
        public User(long id, String name){
            this.id = id;
            this.name = name;
        }

        public Long getId() {
            return id;
        }

        public void setId(Long id) {
            this.id = id;
        }

        public String getName() {
            return name;
        }

        public void setName(String name) {
            this.name = name;
        }
    }
```

2. Then, we create a slow `UserBean` object to return `User`:

```
@Stateless
public class UserBean {
    public User getUser(){
        long id = new Date().getTime();

        try {
            TimeUnit.SECONDS.sleep(5);
            return new User(id, "User " + id);
        } catch (InterruptedException ex) {
            System.err.println(ex.getMessage());
            return new User(id, "Error " + id);
        }
    }
}
```

3. Finally, we create our asynchronous servlet:

```
@WebServlet(name = "UserServlet", urlPatterns = {"/UserServlet"},
asyncSupported = true)
public class UserServlet extends HttpServlet {

    @Inject
    private UserBean userBean;
    private final Jsonb jsonb = JsonbBuilder.create();
```

```
@Override
protected void doGet(HttpServletRequest req,
HttpServletResponse resp) throws ServletException,
IOException {
    AsyncContext ctx = req.startAsync();
    ctx.start(() -< {
        try (PrintWriter writer =
        ctx.getResponse().getWriter()){
            writer.write(jsonb.toJson(userBean.getUser()));
        } catch (IOException ex) {
            System.err.println(ex.getMessage());
        }
        ctx.complete();
    });
}

@Override
public void destroy() {
    try {
        jsonb.close();
    } catch (Exception ex) {
     System.err.println(ex.getMessage());
    }
}

}
```

How it works...

First, we start with a simple annotation:

```
asyncSupported = true
```

This tells the application server that this servlet supports asynchronous features. You need to use this throughout the entire servlet chain (including in filters, if there are any); otherwise, the application server will not work.

As the servlets are instantiated by the server, we can inject other context members onto it, such as our stateless bean:

```
@Inject
private UserBean userBean;
```

The main servlet method holds the actual request and response references and the request gives the context reference to the `async` API:

```
AsyncContext ctx = req.startAsync();
```

Then, we can execute the preceding blocking function in a non-blocking way:

```
ctx.start(() -< {
    ...
  ctx.complete();
});
```

See also

The full source code for this recipe can be found at `https://github.com/eldermoraes/javaee8-cookbook/tree/master/chapter10/ch10-async-servlet`.

Building reactive applications using events and observers

Using events and observers is a great way of writing code in a reactive way without thinking too much about it, thanks to the great work done by the Jakarta **Contexts and Dependency Injection(CDI)** specification.

This recipe shows you how easy it is to use it to improve the user experience of your application.

Getting ready

Let's first add our Jakarta EE 8 dependency:

```
<dependency<
    <groupId<javax</groupId<
    <artifactId<javaee-api</artifactId<
    <version<8.0</version<
    <scope<provided</scope<
</dependency<
```

How to do it...

Take the following steps to complete this recipe:

1. First, let's create a `User` POJO:

```
public class User implements Serializable{

    private Long id;
    private String name;
    public User(long id, String name){
        this.id = id;
        this.name = name;
    }

    public Long getId() {
        return id;
    }

    public void setId(Long id) {
        this.id = id;
    }

    public String getName() {
        return name;
    }

    public void setName(String name) {
        this.name = name;
    }
}
```

2. Then, let's create a REST endpoint with the event and observer features:

```
@Stateless
@Path("asyncService")
public class AsyncService {
    @Inject
    private Event<User< event;
    private AsyncResponse response;
    @GET
    public void asyncService(@Suspended AsyncResponse response){
        long id = new Date().getTime();
        this.response = response;
        event.fireAsync(new User(id, "User " + id));
    }

        public void onFireEvent(@ObservesAsync User user){
        response.resume(Response.ok(user).build());
```

```
        }
    }
```

How it works...

First, we ask the application server to create an `Event` source for the `User` POJO:

```
@Inject
private Event<User< event;
```

This means that it listens to any events fired against any `User` object. So, we need to create a method to deal with it:

```
public void onFireEvent(@ObservesAsync User user){
    response.resume(Response.ok(user).build());
}
```

So, this method is now the correct listener; the `@ObserversAsync` annotation guarantees this. Once an asynchronous event is fired, it does whatever we ask (or code).

Then, we create a simple asynchronous endpoint to fire it:

```
@GET
public void asyncService(@Suspended AsyncResponse response){
    long id = new Date().getTime();
    this.response = response;
    event.fireAsync(new User(id, "User " + id));
}
```

See also

The full source code for this recipe can be found at `https://github.com/eldermoraes/javaee8-cookbook/tree/master/chapter10/ch10-event-observer`.

Building reactive applications using WebSocket

Using WebSocket is a great way of creating decoupled communication channels for your applications. Doing so asynchronously is even better and cooler for non-blocking features.

This recipe shows you how to use it.

Getting ready

Let's first add our Jakarta EE 8 dependency:

```
<dependency<
    <groupId<javax</groupId<
    <artifactId<javaee-api</artifactId<
    <version<8.0</version<
    <scope<provided</scope<
</dependency<
```

How to do it...

You will need to take the following steps to complete this recipe:

1. The first thing we need is our server endpoint:

```
@Singleton
@ServerEndpoint(value = "/asyncServer")
public class AsyncServer {
    private final List<Session< peers =
Collections.synchronizedList(new ArrayList<<());
    @OnOpen
    public void onOpen(Session peer){
        peers.add(peer);
    }
    @OnClose
    public void onClose(Session peer){
        peers.remove(peer);
    }
    @OnError
    public void onError(Throwable t){
        System.err.println(t.getMessage());
    }
    @OnMessage
```

```
        public void onMessage(String message, Session peer){
            peers.stream().filter((p) -<
            (p.isOpen())).forEachOrdered((p) -< {
                p.getAsyncRemote().sendText(message +
                " - Total peers: " + peers.size());
            });
        }
    }
```

2. Then, we need a client to communicate with the server:

```
@ClientEndpoint
public class AsyncClient {

    private final String asyncServer = "ws://localhost:8080
    /ch10-async-websocket/asyncServer";

    private Session session;
    private final AsyncResponse response;

    public AsyncClient(AsyncResponse response) {
        this.response = response;
    }

    public void connect() {
        WebSocketContainer container =
        ContainerProvider.getWebSocketContainer();
        try {
            container.connectToServer(this, new URI(asyncServer));
        } catch (URISyntaxException | DeploymentException |
          IOException ex) {
            System.err.println(ex.getMessage());
        }

    }

    @OnOpen
    public void onOpen(Session session) {
        this.session = session;
    }

    @OnMessage
    public void onMessage(String message, Session session) {
        response.resume(message);
    }

    public void send(String message) {
        session.getAsyncRemote().sendText(message);
```

```
        }

    public void close(){
        try {
            session.close();
        } catch (IOException ex) {
            System.err.println(ex.getMessage());
        }
    }
}
```

3. Finally, we need a simple REST endpoint to talk to the client:

```
@Stateless
@Path("asyncService")
public class AsyncService {
    @GET
    public void asyncService(@Suspended AsyncResponse response){
        AsyncClient client = new AsyncClient(response);
        client.connect();
        client.send("Message from client " + new Date().getTime());
        client.close();
    }
}
```

How it works...

The first important thing in our server is the following annotation:

```
@Singleton
```

Of course, we need to ensure that we only have one instance of the server endpoint. This ensures that all peers are managed under the same umbrella.

```
private final List<Session< peers = Collections.synchronizedList
(new ArrayList<<());
```

The list that holds these objects is a synchronized list. This is important because you add/remove peers when iterating on the list, so things could get messed up if you don't protect it.

All the default WebSocket methods are managed by the application server:

```
@OnOpen
public void onOpen(Session peer){
    peers.add(peer);
}
@OnClose
public void onClose(Session peer){
    peers.remove(peer);
}
@OnError
public void onError(Throwable t){
    System.err.println(t.getMessage());
}
@OnMessage
public void onMessage(String message, Session peer){
    peers.stream().filter((p) -< (p.isOpen())).forEachOrdered((p) -<
    {
        p.getAsyncRemote().sendText(message + " - Total peers: "
        + peers.size());
    });
}
```

Let's also give a special mention to the code on our onMessage method:

```
@OnMessage
public void onMessage(String message, Session peer){
    peers.stream().filter((p) -< (p.isOpen())).forEachOrdered((p)
    -< {
        p.getAsyncRemote().sendText(message + " - Total peers: "
        + peers.size());
    });
}
```

We only send a message to the peer if it is open.

Now, looking at our client, we have a reference to the server URI:

```
private final String asyncServer = "ws://localhost:8080/
ch10-async-websocket/asyncServer";
```

Note that the protocol is ws, which is specific to WebSocket communication.

Then, we have a method to open the connection with the server endpoint:

```
public void connect() {
    WebSocketContainer container =
    ContainerProvider.getWebSocketContainer();
```

```
    try {
        container.connectToServer(this, new URI(asyncServer));
    } catch (URISyntaxException | DeploymentException | IOException ex) {
        System.err.println(ex.getMessage());
    }
}
```

Once we receive the message confirmation from the server, we can do something about it:

```
@OnMessage
public void onMessage(String message, Session session) {
    response.resume(message);
}
```

This response appears on the endpoint that calls the client:

```
@GET
public void asyncService(@Suspended AsyncResponse response){
    AsyncClient client = new AsyncClient(response);
    client.connect();
    client.send("Message from client " + new Date().getTime());
}
```

We pass the reference to the client so that the client can use it to write the message on it.

See also

The full source code for this recipe can be found at `https://github.com/eldermoraes/javaee8-cookbook/tree/master/chapter10/ch10-async-websocket`.

Building reactive applications using message-driven beans

The **Java Messaging Service** (**JMS**) API is one of the oldest Jakarta EE APIs and it has been reactive since day 1— just read the manifesto linked in the introduction of this chapter.

This recipe shows you how to use **Message-Driven Beans** (**MDBs**) to deliver and use asynchronous messages with just a few annotations.

Getting ready

Let's first add our Java EE 8 dependency:

```
<dependency<
    <groupId<javax</groupId<
    <artifactId<javaee-api</artifactId<
    <version<8.0</version<
    <scope<provided</scope<
</dependency<
```

For more details about the queue setup in Eclipse GlassFish 5.1, please refer to the *Using messaging services for asynchronous communication* recipe in `Chapter 5`, *Security of the Enterprise Architecture.*

How to do it...

Take the following steps to complete this recipe:

1. First, we create a `User` POJO:

    ```
    public class User implements Serializable{

        private Long id;
        private String name;
        public User(long id, String name){
            this.id = id;
            this.name = name;
        }

        public Long getId() {
            return id;
        }

        public void setId(Long id) {
            this.id = id;
        }

        public String getName() {
            return name;
        }

        public void setName(String name) {
            this.name = name;
        }
    }
    ```

2. Then, we create a message sender:

```
@Stateless
public class Sender {
    @Inject
    private JMSContext context;
    @Resource(lookup = "jms/JmsQueue")
    private Destination queue;
    public void send(User user){
        context.createProducer()
                .setDeliveryMode(DeliveryMode.PERSISTENT)
                .setDisableMessageID(true)
                .setDisableMessageTimestamp(true)
                .send(queue, user);
    }
}
```

3. Now, we create a message consumer. This is our MDB:

```
@MessageDriven(activationConfig = {
    @ActivationConfigProperty(propertyName = "destinationLookup",
    propertyValue = "jms/JmsQueue"),
    @ActivationConfigProperty(propertyName = "destinationType",
    propertyValue = "javax.jms.Queue")
})
public class Consumer implements MessageListener{

    @Override
    public void onMessage(Message msg) {
        try {
            User user = msg.getBody(User.class);
            System.out.println("User: " + user);
        } catch (JMSException ex) {
            System.err.println(ex.getMessage());
        }
    }
}
```

4. Finally, we create an endpoint just to send a mock user to the queue:

```
@Stateless
@Path("mdbService")
public class MDBService {
    @Inject
    private Sender sender;
    public void mdbService(@Suspended AsyncResponse response){
        long id = new Date().getTime();
        sender.send(new User(id, "User " + id));
```

```
                response.resume("Message sent to the queue");
        }
    }
```

How it works...

We start by asking the application server for a JMS context instance:

```
@Inject
private JMSContext context;
```

We also send a reference to the queue that we want to work with:

```
@Resource(lookup = "jms/JmsQueue")
private Destination queue;
```

Then, using the context, we create a producer to send the message to the queue:

```
context.createProducer()
        .setDeliveryMode(DeliveryMode.PERSISTENT)
        .setDisableMessageID(true)
        .setDisableMessageTimestamp(true)
        .send(queue, user);
```

Pay attention to the following three methods:

- setDeliveryMode: This method can be PERSISTENT or NON_PERSISTENT. If you use PERSISTENT, the server will take special care of the message and will not lose it.
- setDisableMessageID: This method is used to create MessageID, which increases the server's effort to create and deliver the message, as well as increases its size. This property (true or false) gives a hint to the server about whether you are going to need or use it so that it can improve the process.
- setDisableMessageTimestamp: This method works the same as for setDisableMessageID.

Also, note that we send a User instance to the queue. So, we can easily send object instances, not just text messages, as long as they implement the Serializable interface.

The MDB itself, or our message consumer, is basically made up of a few annotations and interface implementation.

Here is its annotation:

```
@MessageDriven(activationConfig = {
    @ActivationConfigProperty(propertyName = "destinationLookup",
    propertyValue = "jms/JmsQueue"),
    @ActivationConfigProperty(propertyName = "destinationType",
    propertyValue = "javax.jms.Queue")
})
```

Here, we use two properties:

- One to define which queue we look up (destinationLookup)
- One to define what queue type we use (destinationType)

Here is the implementation:

```
@Override
public void onMessage(Message msg) {
    try {
        User user = msg.getBody(User.class);
        System.out.println("User: " + user);
    } catch (JMSException ex) {
        System.err.println(ex.getMessage());
    }
}
```

Note that it is easy to get the User instance from the message body:

```
User user = msg.getBody(User.class);
```

No heavy lifting is required at all!

The endpoint used to send the message couldn't be simpler. We first inject Sender (which is a stateless bean):

```
@Inject
private Sender sender;
```

Then, we call an asynchronous method:

```
public void mdbService(@Suspended AsyncResponse response){
    long id = new Date().getTime();
    sender.send(new User(id, "User " + id));
    response.resume("Message sent to the queue");
}
```

See also

You can find the full source code for this recipe at `https://github.com/eldermoraes/ javaee8-cookbook/tree/master/chapter10/ch10-mdb`.

Building reactive applications using Jakarta RESTful Web Services

Jakarta RESTful Web Services also has some great features for event-driven programming. This recipe shows you how you can use an asynchronous invoker from the request to write responses through callbacks.

Getting ready

Let's first add our Jakarta EE 8 dependency:

```
<dependency<
    <groupId<javax</groupId<
    <artifactId<javaee-api</artifactId<
    <version<8.0</version<
    <scope<provided</scope<
</dependency<
```

How to do it...

Take the following steps to complete this recipe:

1. First, we create a `User` POJO:

```
public class User implements Serializable{

    private Long id;
    private String name;
    public User(long id, String name){
        this.id = id;
        this.name = name;
    }

    public Long getId() {
        return id;
```

```
        }

        public void setId(Long id) {
            this.id = id;
        }

        public String getName() {
            return name;
        }

        public void setName(String name) {
            this.name = name;
        }
    }
```

2. Here, we define `UserBean`, which acts as a remote endpoint:

```
@Stateless
@Path("remoteUser")
public class UserBean {

    @GET
    public Response remoteUser() {
        long id = new Date().getTime();
        try {
            TimeUnit.SECONDS.sleep(5);
            return Response.ok(new User(id, "User " + id))
            .build();
        } catch (InterruptedException ex) {
            System.err.println(ex.getMessage());
            return Response.ok(new User(id, "Error " + id))
            .build();
        }
    }

}
```

3. Then, finally, we define a local endpoint that consumes the remote one:

```
@Stateless
@Path("asyncService")
public class AsyncService {
    private Client client;
    private WebTarget target;

    @PostConstruct
    public void init() {
        client = ClientBuilder.newBuilder()
```

```
                .readTimeout(10, TimeUnit.SECONDS)
                .connectTimeout(10, TimeUnit.SECONDS)
                .build();
        target = client.target("http://localhost:8080/
        ch10-async-jaxrs/remoteUser");
    }

    @PreDestroy
    public void destroy(){
        client.close();
    }
    @GET
    public void asyncService(@Suspended AsyncResponse response){
        target.request().async().get(new
        InvocationCallback<Response<() {
            @Override
            public void completed(Response rspns) {
                response.resume(rspns);
            }

            @Override
            public void failed(Throwable thrwbl) {
                response.resume(Response.status(Response.Status.
                INTERNAL_SERVER_ERROR).entity(thrwbl.getMessage())
                .build());
            }
        });
    }
}
```

How it works...

We start the bean by creating its communication with the remote endpoint right in the bean instantiation. Doing this avoids the overhead of doing it later while the invocation takes place. Refer to the following code:

```
private Client client;
private WebTarget target;

@PostConstruct
public void init() {
    client = ClientBuilder.newBuilder()
            .readTimeout(10, TimeUnit.SECONDS)
            .connectTimeout(10, TimeUnit.SECONDS)
            .build();
    target = client.target("http://localhost:8080/
```

```
        ch10-async-jaxrs/remoteUser");
    }
```

Then, we create an anonymous `InvocationCallback` implementation within our `async` invoker:

```
target.request().async().get(new InvocationCallback<Response<()
{
    @Override
    public void completed(Response rspns) {
        response.resume(rspns);
    }


    @Override
    public void failed(Throwable thrwbl) {
        System.err.println(thrwbl.getMessage());
    }
});
```

This way, we rely on the `completed` and `failed` events and deal with them properly.

See also

You can find the full source code for this recipe at `https://github.com/eldermoraes/javaee8-cookbook/tree/master/chapter10/ch10-async-jaxrs`.

Building reactive applications using asynchronous session beans

Session beans can also become reactive and event-driven just by using annotations. This recipe shows you how to do this.

Getting ready

Let's first add our Jakarta EE 8 dependency:

```
<dependency<
    <groupId<javax</groupId<
    <artifactId<javaee-api</artifactId<
    <version<8.0</version<
```

```
    <scope<provided</scope<
</dependency<
```

How to do it...

You will need to perform the following steps to try this recipe:

1. First, we create a `User` POJO:

```
public class User implements Serializable{

    private Long id;
    private String name;
    public User(long id, String name){
        this.id = id;
        this.name = name;
    }

    public Long getId() {
        return id;
    }

    public void setId(Long id) {
        this.id = id;
    }

    public String getName() {
        return name;
    }

    public void setName(String name) {
        this.name = name;
    }
}
```

2. Then, we create our asynchronous session bean:

```
@Stateless
public class UserBean {
    @Asynchronous
    public Future<User< getUser(){
        long id = new Date().getTime();
        User user = new User(id, "User " + id);
        return new AsyncResult(user);
    }
    @Asynchronous
```

```
public void doSomeSlowStuff(User user){
    try {
        TimeUnit.SECONDS.sleep(5);
    } catch (InterruptedException ex) {
        System.err.println(ex.getMessage());
    }
}
}
```

3. Finally, we create the endpoint that calls the bean:

```
@Stateless
@Path("asyncService")
public class AsyncService {
    @Inject
    private UserBean userBean;
    @GET
    public void asyncService(@Suspended AsyncResponse response){
        try {
            Future<User< result = userBean.getUser();
            while(!result.isDone()){
                try {
                    TimeUnit.SECONDS.sleep(1);
                } catch (InterruptedException ex) {
                    System.err.println(ex.getMessage());
                }
            }
            response.resume(Response.ok(result.get()).build());
        } catch (InterruptedException | ExecutionException ex) {
            System.err.println(ex.getMessage());
        }
    }
}
```

Now, you can try it out by calling the following URL:

```
http//localhost:8080/ch10-async-bean/asyncService
```

How it works...

Let's first check the `getUser` method from the session bean:

```
@Asynchronous
public Future<User< getUser(){
    long id = new Date().getTime();
    User user = new User(id, "User " + id);
    return new AsyncResult(user);
}
```

Once we use the `@Asynchronous` annotation, we have to turn its returning value into a `Future` instance of something (in our case, `User`).

We have also created a `void` method to show you how to create a non-blocking code with session beans:

```
@Asynchronous
public void doSomeSlowStuff(User user){
    try {
        TimeUnit.SECONDS.sleep(5);
    } catch (InterruptedException ex) {
        System.err.println(ex.getMessage());
    }
}
```

Finally, we create our calling endpoint:

```
@GET
public void asyncService(@Suspended AsyncResponse response){
    try {
        Future<User< result = userBean.getUser();
        while(!result.isDone()){
            try {
                TimeUnit.SECONDS.sleep(1);
            } catch (InterruptedException ex) {
                System.err.println(ex.getMessage());
            }
        }
        response.resume(Response.ok(result.get()).build());
    } catch (InterruptedException | ExecutionException ex) {
        System.err.println(ex.getMessage());
    }
}
```

As `getUser` returns `Future`, we can work with an async status check. Once this is done, we write the results in the response (also asynchronous).

See also

You can find the full source code for this recipe at `https://github.com/eldermoraes/javaee8-cookbook/tree/master/chapter10/ch10-async-bean`.

Using lambdas and CompletableFuture to improve reactive applications

The Java language has always had a reputation for being a verbose language. However, since the advent of lambdas, this issue has improved a lot.

We can use lambdas and bring `CompletableFuture` to the party to improve not only the coding but also the behavior of reactive applications. This recipe shows you how to do this.

Getting ready

Let's first add our Jakarta EE 8 dependency:

```
<dependency<
    <groupId<javax</groupId<
    <artifactId<javaee-api</artifactId<
    <version<8.0</version<
    <scope<provided</scope<
</dependency<
```

How to do it...

Take the following steps to complete this recipe:

1. First, we create a `User` POJO:

```
public class User implements Serializable{

    private Long id;
    private String name;
    public User(long id, String name){
        this.id = id;
        this.name = name;
    }
```

```
        public Long getId() {
            return id;
        }

        public void setId(Long id) {
            this.id = id;
        }

        public String getName() {
            return name;
        }

        public void setName(String name) {
            this.name = name;
        }
    }
```

2. Then, we call `UserBean` to return a `User` instance:

```
@Stateless
public class UserBean {

    public User getUser() {
        long id = new Date().getTime();
        try {
            TimeUnit.SECONDS.sleep(5);
            return new User(id, "User " + id);
        } catch (InterruptedException ex) {
            System.err.println(ex.getMessage());
            return new User(id, "Error " + id);
        }
    }

}
```

3. Finally, we create an async endpoint to call the bean:

```
@Stateless
@Path("asyncService")
public class AsyncService {

    @Inject
    private UserBean userBean;

    @GET
    public void asyncService(@Suspended AsyncResponse response)
    {
        CompletableFuture
```

```
            .supplyAsync(() -< userBean.getUser())
            .thenAcceptAsync((u) -< {
                response.resume(Response.ok(u).build());
            }).exceptionally((t) -< {
                response.resume(Response.status
                (Response.Status.
                INTERNAL_SERVER_ERROR).entity(t.getMessage())
                .build());
                return null;
            });
    }
}
```

Now, you can try it out by calling the following URL:

```
http//localhost:8080/ch10-completable-future/asyncService
```

How it works...

We use two `CompletableFuture` methods:

- `supplyAsync`: This starts an async call to whatever you put inside it. Here, we put in a lambda call.
- `thenAcceptAsync`: Once the async process is complete, the returning value comes out here. Thanks to lambdas, we can call this returning value u (but it could be whatever you want). Then, we use it to write it down to the asynchronous response.

See also

You can find the full source code for this recipe at `https://github.com/eldermoraes/javaee8-cookbook/tree/master/chapter10/ch10-completable-future`.

11
Rising to the Cloud - Jakarta EE, Containers, and Cloud Computing

Two things have happened in the computer industry that have changed it for good – **cloud computing** and **containers**. Cloud computing came first and changed the way we look at infrastructure, the way we consume software, and the way we should grow many businesses. Now, computation is a commodity.

Containers change, and they are also changing the way we build and deliver software. They are also the essential glue for DevOps and the way to take **Continuous Integration/Continuous Delivery (CI/CD)** to another level.

Put them together and you will have one of the most powerful environments in IT. But can Jakarta EE take advantage of it? Of course! If an application server is an abstraction for Jakarta EE applications, containers are an abstraction for the server, and once you have them built in a standard such as Docker, you have the power to use such tools to manage an application server.

This chapter will show you how to put your Jakarta EE application inside a container and how to deliver this container with some of the best providers we have today.

This chapter contains the following recipes:

- Building Jakarta EE containers using Docker
- Using Oracle Cloud Infrastructure for container orchestration in the cloud
- Using Jelastic for container orchestration in the cloud
- Using OpenShift for container orchestration in the cloud
- Using AWS for container orchestration in the cloud

Let's get started.

Building Jakarta EE containers using Docker

Since day one, Jakarta EE has been based on containers. If you're in any doubt about this, just have a look at the following diagram:

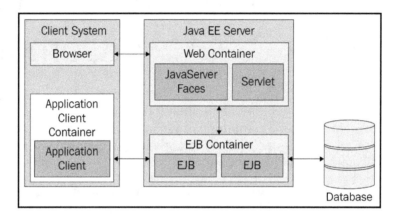

Java EE architecture: https://docs.oracle.com/javaee/6/tutorial/doc/bnacj.html

It belongs to Oracle's former official documentation for Java EE 6 and has been much the same architecture since the times of Sun. It's here to show that this is not new at all.

As you can see, there are different containers – a web container, an **Enterprise Java Beans (EJB)** container, and an application client container. In other words, the applications developed under those containers will rely on many features and services provided by them.

When we take the Jakarta EE application server and put it inside a Docker container, we are doing the same thing – it is relying on some of the features and services provided by the Docker environment.

This recipe will show you how to deliver a Jakarta EE application in a container bundle, which is called an **appliance**.

Getting ready

First, you need the Docker platform to be installed in your environment. There are plenty of options, so I suggest that you go the following link for more details: `https://docs.docker.com/install/`.

If you are not familiar with Docker commands, I recommend that you have a look at this beautiful cheat sheet: `https://zeroturnaround.com/rebellabs/docker-commands-and-best-practices-cheat-sheet/`.

You'll also need to create an account at Docker Hub so that you can store your images. Check it out: `https://hub.docker.com/`. It's free for public images.

How to do it...

To build your Jakarta EE container, you'll need a Docker image. Let's learn how to build one:

1. You'll need a Dockerfile such as the following one to build a Docker image:

```
FROM openjdk:8-jdk

ENV GLASSFISH_HOME /usr/local/glassfish
ENV PATH ${GLASSFISH_HOME}/bin:$PATH
ENV GLASSFISH_PKG glassfish-5.1.0.zip
ENV GLASSFISH_URL
https://www.eclipse.org/downloads/download.php?file=/glassfish/glassfish-5.1.0.zip&r=1

RUN mkdir -p ${GLASSFISH_HOME}

WORKDIR ${GLASSFISH_HOME}

RUN set -x \
  && curl -fSL ${GLASSFISH_URL} -o ${GLASSFISH_PKG} \
    && unzip -o $GLASSFISH_PKG \
    && rm -f $GLASSFISH_PKG \
  && mv glassfish5/* ${GLASSFISH_HOME} \
    && rm -Rf glassfish5

RUN addgroup glassfish_grp \
    && adduser --system glassfish \
    && usermod -G glassfish_grp glassfish \
    && chown -R glassfish:glassfish_grp ${GLASSFISH_HOME} \
    && chmod -R 777 ${GLASSFISH_HOME}
```

```
COPY docker-entrypoint.sh /
RUN chmod +x /docker-entrypoint.sh

USER glassfish

ENTRYPOINT ["/docker-entrypoint.sh"]

EXPOSE 4848 8080 8181
CMD ["asadmin", "start-domain", "-v"]
```

2. This image will be our base image. We will use it to construct other images in this chapter. Now, we need to build it:

   docker build -t eldermoraes/gf-jakartaee-jdk8 .

3. Now, you need to log into your Docker Hub account:

   docker login

4. Go ahead and push it to your Docker registry at Docker Hub:

   docker push eldermoraes/gf-jakartaee-jdk8

5. Now, you can create another image by customizing the preceding one, and then put your app on it:

   FROM eldermoraes/gf-jakartaee-jdk8

   ENV DEPLOYMENT_DIR
   ${GLASSFISH_HOME}/glassfish/domains/domain1/autodeploy/

   COPY app.war ${DEPLOYMENT_DIR}

6. In the same folder, we have a Jakarta EE application file (app.war) that will be deployed inside the container. Check the *See also* section to download all the files.

7. Once you've save your Dockerfile, you can build your image:

   docker build -t eldermoraes/gf-jakartaee-cookbook .

8. You can push this new image to Docker Hub for later use:

   docker login
   docker push eldermoraes/gf-jakartaee-cookbook

9. Now, you can create the container:

```
docker run -d --name gf-jakartaee-cookbook \
    -h gf-jakartaee-cookbook \
    -p 80:8080 \
    -p 4848:4848 \
    -p 8686:8686 \
    -p 8009:8009 \
    -p 8181:8181 \
    eldermoraes/gf-jakartaee-cookbook
```

10. Wait a few seconds and open the following URL in your browser:

```
http://localhost/app
```

How it works...

Let's understand our first Dockerfile:

```
FROM openjdk:8-jdk
```

The FROM keyword will ask Docker to pull the openjdk:8-jdk image, but what does this mean?

This means that there's a registry somewhere where Docker will find prebuilt images. If there's no image registry in your local environment, it will search for it in Docker Hub, the official and public Docker registry in the cloud.

When you say that you are using a pre-built image, this means that you don't need to build the whole Linux container from scratch. There's already a template that you can rely on:

```
ENV GLASSFISH_HOME /usr/local/glassfish
ENV PATH ${GLASSFISH_HOME}/bin:$PATH
ENV GLASSFISH_PKG glassfish-5.1.0.zip
ENV GLASSFISH_URL
https://www.eclipse.org/downloads/download.php?file=/glassfish/glassfish-5.
1.0.zip&r=1

RUN mkdir -p ${GLASSFISH_HOME}

WORKDIR ${GLASSFISH_HOME}
```

Here are just some environment variables to help with the coding process:

```
RUN set -x \
  && curl -fSL ${GLASSFISH_URL} -o ${GLASSFISH_PKG} \
```

```
    && unzip -o $GLASSFISH_PKG \
    && rm -f $GLASSFISH_PKG \
    && mv glassfish5/* ${GLASSFISH_HOME} \
    && rm -Rf glassfish5
```

The RUN clause in Dockerfiles executes some bash commands inside the container when it has been created. Here, GlassFish is being downloaded and then prepared in the container:

```
RUN addgroup glassfish_grp \
    && adduser --system glassfish \
    && usermod -G glassfish_grp glassfish \
    && chown -R glassfish:glassfish_grp ${GLASSFISH_HOME} \
    && chmod -R 777 ${GLASSFISH_HOME}
```

For safety, we define the user that will hold the permissions for GlassFish files and processes:

```
COPY docker-entrypoint.sh /
RUN chmod +x /docker-entrypoint.sh
```

Here, we are including a bash script inside the container so that we can perform some GlassFish administrative tasks:

```
#!/bin/bash

if [[ -z $ADMIN_PASSWORD ]]; then
  ADMIN_PASSWORD=$(date| md5sum | fold -w 8 | head -n 1)
  echo "#########GENERATED ADMIN PASSWORD: $ADMIN_PASSWORD
  ##########"
fi

echo "AS_ADMIN_PASSWORD=" > /tmp/glassfishpwd
echo "AS_ADMIN_NEWPASSWORD=${ADMIN_PASSWORD}" >> /tmp/glassfishpwd

asadmin --user=admin --passwordfile=/tmp/glassfishpwd change-admin-password
--domain_name domain1
asadmin start-domain

echo "AS_ADMIN_PASSWORD=${ADMIN_PASSWORD}" > /tmp/glassfishpwd

asadmin --user=admin --passwordfile=/tmp/glassfishpwd enable-secure-admin
asadmin --user=admin stop-domain
rm /tmp/glassfishpwd

exec "$@"
```

After copying the bash file into the container, we can go to the final block:

```
USER glassfish

ENTRYPOINT ["/docker-entrypoint.sh"]

EXPOSE 4848 8080 8181
CMD ["asadmin", "start-domain", "-v"]
```

From the preceding code, we can see the following:

- The USER clause defines the user that will be used from this point in the file. This is great because, from there, all the tasks will be completed by the glassfish user.
- The ENTRYPOINT clause will execute the docker-entrypoint.sh script.
- The EXPOSE clause will define the ports that will be available for containers that use this image.
- The CMD clause will call the GlassFish script that will initialize the container.

Now, let's understand our second Dockerfile:

```
FROM eldermoraes/gf-jakartaee-jdk8
```

We need to take the same considerations regarding the prebuilt image into account, but here, the image was made by you. Congratulations!

```
ENV DEPLOYMENT_DIR ${GLASSFISH_HOME}/glassfish/domains/domain1/autodeploy/
```

Here, we are building an environment variable to help with the deployment process. This is done in the same way as it's done for Linux systems:

```
COPY app.war ${DEPLOYMENT_DIR}
```

This COPY command will literally copy the app.war file to the folder defined in the DEPLOYMENT_DIR environment variable.

From here, you are ready to build an image and create a container. The image builder is self-explanatory:

```
docker build -t eldermoraes/gf-jakartaee-cookbook .
```

Let's check the docker run command:

```
docker run -d --name gf-jakartaee-cookbook \
    -h gf-jakartaee-cookbook \
    -p 80:8080 \
```

```
-p 4848:4848 \
-p 8686:8686 \
-p 8009:8009 \
-p 8181:8181 \
eldermoraes/gf-jakartaee-cookbook
```

If we break this down, this is what the various elements of the command mean:

- `-h`: Defines the hostname of the container.
- `-p`: Defines which ports will be exposed and how this will be done. This is useful, for example, when more than one container is using the same port by default – you just use them differently.
- `eldermoraes/gf-jakartaee-cookbook`: The reference to the image you just built.

See also

The source code and files that were used in this recipe can be found at `https://github.com/eldermoraes/javaee8-cookbook/tree/master/chapter11/ch11-docker`.

Using Oracle Cloud Infrastructure for container orchestration in the cloud

The best way to use containers in the cloud is by using a provider. Why? Because they can provide good infrastructure and a nice service for a small price.

This recipe will show you how to get the container we created in the first recipe of this chapter and deliver it using **Oracle Cloud Infrastructure (OCI)**.

Getting ready

If you don't have an account with OCI, you can register for a free trial at `https://cloud.oracle.com/tryit`.

That's all you need, beyond creating the Docker image in the first recipe of this chapter.

So that you can deploy your application, create a file called `app.yaml` and put the following content into it:

```
kind: Service
apiVersion: v1
metadata:
  name: gf-jakartaee-cookbook
  labels:
    app: gf-jakartaee-cookbook
spec:
  type: NodePort
  selector:
    app: gf-jakartaee-cookbook
  ports:
  - port: 80
    targetPort: 8080
    name: http
  - port: 4848
    targetPort: 4848
    name: admin
  - port: 8686
    targetPort: 8686
    name: jmx
  - port: 8009
    targetPort: 8009
    name: ajp
  - port: 8181
    targetPort: 8181
    name: https
---
kind: Deployment
apiVersion: extensions/v1beta1
metadata:
  name: gf-jakartaee-cookbook
spec:
  replicas: 1
  template:
    metadata:
      labels:
        app: gf-jakartaee-cookbook
        version: v1
    spec:
      containers:
      - name: gf-jakartaee-cookbook
        image: eldermoraes/gf-jakartaee-cookbook
        imagePullPolicy: IfNotPresent
        ports:
        - containerPort: 8080
```

How to do it...

To complete this recipe, perform the following steps:

1. After logging in, you will see the OCI dashboard, as shown in the following screenshot:

2. Click on the three horizontal lines at the top left of the screen, go to the **Developer Services** option, and then click on **Container Cluster (OKE)**, as shown in the following screenshot:

3. Now, you will be on the main page of the **Oracle Kubernetes Engine** (**OKE**):

As you may have already noticed, OCI hosts containers by using Kubernetes. So, we need to create a Kubernetes cluster under the OCI infrastructure.

There are some prerequisites for this, and you can check and perform them by clicking on **Preparing for Container Engine for Kubernetes** (refer to the preceding screenshot). We could put the instructions here in this book, but the vendor can change them at any time, so it's better to follow their updated instructions.

This is also a good time to say that this book doesn't have the intention of teaching you in-depth details about Kubernetes! We will just use it to deploy our containers when this is the way defined by our vendors. If you want to learn more about this (and I truly believe that you should!), please find the right references.

So, let's create our cluster! After following the preparing instructions, click on the **Create Cluster** button.

4. Now, you will be taken to the **Cluster Creation** form:

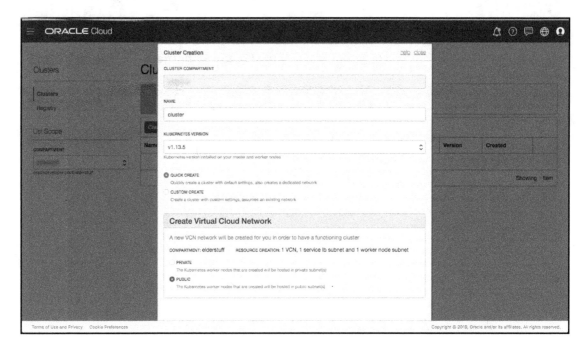

Here, fill in the following fields:

- **CLUSTER COMPARTMENT**: Use the default
- **NAME**: Name your cluster
- **KUBERNETES VERSION**: Use the default
- **QUICK CREATE**: Keep it selected
- **Create Virtual Cloud Network**: Select **PUBLIC**

5. Then, scroll down to the **Create Node Pool** section:

Keep all the default values for these fields. Also, paste your **Secure Shell (SSH)** public key into the **PUBLIC SSH KEY** field. If you are not familiar with SSH keys, please refer to this article: `https://www.ssh.com/ssh/key/`.

6. Scroll down until the end of the form and click on the **Create** button. Now, your cluster dashboard will look like this on the **OKE Overview** page:

7. Now, click on the name of your cluster to open a page containing its details:

8. Click on the **Access Kubeconfig** button and follow the instructions for setting up your local environment so that you can access your remote cluster. Once you are done, you are ready to deploy your Eclipse Glassfish container and run your Jakarta EE application on your Kubernetes cluster.

9. Open Terminal (or Command Prompt), go to the folder where you created the app.yaml file (as shown in the *Getting ready* section of this recipe), and execute the following command:

    ```
    kubectl create -f app.yaml
    ```

    This will deploy your application.

10. Now, you need to expose it so you can access it on the internet:

    ```
    kubectl expose deployment gf-jakartaee-cookbook --type=LoadBalancer
    --name=gf-jakartaee-cookbook-lb
    ```

11. Open a local proxy with your remote cluster:

    ```
    kubectl proxy &
    ```

12. Open the Kubernetes dashboard by going
    to `http://localhost:8001/api/v1/namespaces/kube-system/services/`
    `https:kubernetes-dashboard:/proxy/`. The Kubernetes dashboard should
    look something like this:

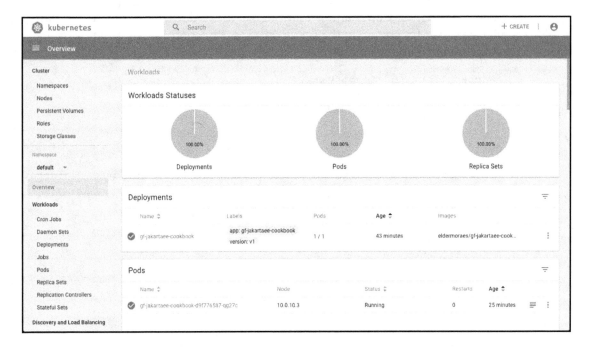

13. If you scroll down the page, you will find the **Services** section, as shown in the
    following screenshot:

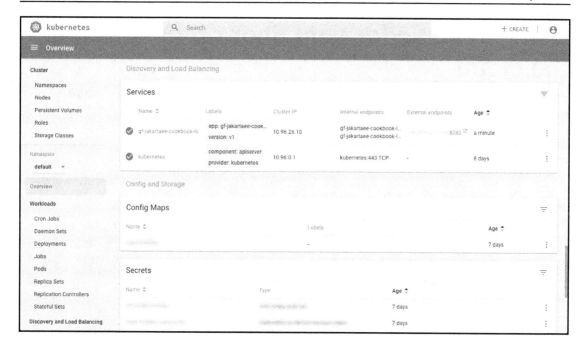

14. Check the `gf-jakartaee-cookbook-lb` service. In the same line, in the **External endpoints** column, you'll find its external address. Copy and use it to open the application in a browser, like this: `http://[external address]:8080/app/`.

15. If everything went well, you should see a page like this:

> ## The request is being answered by:
>
> IP: 10.244.1.121
>
> HostName: gf-jakartaee-cookbook-d9f776587-qg27c
>
> Session ID: 37d1c8988b371be608d94347ee6c

With that, you've made it! Now, your container has been orchestrated in the cloud using a Kubernetes cluster with OCI.

Using Jelastic for container orchestration in the cloud

The best way to use containers in the cloud is by using a provider. Why? Because they can provide you with good infrastructure and a nice service for a small price.

This recipe will show you how to get the container we created in the first recipe of this chapter and deliver it using Jelastic.

Getting ready

If you don't have an account with Jelastic, you can sign up for a free trial at `https://jelastic.com/`. Refer to the *Building Jakarta EE containers using Docker* recipe to get the container we will be using in this recipe.

How to do it...

To complete this recipe, please perform the following steps:

1. After logging in, you will be taken to the main page of Jelastic, as shown in the following screenshot:

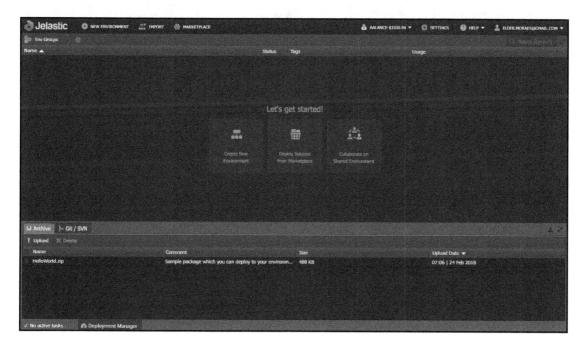

2. First things first: click on the **Settings** button (top right). This will open the **User Settings** section (bottom left):

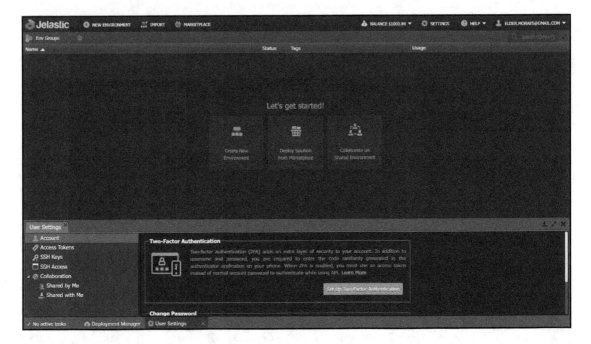

3. Click on **Public** inside **SSH Keys** and upload your public SSH key:

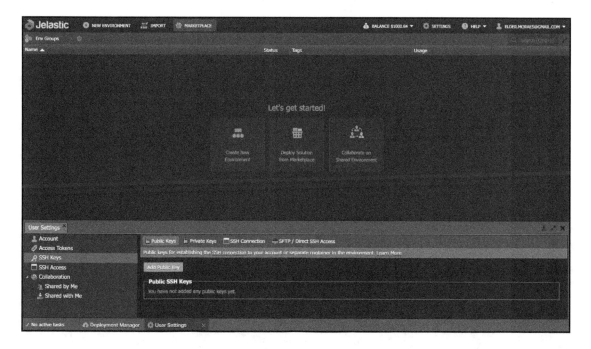

4. Make sure your SSH key has been uploaded; otherwise, you won't be able to log into the platform using SSH:

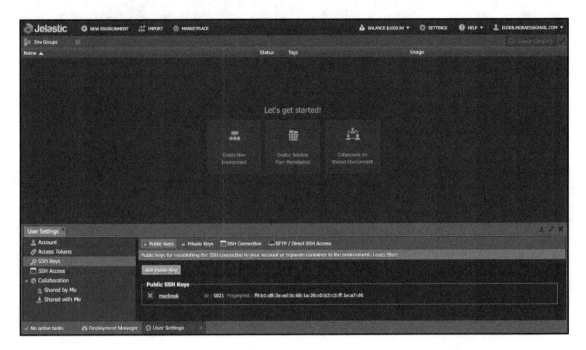

5. At the top of the page, click on the **Marketplace** button. Find the **Docker Engine CE** option. Then, click on **Install**:

6. Give this environment a name and click on **Install**. The following screenshot shows the **Docker Engine CE** configuration pop-up:

Wait until the installation is complete:

7. Once installed, a pop-up will appear and provide you with the command you'll have to use to log into the platform. Copy it. The following screenshot shows the installation confirmation pop-up and the commands for connecting:

8. When you are back on the dashboard, click on **Engine Node** and then the **Config** icon:

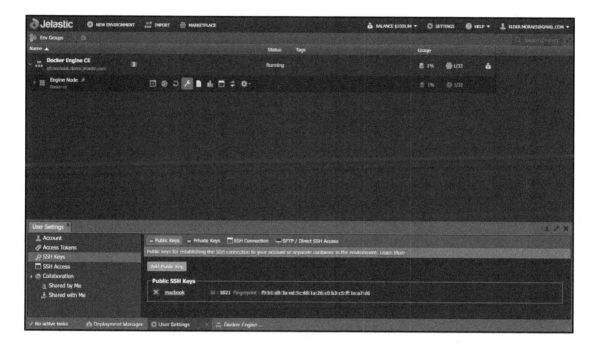

9. This will open a tab panel at the bottom of the page. Click on the **SFTP/SSH Gate** tab. Copy the command from the **SSH Gate Command** field:

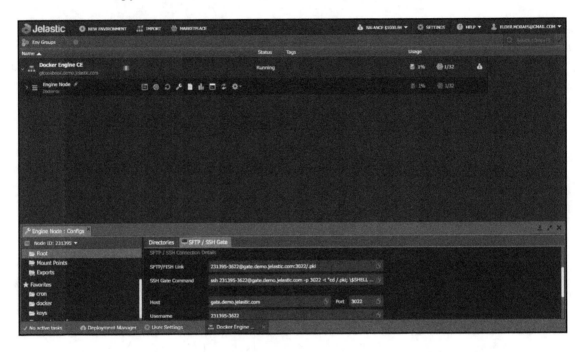

10. Open Terminal (or Command Prompt) on your machine and paste it in:

```
Elders-MacBook-Pro-2:~ eldermoraes$ ssh 231395-3622@gate.demo.jelastic.com -p 3022 -t "cd /.pki; \$SHELL --login"
/etc/profile.d/lang.sh: line 19: warning: setlocale: LC_CTYPE: cannot change locale (UTF-8): No such file or directory
root@node231395-gfcookbook /:pki $ █
```

11. Now, you can just run your command to create a container:

```
docker run -d --name gf-jakartaee-cookbook \
    -h gf-jakartaee-cookbook \
    -p 80:8080 \
    -p 4848:4848 \
    -p 8686:8686 \
    -p 8009:8009 \
    -p 8181:8181 \
    eldermoraes/gf-jakartaee-cookbook
```

12. Check out the container log's output:

```
●○○                          eldermoraes — ssh 231395-3622@gate.demo.jelastic.com -p 3022 -t cd /
root@node231395-gfcookbook /.pki $ docker run -d --name gf-jakartaee-cookbook \
>      -h gf-jakartaee-cookbook \
>      -p 80:8080 \
>      -p 4848:4848 \
>      -p 8686:8686 \
>      -p 8009:8009 \
>      -p 8181:8181 \
>      eldermoraes/gf-jakartaee-cookbook
Unable to find image 'eldermoraes/gf-jakartaee-cookbook:latest' locally
latest: Pulling from eldermoraes/gf-jakartaee-cookbook
a4d8138d0f6b: Pull complete
dbdc36973392: Pull complete
f59d6d019dd5: Pull complete
aaef3e026258: Pull complete
5e86b04a4500: Pull complete
1a6643a2873a: Pull complete
2ad1e30fc17c: Pull complete
7e10bc6570f3: Pull complete
a6a23a84cc16: Pull complete
c5fbb211527a: Pull complete
4c95339b6ac2: Pull complete
efdcc99ae76c: Pull complete
392535908804: Pull complete
Digest: sha256:57c4f75737b75f221bf9c4bd63b9a3550ee80e7f7c75c8efa5aa77027e0caefa
Status: Downloaded newer image for eldermoraes/gf-jakartaee-cookbook:latest
a9a7d75eac4040cd69043fa1c16b98db45e0afb7628193413cd80864f15a173e
root@node231395-gfcookbook /.pki $
```

This is similar to if you were running in your local machine, but you are running on the Jelastic platform.

13. Now, if you go back to the main page, you will see your environment up and running with the node you created:

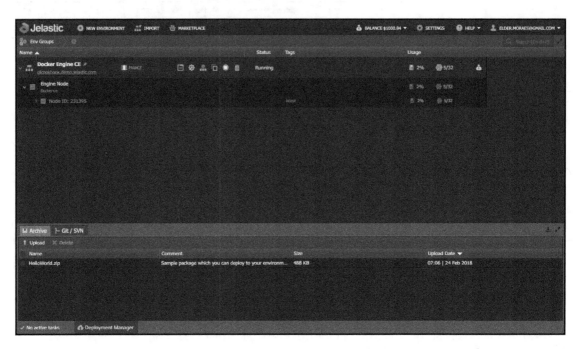

14. Under the **Docker Engine CE** label, you can find the URL of your environment. Just click on it and add `/app` to the end of it:

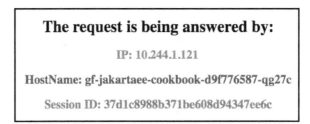

If you can see this page, then congratulations! Your application has been deployed on Jelastic.

Using OpenShift for container orchestration in the cloud

The best way to use containers in the cloud is by using a provider. Why? Because they can provide you with good infrastructure and a nice service for a small price.

This recipe will show you how to get the container we created in the first recipe of this chapter and deliver it using OpenShift.

Getting ready

If you don't have an account with OpenShift, you can sign up for a free trial at `https://www.openshift.com/`. Click on **Sign up for free** to complete this process. Refer to the *Building Jakarta EE containers using Docker* recipe to get the container we will be using in this recipe.

How to do it...

To complete this recipe, please perform the following steps:

1. After logging in, you will see the main page of OpenShift, as shown in the following screenshot:

2. Click on the **Create Project** button and fill in the fields provided. Then, click on **Create**:

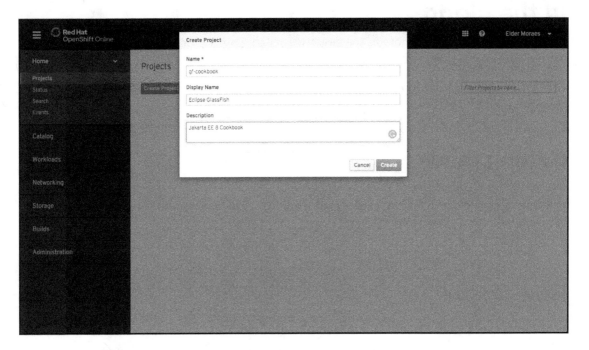

3. Once your project has been created, it will be automatically loaded onto the screen:

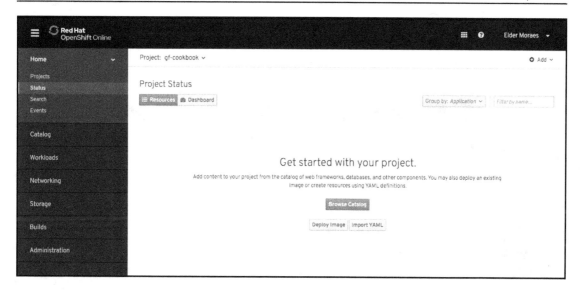

4. On the open page, click on **Add** (top right) and then **Deploy Image**:

5. From the pop-up, select **Image Name**, fill in the form with our pre-built image (`eldermoraes/gf-jakartaee-cookbook`), and click on the **Search** icon. The following screenshot shows the **Image deployment** page:

6. Scroll down to the bottom of the page and click on **Deploy**:

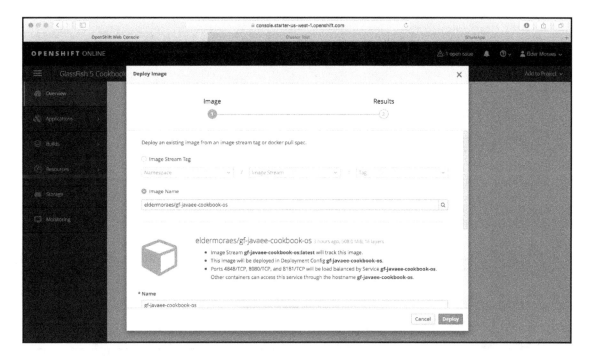

7. Watch the following page until the pod count is **1 of 1 pods**. The following screenshot shows us monitoring the pod's creation:

8. Navigate through the left-hand menu until you find the **Networking | Routes** option. Click on it:

9. Then, click on the **Create Route** button.

10. On the new page that appears, fill in the provided fields, as shown in the following screenshot:

11. Click on the **Create** button.

12. This will open the following page. Under the **Location** label, you can find the route to your application. Click on it:

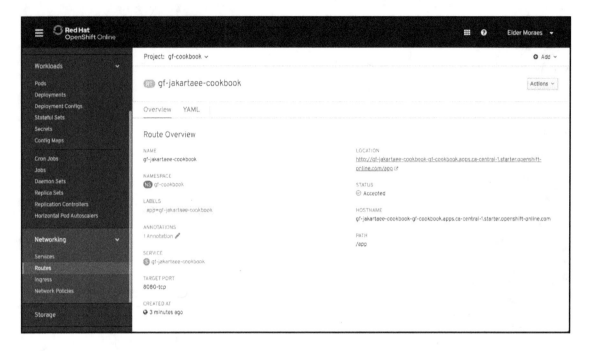

The preceding screenshot shows the route being confirmed.

13. After running it, we will see the following test page for our application:

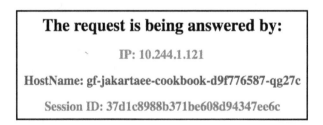

If you can see this page, then congratulations! You are now orchestrating your container in OpenShift.

Using AWS for container orchestration in the cloud

The best way to use containers in the cloud is by using a provider. Why? Because they can provide you with good infrastructure and a nice service for a small price.

This recipe will show you how to get the container we created in the first recipe of this chapter and deliver it using **Amazon Web Services** (**AWS**).

Getting ready

If you don't have an account with AWS, register for a free trial at `https://aws.amazon.com/free`. Refer to the *Building Jakarta EE containers using Docker* recipe to get the container that we will use in this recipe.

How to do it...

You need to perform the following steps to complete this recipe:

1. Once you've logged in, you will see the main page for AWS, as shown in the following screenshot:

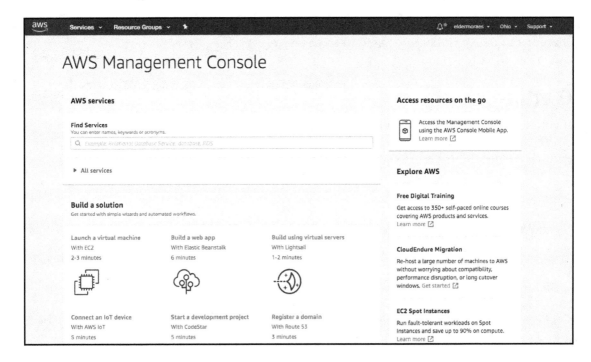

2. Click on the **Services** menu (top left) and then **Compute** | **ECS** :

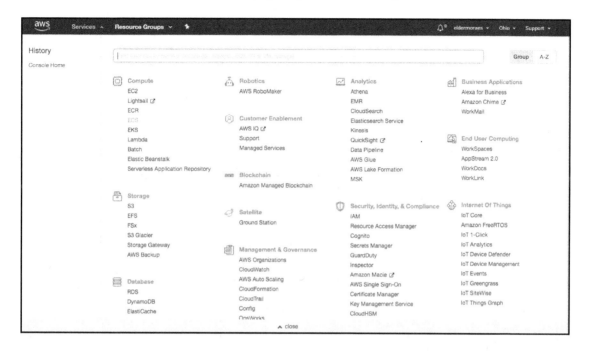

3. On the page that opens, click on **Get started**:

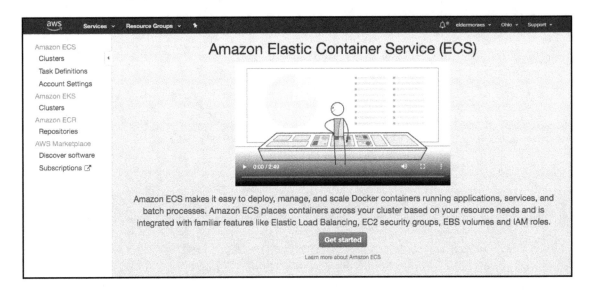

4. From the **Container definition** section, select **custom** and then **Configure**:

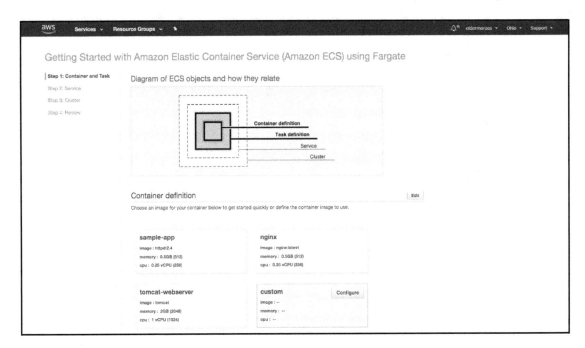

5. Fill in the fields that appear. Pay special attention to the **Image** field, since this is where you will use our prebuilt image. Click on **Update**:

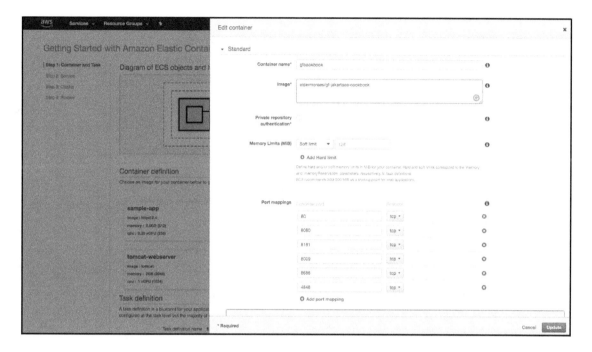

6. Scroll down the page until you get to **Port mappings**. Click on **Next**:

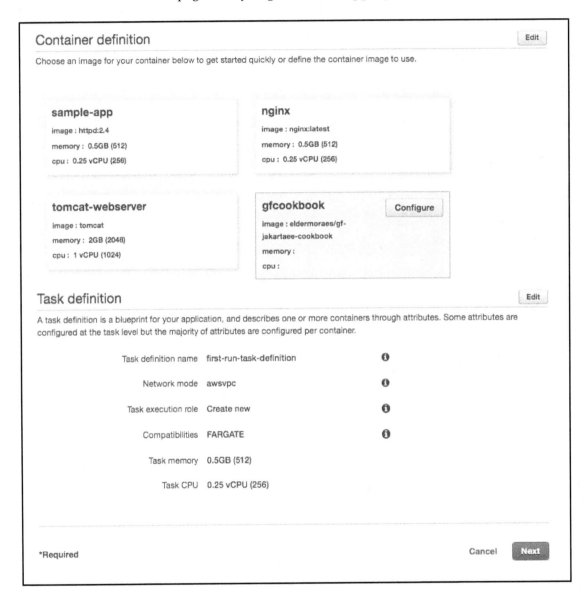

7. In the **Define your service** section, click on **Edit.** The following screenshot shows the service and its network configuration:

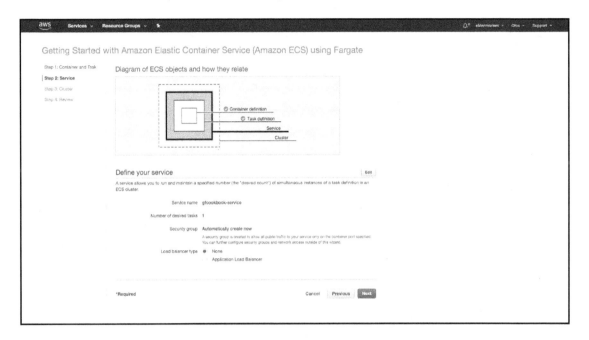

8. Select **Application Load Balancer** and then change **Load balancer listener port** to 8080. Click on **Save**:

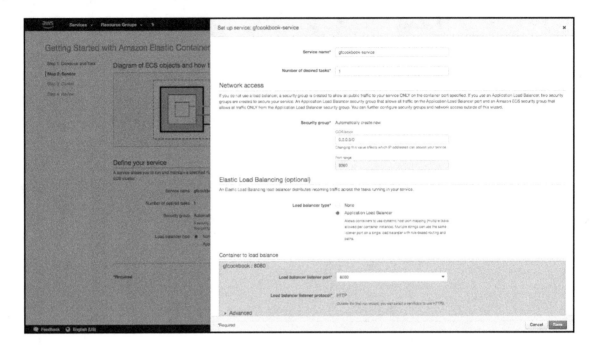

9. After that, click on **Next**:

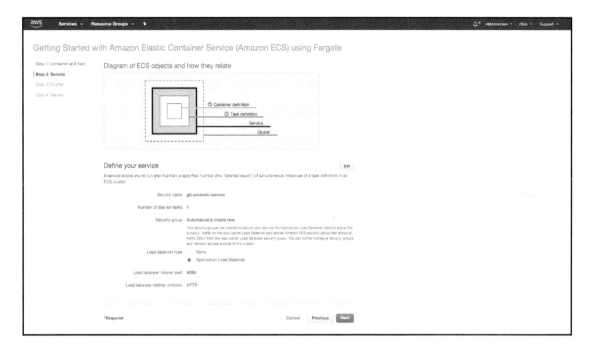

10. Configure the cluster, as follows:

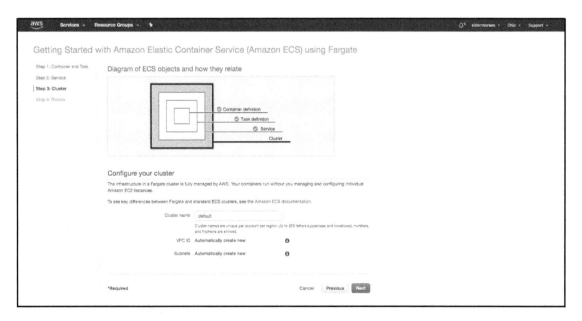

11. Scroll down until you get to the launch instance and click on **Create**:

Review

Review the configuration you've set up before creating your task definition, service, and cluster.

Task definition   Edit

Task definition name	first-run-task-definition
Network mode	awsvpc
Task execution role	Create new
Container name	gfcookbook
Image	eldermoraes/gf-jakartaee-cookbook
Memory	512
Port	8080
Protocol	HTTP

Service   Edit

Service name	gfcookbook-service
Number of desired tasks	1
Load balancer listener port	8080
Load balancer listener protocol	HTTP

Cluster   Edit

Cluster name	default
VPC ID	Automatically create new
Subnets	Automatically create new

*Required   Cancel   Previous   Create

12. You can follow the status of the process on the following page. When it's complete, click on the **View service** button:

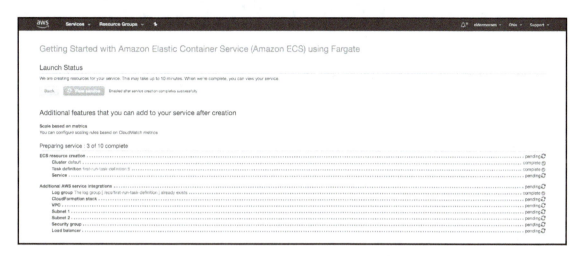

13. You'll see the details of your service on the following page. Click on **default > label**:

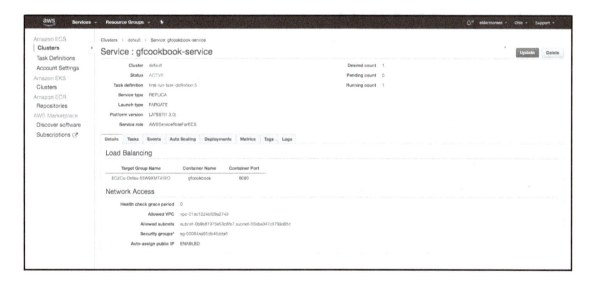

14. On the page that opens, you can view more details about the cluster:

15. Click on the **Tasks** tab to see information about the tasks and the containers that were created. Click on the task label (the first column):

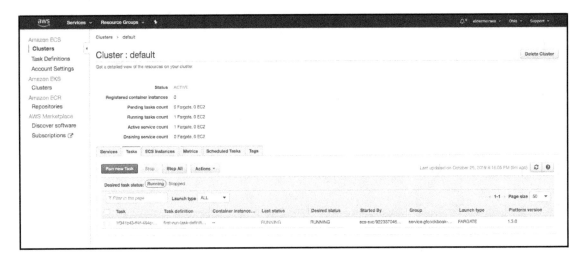

16. From here, you can see details about the task that has been created. Copy the **Public IP** address (under the **Network** section):

17. Port `8080` has been mapped, so you will need to use `http://[public-ip]:8080/app` to try it out:

> # The request is being answered by:
>
> ## IP: 10.244.1.121
>
> ## HostName: gf-jakartaee-cookbook-d9f776587-qg27c
>
> ## Session ID: 37d1c8988b371be608d94347ee6c

If you can see this page, then congratulations! You are now orchestrating your container in AWS.

12
Appendix - The Power of Sharing Knowledge

This appendix covers the following topics:

- Why contributing to the Adopt a JSR program can make you a better professional.
- The secret to unsticking your career, your project, and even your life!

Introduction

Wait—covering careers, knowledge sharing, and the community...all in a cookbook?

Well, you should thank my editors for this addition, as they have surrendered to my charm (and insistence) and allowed me to include this chapter in this book.

The reasons why I am so concerned with these topics are as follows:

- I am sure that this content is quite important and can be life-changing both to you personally and to your career.
- I don't know if or when I'll write another book, so I wanted to take the chance to talk about these topics now.

I consider this content as important as the rest of the content in this book. If you apply its principles to your career, you could soon be the one writing a book!

Why contributing to the Adopt a JSR program can make you a better professional

Have you ever heard the phrase "Help others to help yourself?" This section is all about this. Believe me, I wrote that.

Perhaps you've never heard of the *Adopt a JSR program*, or perhaps you've heard about it but have no idea what it is. Or maybe you do know of it, but don't know how it has anything to do with your career.

Allow me to have your attention for the next few pages—and enjoy the ride!

Understanding the Adopt a JSR program

First of all, what is the Adopt a JSR program?

Adopt a JSR is an initiative that intends to bring the Java community closer together while evolving Java. By community, we mean **Java User Groups** (**JUGs**)—that is, individuals and any kind of organization.

To understand this term, maybe we should hold on for a second and try to understand the Java evolution process.

Java technology has a set of standards called **Java Specification Requests** (**JSRs**). Every **Application Programming Interface** (**API**), and any other aspects of the language, have to be written in some form of JSR.

Every JSR has a spec leader, which is the individual in charge of leading the process of building that specification. Each spec leader works with an **Expert Group** (**EG**) that does all the heavy lifting of creating and/or evolving a JSR.

In each JSR, there are also contributors—people from the community who volunteer to collaborate with a JSR. They don't have the same role as the spec leader or the EG, but can also do a lot for this process.

For each JSR, there's a **Reference Implementation** (**RI**). The RI is the code that JSR is working on as real Java code. It exists to bring all those conceptual lines of a specification to the real world. It's vital for proving that what was once specified works.

Some examples of RIs in the former Java **Enterprise Edition** (**EE**) world are Mojarra for **JavaServer Faces** (**JSF**), Soteria for security, and GlassFish for Java EE.

When we say that the RI is proof that some JSRs work, this is not just on a conceptual level—it is really tested. That's why we have **Technology Compatibility Kits** (**TCKs**).

TCKs are a set of tests designed to test the implementations specified in the JSR. So, when an RI is written, it should pass in the TCKs to prove that it works (at least, in theory).

Those three parts—the JSR, the RI, and the TCK—are the pieces ratified by the **Java Community Process** (**JCP**).

So, in the JCP, you have all the working JSRs and their own processes monitored by the **Executive Committee** (**EC**), a group formed of companies, individuals, and JUGs that ensures that all the JSRs work under the best practices defined by the JCP and move toward the best results for the Java ecosystem and the community that relies on it.

So, the next time you think *"how can I contribute to Java? How can I make my contribution?"*—or, more specific to this section, *"how can I adopt a JSR?"*—know that you can do so by doing the following things:

- Join some JSRs as a contributor. Most spec leaders will be happy to accept help with the hard work of evolving a JSR.
- Help write the specification—or, at least, help with useful suggestions.
- Write tests for TCKs or help solve issues found in the TCK tests.
- Code for the RIs.

You can do all of these things by yourself, but it is much more productive (and fun!) if you do them with a community. You can do so by joining a JUG or starting a small group in your company (or wherever you can find some people to work together). It's a lot of work, so it's better to have some company!

For more information about adopting a JSR program, you can check out the following links:

- `https://jcp.org/aboutJava/communityprocess/community/JCPAdoptJSR.pdf`
- `https://github.com/Adopt-a-JSR`
- `https://developercareers.wordpress.com/2011/11/01/give-your-career-a-boost-by-adopting-a-jsr/`

To get to work, visit `https://jcp.org` or `https://github.com/jakartaee`.

Collaborating on the future of Jakarta EE

So, if you are reading this book, I believe that you are interested in Jakarta EE. If you have reached this very line, I hope that I have started to convince you that you can help Jakarta EE to move forward and how it can help your career.

Yes—you can help Jakarta EE move forward and, talking from my own experience, I can assure you that you should start doing so right now! But, in terms of the process, things are slightly different for Jakarta EE.

In 2017, Oracle decided to transfer Java EE to the Eclipse Foundation. Now, we have Jakarta EE, but other Java specifications will continue under the JCP (at least for now).

What does this change for you in terms of collaboration? Nothing. There are still groups, specifications, tests, and so on. The things that have changed are as follows:

- The names (mainly because of branding)
- The process, as it is now owned by the Eclipse Foundation

So, Java EE was transferred to Eclipse as **Eclipse Enterprise for Java (EE4J)**. It's the project umbrella that holds all the other projects under it; these other projects are the former JSRs. More details about EE4J can be found at `https://projects.eclipse.org/projects/ee4j/charter`.

About the EE4J itself, you will find a lot of answers to your questions at `https://www.eclipse.org/ee4j/faq.php`.

The project in Eclipse is led by the **Project Management Committee (PMC)**, as with the EC in the JCP. More details about the PMC can be found at `https://projects.eclipse.org/projects/ee4j/pmc`.

The bottom line here is that you can—and, I believe, you should—make your contribution to the future of Jakarta EE. Maybe you think that you don't have what it takes. Yes, you do! Every suggestion counts—every good idea, every line of working code, and every test that passes. Give it a shot and see the results!

Setting yourself up for collaboration

There are some things you need to do to collaborate on the future of Java EE.

Setting aside a specific time for it

If you plan to just do it when you have time for it, you may never do it! So, make time. Define some time that you are willing to dedicate to the task per week (such as 1 hour per day, 3 hours per week, and so on). Write this plan down and make an appointment for it.

Choosing where you'll concentrate your efforts

It's useless to start sending emails to dozens of spec leaders asking them to join the group and collaborate. I know—I've done this before.

Instead, take a step back, think about what you are interested in, and choose one single specification to start. Join the mailing list, find its repository on GitHub, and start using it.

A great way to start collaboration on any open source project is with documentation. This is important, but often, people involved with writing specifications and coding don't have enough time to go deeper into the documentation. So, they are usually glad when somebody else is willing to do so.

I know many people who started collaborating this way that today work on some of the biggest open source projects.

Do it!

Any plan makes sense if you just do something about it. So, stop procrastinating and get to work! Don't wait until Monday, after the vacation, after the end of college, when you get a better job, or use any other excuse.

Keep in mind that you will probably never feel like you are ready for it. So, stop waiting for the right feeling and start doing it, even if you don't feel like it. If you do the hard work, the results will come—you can be assured of that!

The secret to unsticking your career, your project, and even your life!

Do you feel stuck in your career? I've felt that way, too. Let me tell you a story about a secret that made my career explode.

It was 2002. I was at The American Chamber of Commerce in San Paolo, attending the *Sun Tech Days developer* conference. The venue was full and I was a little lost.

Maybe "lost" doesn't define my state very well. "Out of place" works much better. After all, I was just a tech newbie in the midst of giants.

I saw some well-known faces—Bruno Souza and Fabio Velloso. *"Should I introduce myself?"*, I thought.

Of course not...who was I? I should leave the guys alone—they must always be busy at conferences such as this.

I read the program and saw that there was a keynote speech taking place in the main room. It looked like it was by someone important, called James Gosling. I had no idea who he was, but I went to room.

I was the first in line. Of course I was—I was a newbie! Everyone was deep in conversation while I was there alone standing in front of the door. What were they all talking about? Definitely having some super-technical discussion that I wouldn't be able to understand. Better to stay there and wait.

Five minutes before they opened the doors, there were 200 people lined up behind me. Hey, looks like I was a lucky newbie, huh?!

I walked in and took a seat in the second row, waiting for the keynote speech to start.

Holy God, James Gosling is the creator of Java! What a silly newbie I was.

His talk was awesome! You know, he is not the best speaker in the world, but there were some things that he mentioned in his speech that amazed everyone in the room. Maybe it was his passion, his knowledge, or even the super-cool project that he revealed he was working on—the operating system for a remote-controlled Mars rover. Wow!

It was already the end of the second day of the conference and I felt disturbed—there were so many things to do with this Java thing. I'd tried it out a little by myself, but seeing all those Sun evangelists talking about real-life and cool projects took me to a whole new world of possibilities. My career needed to go in that direction.

After a few days out of the office, I returned and couldn't help myself—I needed to tell everybody what I'd just seen. Most of us who worked there worked with Visual Basic and Delphi, but Java would bring a whole new set of possibilities to our projects.

Just 6 months after I attended the *Sun Tech Days* conference I was working on my first Java project. That's right—the company outsourced a project and asked me to work on it with our partner!

What a terrible idea! Our partner's lead developer knew about as much about Java as I did, but I thought "*OK, let's do this.*" At least I would have the opportunity to work on a real Java project.

In 2004, I found myself about to talk at a big conference for the first time ever. I had to admit, I was terrified. But, actually, a new friend, Mauricio Leal, was joining me for the talk. He was one of the top Java influencers in Brazil and agreed to give a talk with me at the Just Java conference. Or, was it me that agreed to do the talk with him? Well, it doesn't matter now.

It was very hard for me to go to the conference as my mother had started her fight against cancer just a few months before. I was not only very concerned about her, but I also didn't have enough time to prepare for the conference. However, she encouraged me to go and said that she was proud of her child talking at a big event. Thanks, Mom!

We gave our talk and it was great! I had a lot to learn from Mauricio and all of his Java friends. I needed to keep going with this community thing—events, open source, talks, and so on.

In 2005, I decided to join a big project at the same company that I had been working with for the last 3 years. No, not a Java project, but a project so big that I couldn't miss the chance to be a part of it. It would be good for my career and I would get some good opportunities as a project manager.

By June 2006, my mother had just lost her fight against cancer. I was destroyed. I never thought, in my entire life, that I would lose her when she was only 58 and I was 26. Who cares about my career? Who cares about my job? Who cares about anything?

In December 2015, I was driving my car, with my wife at my side and my baby daughter in the back seat. I was telling my wife that I felt very concerned about my career.

I realized that I was no longer a kid. I was 36 and I had a good job that I was earning decent money from—but, I felt...stuck. Since when—2004? I know—it was a big mistake to join that project, even though it was a big one. We had all failed in it.

I told my wife "*you know, I have to do something...*"

After a couple of sleepless nights, some hours of research on the internet, and reading some reference books, I thought I had put a good list together for someone who had done nothing for years. Here it was:

- Write a technical article to be published.
- Give a tech talk at a small event.
- Get a Java EE Architect certificate.

I decided to stick with Java until the end. I knew a lot about it—I'd been studying and working with it for many years. I had to focus on it and I knew I could do it.

Suddenly, in the middle of all of this big confusion and a lot of doubt, I'd made it. I'd become a partner in the company!

"Well, maybe I've done something right, huh?!", I thought. All those years of hard work and study had finally paid off.

But, what was I thinking? I hated sales, I hated dealing with clients, I hated negotiations, I hated wearing a suit, and I hated chasing money. I hated this partner stuff!

To have my own business was always a dream of mine, but my life at that time felt more like a nightmare. This wrong decision made everything fall apart. The situation was unbearable, to the point where I now needed to take medication for depression.

All this poison in my mind made me think *"what the hell am I doing with my life? That's not the path I want to follow."* I mean, yes, the company was great and they were doing great things, but not in a way that worked for me.

I needed a change. I needed to make a move. If I didn't, what about my family's future? What kind of support would I be able to give my wife and daughter when I got old and retired?

It's was another terrible day when I got an email from... Bruno Souza? The Brazilian Java-man? How the heck did this guy have my email address? Oh, yes, I had subscribed to some sort of mailing list.

In his email, he talked about dreams, saying that one of his friends was helping him with a career dream this year, so he had decided to help others, too. He said *"tell me your career dreams for 2016 and I'll try to help you with them."*

Well, I was sure this guy wouldn't even read my email, but I thought I would reply to it anyway. At least writing down my dreams for the year would help me visualize them. I used the list that I had showed to my wife a few weeks ago.

Just half an hour later, he had replied!

He said that he could help me in the following ways:

- **With the article**: He could help me find a good topic and publish it with the **Oracle Technology Network (OTN)**. Was he being serious? I was just thinking about writing a blog post or something!
- **With the talk**: Once I had written the article, he could help me turn it into a talk. OK, that sounded interesting.
- **With the certification**: He wouldn't help me with this at all. I should sit down and study. Yeah, that made sense.

From all of the conversations I had with Bruno, one thing always stood out—sharing. Share your knowledge, share what you know, and share to help others—share, share, share. It seemed like this guy really wanted to help people.

So, I managed to leave the company (and the partnership) and finally got a position that I wanted—systems architect!

That's it—I loved architecture and I loved to deal with all the different trade-offs when planning an application from scratch or scaling/refactoring some legacy applications. I had found my place!

Not so fast, pal, not so fast. Within a month or so, the company changed its CEO and the new guy decided that Java would die there and then. The focus now would be .NET. OK, let's try it out.

In the meantime, Bruno and I published our first article on the OTN and it got thousands of views in just a few days. That was awesome!

We created a proposal on the same subject to present at The Developer's Conference (the biggest developer event in Latin America) and *JavaOne Latin America*. We were accepted to both conferences and I had the opportunity to present with Bruno to hundreds of people at these events.

We later worked on submitting our proposal to JavaOne San Francisco. However, on the last day before submitting it, I decided to give up on it. I couldn't afford it. Bruno almost kicked my ass and said "*Come on! Submit it! If it gets approved, you can figure out how to afford it.*"

The talk was approved and Cristina Saito, a former boss (and partner!) sent me a gift—airplane tickets to get to *JavaOne*. She said she was proud of me. I could probably never thank her enough for her kindness and generosity, and I hope this mention here goes some way toward that thanks.

It was hard to believe what had happened. Just 10 months after opening Bruno's email, 10 months after starting to take depression medication, and 10 months after the lowest moment of my career, I was in San Francisco, California. In a couple of minutes, I would be giving a talk with Bruno at *JavaOne*, the biggest Java event in the world. It was like a movie played through my mind and now I was here.

The talk was great! Some stuff went wrong, but we made it! It seemed as though this idea of sharing was working. I was feeling confident and couldn't wait to be back in Brazil and get back to work, getting things done and climbing my success mountain.

So, I landed in Brazil, went to the office, and... I was fired. Really? I thought that all this sharing stuff would help me, not cause me to lose my job... somebody lied to me!

OK, OK—let's take a deep breath...you know, I felt more confident now. No, I wasn't prepared for something such as getting fired after achieving the biggest accomplishment of my career up to now; but, I thought, I would figure something out.

It didn't take long until I got a position at Summa Technologies. Yes, sharing was working—I didn't even need to send in a resume. They had heard about me (because of my sharing) and there I was, working with the software that I had been talking and writing about.

The company was great, the team was highly skilled, and the project was challenging. But, you know, 6 months later it looked like I was getting stuck again. The results were just OK, the project was just OK, and there was nothing big to learn or to do here.

It was May 2017. In a few months, Java EE 8 would be released. What if we interviewed some top Java EE influencers from all over the world and shared all the information, expectations, and news they had about it? Sounds good. We thought we'd call this project *Java EE 8—The Next Frontier*.

Bruno was skilled enough to convince me to work with this Java EE 8 stuff and SouJava would give me all the support I needed. This was a SouJava initiative from the very first moment.

But, come on, why would all those Java EE experts give me an interview? Who was I?

It had been just 3 months since I'd started working with SouJava for the Java EE project. We'd already interviewed 15 of the top Java EE influencers. Thousands of developers from almost 70 countries saw the interviews. Our playlist on YouTube was featured on the official Java channel. All of the content got thousands of views a month.

I have to be honest—I would never have imagined that the Java EE community would be so open to this initiative. I mean, it's like they were expecting this content. They were willing to consume it.

The thing I was lacking this entire time? Focus! Anything you do without focus is almost useless. It can be helpful, but you won't have continuity.

These projects led me to write the book that you are reading right now. In one of my conversations with Packt, I asked them how they found me. They said: *"Well, you've been sharing a lot of Java EE 8 content... that's what we need."*

Just a few days after signing a deal with Packt, I got a call from Oracle. Yes, *that* Oracle!

So, right now, as I write these lines and am working at one of the biggest companies in the world, I'm doing exactly what I told you to do in this chapter—sharing my knowledge.

I tell you—if sharing my knowledge changed my career, it can also change yours. Don't think you don't have what it takes for it—you do! I can assure you that you know many things that other people would love to learn.

Why don't you find some good ways to help others? I can give you some suggestions on how you can help others based on what you just read here. Here they are:

- You can write a short block of code based on something you learned in this book. Share it on Twitter or on a blog post.
- Record a video explaining some of the insights you had when reading something in this book. Share it!
- If you don't want to put yourself out there at this point, email me telling me anything that this book has taught you. I'd love to read it! Send an email to elder@eldermoraes.com.

Sharing is a habit. Exercise it!

To add more to this, we have a new version of Jakarta EE coming soon and you can refer to the next Appendix to know more about this new release!

Other Books You May Enjoy

If you enjoyed this book, you may be interested in these other books by Packt:

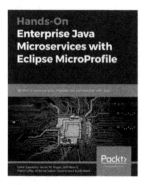

Hands-On Enterprise Java Microservices with Eclipse MicroProfile

Cesar Saavedra, Heiko W. Rupp, Jeff Mesnil, Pavol Loffay, Antoine Sabot-Durand, Scott Stark

ISBN: 978-1-83864-310-2

- Understand why microservices are important in the digital economy
- Analyze how MicroProfile addresses the need for enterprise Java microservices
- Test and secure your applications with Eclipse MicroProfile
- Get to grips with various MicroProfile capabilities such as OpenAPI and Typesafe REST Client
- Explore reactive programming with MicroProfile Stream and Messaging candidate APIs
- Discover and implement coding best practices using MicroProfile

Hands-On Cloud-Native Applications with Java and Quarkus

Francesco Marchioni

ISBN: 978-1-83882-147-0

- Build a native application using Quarkus and GraalVM
- Secure your applications using Elytron and the MicroProfile JWT extension
- Manage data persistence with Quarkus using PostgreSQL
- Use a non-blocking programming model with Quarkus
- Learn how to get Camel and Infinispan working in native mode
- Deploy an application in a Kubernetes-native environment using Minishift
- Discover Reactive Programming with Vert.x

Leave a review - let other readers know what you think

Please share your thoughts on this book with others by leaving a review on the site that you bought it from. If you purchased the book from Amazon, please leave us an honest review on this book's Amazon page. This is vital so that other potential readers can see and use your unbiased opinion to make purchasing decisions, we can understand what our customers think about our products, and our authors can see your feedback on the title that they have worked with Packt to create. It will only take a few minutes of your time, but is valuable to other potential customers, our authors, and Packt. Thank you!

Index

MVC 1.0 code
  executing 37, 38
  reference link 40
  working 40

O

observers
  used, for building reactive applications 265, 266,
  267
OpenAPI
  URL 225
OpenShift
  using, for container orchestration in cloud 317,
  318, 319, 320, 321, 322, 324
Oracle Cloud Infrastructure (OCI)
  about 294
  using, for container orchestration in cloud 294,
  296, 297, 298, 299, 300, 301, 302, 303
Oracle Kubernetes Engine (OKE) 297
Oracle Technology Network (OTN) 347

P

Payara Micro
  about 199
  URL 199
Persistence Unit (PU) 71
Plain Old Java Object (POJO) 262
programmatic security
  about 37, 137
  using 145, 146, 148, 149, 151
Project Management Committee (PMC)
  about 342
  reference link 342
Project Object Model (POM) 209

Q

Quality Assurance (QA) 214

R

reactive applications
  building, with asynchronous servlets 262, 263,
  264
  building, with asynchronous session beans 280,
  281, 282, 283
  building, with events and observers 265, 266,

  267
  building, with Jakarta RESTful Web Services
  277, 278, 279
  building, with message-driven beans (MDBs)
  272, 274, 275, 276
  building, with WebSocket 268, 269, 270, 271
  improving, with CompletableFuture 284, 286
  improving, with lambdas 284, 286
readiness
  about 217
  versus liveness 217
Red Hat WildFly
  about 180, 181, 183, 184
  download link 180
  URL 184
Reference Implementation (RI) 175, 340
request and response management
  with Jakarta Servlet 52, 53, 54
Request for Comments (RFC) 28
response performance
  improving, with Server Push 114, 115, 116
rights
  granting, through authorization 125, 127, 129,
  131, 133, 134

S

Secure Shell (SSH) 299
Secure Sockets Layer (SSL) 134
security 119
Selenium Webdriver
  reference link 214
self-managed beans
  avoiding 67
Server Push
  PushBuilder 59
  response performance, improving 114, 115, 116
  used, for pushing resources in request 55, 56,
  57, 59
Server-Sent Event (SSE) 18
Server-Side Event (SSE)
  about 91
  building, with JAX-RS 83, 86, 88, 89, 91
service's capabilities
  improving, with Jakarta CDI 92, 93, 95, 96
  improving, with JAX-RS 92, 93, 95, 96

servlet
  life cycle 164, 165, 166
  using, for request and response management
    105, 106, 108
  with init params 110
Sonatype Nexus
  about 208
  reference link 212
SSL/TLS
  used, for protecting data confidentiality and
    integrity 134, 136

T

Technology Compatibility Kits (TCKs) 341
Thoairntl
  about 200
  URL 200
transaction management
  about 166, 168, 169, 170
  with EJB 60, 62, 63, 64
  with Java Transaction API (JTA) 60, 61, 63, 64

transactions
  using, with asynchronous tasks 236, 238, 240,
    241, 242
Transport Layer Security (TLS) 135

U

user microservice
  reference link 200
UserAddress microservice
  reference link 200
UserService
  reference link 205

V

View (V) 38

W

Web Application Resource (WAR) 172
WebSocket
  used, for building reactive applications 268, 269,
    270, 271

www.ingramcontent.com/pod-product-compliance
Lightning Source LLC
LaVergne TN
LVHW081514050326
832903LV00025B/1478